REINTRODUCING ROBERT K. MERTON

This book reintroduces the work of Robert K. Merton as a bridge between classical sociology and modern sociology. Founded in the sociological classics but developing a modern approach to the advancement of theory and research methodology, Merton's thought helped to construct modern sociology in its coverage of many of the social institutional areas of contemporary society. Recovering and analysing the system of 'structural analysis', which Merton progressively developed – a system largely overlooked due to the tendency among commentators to stereotype him as a 'functionalist' – the author considers the applications of this approach to various substantive fields, particularly science and criminal justice, and examines the effect of Merton's later 'sociological semantics' on his overall schema. A clear and accessible presentation of the array of concepts introduced by Merton to sociology, *Reintroducing Robert K. Merton* will appeal to scholars and students with interests in sociological theory, social research, the history of sociology and the various substantive areas covered in the work of Merton – deviance, science, and communications.

Charles Crothers is Emeritus Professor of Sociology at Auckland University of Technology, New Zealand. He has previously worked at the Town & Country Planning Division of the Ministry of Works, Wellington, Victoria University of Wellington, the University of Auckland, the University of Natal and as Senior Research Associate at the University of Johannesburg. He is the author of *Sociologies of New Zealand*, *Social Structure* and *Robert K. Merton* and was previously editor of *NZ Population Review*, *Sociology in Transition*, *New Zealand Sociology* and *Kotuitui: New Zealand Journal of Social Sciences Online*.

REINTRODUCING...

The 'Reintroducing' series offers concise and accessible books that remind us of the importance of sociological theorists whose work, while constituting a significant and lasting contribution to the discipline, is no longer widely discussed. With each volume examining the major themes in thought of a particular figure and the context in which this work came about, as well as its reception and enduring relevance to contemporary social science, the books in this series will appeal to scholars and students of sociology seeking to rediscover the work of important but often neglected sociologists.

Reintroducing Robert K. Merton
Charles Crothers

For more information about this series, please visit: www.routledge.com/Reintroducing/book-series/RCST

REINTRODUCING ROBERT K. MERTON

Charles Crothers

Routledge
Taylor & Francis Group

LONDON AND NEW YORK

First published 2021
by Routledge
2 Park Square, Milton Park, Abingdon, Oxon OX14 4RN

and by Routledge
52 Vanderbilt Avenue, New York, NY 10017

Routledge is an imprint of the Taylor & Francis Group, an informa business

British Library Cataloguing-in-Publication Data
A catalogue record for this book is available from the British Library

Library of Congress Cataloging-in-Publication Data
Names: Crothers, C., author.
Title: Reintroducing Robert K. Merton / Charles Crothers.
Description: Abingdon, Oxon; New York, NY: Routledge, 2021. |
Series: Reintroducing... | Includes bibliographical references and index.
Identifiers: LCCN 2020039871 (print) | LCCN 2020039872 (ebook) |
ISBN 9780367409678 (paperback) | ISBN 9780367409661 (hardback) |
ISBN 9780367810160 (ebook)
Subjects: LCSH: Merton, Robert King, 1910–2003. |
Sociologists–United States–Biography. | Sociology–United States–History.
Classification: LCC HM479.M47 C76 2021 (print) |
LCC HM479.M47 (ebook) | DDC 301.092 [B]–dc23
LC record available at https://lccn.loc.gov/2020039871
LC ebook record available at https://lccn.loc.gov/2020039872

ISBN: 9780367409661 (hbk)
ISBN: 9780367409678 (pbk)
ISBN: 9780367810160 (ebk)

Typeset in Bembo
by Newgen Publishing UK

This study is dedicated to the memory of Robert K. Merton and to Raewyn Peart who provided valued writing support. I hope that it captures the style and thrust of Merton's work, and provides a sketch of the overview he never presented. I would like to indicate my great debt to the group of Mertonians and even anti-Mertonians who have explored, developed or criticised his thought, including Charles Camic, David Caplovitz, Stephen Cole, Jonathan Cole, Randall Collins, Lewis Coser, Mathieu Deflem, Michel Dupois, Cynthia Epstein, Christian Fleck, Kenneth Fox, Alvin Gouldner, Robert Marsh, Larry Nichols, Nico Stehr, Larry Stern (who provided much valued close feedback on a draft), Peter Simonson, Arthur Stinchcombe, Piotr Sztompka and Harriet Zuckerman.

CONTENTS

ILLUSTRATIONS

Figures

Tables

ACRONYMS

ASA	American Sociological Association
BASR	Bureau of Applied Social Research (at Columbia University)
CUDOS	communism, universalism, disinterestedness, organised skepticism
ISA	International Sociological Association
OBI	obliteration by incorporation
OTSOG	*On the Shoulders of Giants*
SA	sociological ambivalence
SED	socially expected duration
SFP	self-fulfilling prophecy
SS	sociological semantics
SS&A	social structure and anomie
STSS	*Social Theory and Social Structure*
UCA	unintended consequences of purposive action

BIOGRAPHICAL NOTES

I am Emeritus Professor of Sociology at Auckland University of Technology. I have worked as a junior lecturer at Victoria University of Wellington, New Zealand; as a research sociologist in the Town and Country Planning Division, Ministry of Works and Development, Wellington; then a senior lecturer in the Department of Sociology, University of Auckland; and Chair at the Department of Sociology, University of Natal before returning to New Zealand. My research interests span urban and regional sociology, social research methods, social theory, the sociology of social science, and especially, the analysis of New Zealand society and other settler societies. I am also Senior Research Associate at the University of Johannesburg.

In the mid-1960s I attended a greenfields-site new university in a New Zealand service city which was unsure of what to make of this new institution in its midst. The downtown bookstore ordered in some relevant books and I was able to purchase Merton's *Social Theory and Social Structure*, which I sporadically read. We discussed one of Merton's essays in class and a classmate complimented my sociological interest on the basis of Merton's essay and that crystallised my interest. Doing a sociology of science thesis inevitably involved much of Merton writings. At my selection committee discussion about joining the Department of Sociology at University of Auckland some years later, I volunteered that I intended to write a book on Merton. This was negotiated as part of the Ellis Horwood/Tavistock (generically Routledge) series on Key Sociologists under the editorship of Peter Hamilton. My follow-up was to obtain further material on Merton and on the Columbia Tradition which was my research over several years, reporting on both through several articles, chapters and working papers.

The massive range of Merton's work is difficult to accommodate. I feel I've been a dwarf fighting to get onto Merton's shoulders in order to purchase a good view. I hope I've been able to provide an adequate coverage of Merton's extensive range of writings and the further penumbra of writings on, and drawing on,

Merton while also pointing up the patterns and underlying mode. For a (re)introduction I've tried to keep the text as unencumbered with references to the literature as I can, while ensuring that my sources are clearly identified. In particular, this volume does not endeavour to track down the empirical adequacy of Merton's formulations or track the exact contours of his influence, which are tasks for other writings and other writers.

1

THE CASE FOR REINTRODUCING MERTON

The image of Merton's work

Robert K. Merton's death in 2003 was mourned in several newspapers – including, impressively, in *The New York Times*, and in a wide array of more academic obituaries (see Crothers, 2019). The newspaper coverage tended to focus on key concepts which Merton introduced into the discipline, many of which have become widespread in public usage: especially focus groups, role model, and the self-fulfilling prophecy. More academic obituaries usually covered a broader range although some were specifically tied to Merton's contributions to the field covered by that particular journal. Reminiscences were shared by several colleagues (Calhoun et al., 2003) and later Zuckerman et al., 2011 *Robert K. Merton at 100: Reflections and Recollections*.

Merton's work is varyingly covered in both introductory and more advanced sociology textbooks, and to a greater extent than most other theorists since the 'founding fathers'. There are a few, mostly brief, chapters focused on Merton in theory texts (more recent examples of full chapter length treatments are Crothers 2011 and Sztompka 2017), encyclopedia entries, a scattering of critical articles and a large and growing literature drawing on his concepts (see Chapter 7 for detail). He is mainly known as the architect of an alternative structural-functional analysis, as collaborator with Paul Lazarsfeld and co-leader of the Columbia Sociology department, a proponent of middle-range theory, as having developed the field of the sociology of science, and especially for his account of anomie and the modes of adaptation. Zuckerman (2011: 139–140) provides a useful listing of Merton-linked concepts well entrenched in the discipline of sociology and more widely. In addition to 'role model' and 'focus group', other contributions include 'unintended consequences', 'self-fulfilling prophecy', 'middle-range theories', 'role conflict', influentials, 'role set' and the 'Matthew effect'. Much commentary relates to *particular* areas of Merton's expertise, while the analysis of Merton's *general* approach to sociology is slight.

In these accounts, Merton is usually portrayed as a structuralfunctional loyalist, differing only in detail (not least in graciousness of writing style!) from Talcott Parsons as the grand master of structural-functional analysis, whereas on closer examination, Merton's approach is fundamentally different. Even the more detailed of these accounts cover only highly selected portions of Merton's work, and are more concerned to describe, than to analyse, how he constructs his analyses. Some texts explicitly *deny* that "he has produced a systematic theory or a system of sociology" (Bierstedt, 1981: 445). His later-developed cultural sociology or 'sociological semantics' is seldom mentioned, and some earlier work is overlooked. Moreover, readily available coverage largely ignores his empirical and methodological work, the range of studies spread across the many realms of contemporary society, and his underlying moral stance. Such accounts, too, seldom draw on previous exegesis established in the secondary literature on Merton.

My 1987 intellectual biography of Merton provides the foundation for this study. But much has happened since, that has been worked into the text. Most importantly, Merton continued to publish: especially his (delayed a half century) book on *Serendipity* (see Chapter 5). A spate of commentary volumes has appeared over the last three decades (see below) together with a range of shorter studies. The volume of material is sufficiently large that very precise tracing of sources would quickly amass a mountain of documentation, so in this book sources are often only generally indicated. And I have pursued relevant studies of my own. All these are drawn upon in updating the earlier book. This book takes a chronological approach not deployed in the earlier version.

The need for reintroducing Merton

The current standard accounts of the development of American sociology often, but not always, cover Merton, but he is seldom seen as a major proponent in contemporary theoretical debates. This partial silence is a fate shared with a slew of American mid-century theorists. The theoretical grounding of many contemporary 'European' social theorists lies with the `founding fathers' (Marx, Durkheim and Weber) and the complexly intertwined threads of exegesis and extension that stretch from them. The transmission line of major theoretical ideas is seen to mainly bypass those early and mid-twentieth-century decades in which the development of sociological knowledge was largely left in American hands.

Where there is such treatment, it is often deficient. Once various early American theorists have been treated and the 'Chicago School' described, treatment of the sociology of the 1950s and 1960s often falters. North American sociology of the post-war period is usually characterised using one or other, or both, of two labels – 'structural functionalism' and 'empiricism'. The theoretical arm of post-WW2 American sociology is often seen as a 'grand theory', which took a 'structural-functionalist' form, and which was detached from both empirical concerns and the provision of social criticism. Under the theoretical aegis of Talcott Parsons, a complex and terminologically dense conceptual framework is often seen as having developed a conservative-leaning social theory during the 'end of ideology' decades of the 1950s and 1960s. This approach is depicted as seeing social order as emanating from socialised conformity to cultural ideas, with a self-righting, equilibrium-seeking social system quickly restoring any departures from the status quo. But, Parsons's direct influence on sociological theorising and research was perhaps more limited than is often held. After all, his work did not lead to the ready development of research problems or the easy formulation of theoretical explanations. The other arm of post-war American sociology is often seen to involve an 'abstracted empiricism' wherein micro problems about the explanations of the social distribution of attitudes and behaviour were relentlessly attacked through a myriad social survey studies, without sufficient concern for understanding the structural anchoring of these social minutiae in wider societal contexts. But a more granular account would show the more integrated theory–research combination developed at Columbia by Merton and Lazarsfeld and colleagues was a crucial seedbed of many developments over that period and since.

Especially after the upheavals of the 1960s, the picture must be immediately widened to include the 'loyal opposition' of symbolic interactionism, and its associated qualitative field research methodology, which throughout the period was held to be particularly cherished by the scattered remnants of the older 'Chicago School'. To this was added a flowering of Marxisant 'radical sociology'. Both tended to occlude functional sociology, although the research arm of positivist work continued strongly. But, the impetus for social theory then became located in Europe. That social theory tended to have a broad reach examining the social order in abstract terms and not particularly concerned to drive empirical research. Being armed with a more sophisticated account of Merton's and other American sociology would have facilitated an active interface with more recent theory, to the benefit of both.

As a consequence, Merton's concepts–terms continue to fuel the literatures of several fields of sociology and social science, even humanities, but to be offset to some extent from the energies of mainstream sociology. The full extent of Merton's influence may seem to some to be fading, given that his name becomes de-coupled from his terms–concepts, a phenomenon Merton christened 'OBI: obliteration by incorporation in the literature' (1968: 27–28) when concepts seem so well known that their intellectual origin need no longer be acknowledged. Consideration of the possible fading influence of Merton has been raised: for example, it is the query the Elkana et al., 2010 collection is (to some extent) built around, and see also Calhoun (2010). Simonson's considerable work on Merton's media studies has in part (2006) been framed by the rubric 'works deserving renewed attention (GUAWDRAs)' in which category he firmly places Merton's *Mass Persuasion*. However, questions of extent of continuing influence have still to be resolved.

Beyond the inevitable passage of time, there may also be psychosocial mechanisms at work that have acted as barriers to closer attention to Merton's work. He is not yet ancient enough to be extensively mined for historical work. There was no particular occasion on which broader examination was called for, apart from potential centennial 'anniversaries', and perhaps there is a structural resistance arising out of master–apprenticeship ambivalence and similar scholarly patterns (cf. Merton, 1973: 534–535). This ambivalence towards a preceding intellectual generation is nicely pointed up in the preface to Stinchcombe's *Constructing Social Theories*: "Robert K. Merton was another classic writer who ranked with Durkheim, Marx and Trotsky in my earlier intellectual life. I have been a bit bewildered by his becoming a contemporary as I grow older" (1968: vii). While many significant sociologists were spawned out of the Columbia setting, unlike the 'Chicago School(s)', loyalty was not emphasised and few wrote extensively on their teachers (or more specifically their teachers' ideas), albeit often developing those ideas further in their own work.

In sum, Merton played a crucial shaping role in the development of sociology over the post-WW2 'golden period' of its construction, and still has much potential to contribute to contemporary debates. This study is devoted to arguing this case.

Images of Merton's contributions to sociology

In the literature, there are several main lines of interpretation of the nature and extent of Merton's scholarly work. They all agree in recognising that Merton has produced much of value to sociology, but differ in their interpretation. Responses to Merton's work fall along separate axes of the extent to which his work is general v. specific, conservative v. radical and contemporary v. aged.

Merton as orthodox

The 'orthodox' interpretation places Merton as a junior partner of Parsons in the 'structural-functional' enterprise. If pressed, those adopting this viewpoint might point to any, or several, of a wide array of concepts particularly associated with Merton: manifest and latent functions, reference groups, role sets, etc. but these are not seen as constituting an alternative approach, as is argued in this book.

Merton as conservative

A second line of interpretation sees Merton as politically conservative. This line of interpretation is grounded in radical sociological theory and has been advanced particularly by Randall Collins, although several other predecessors in this tradition chose not to: C. Wright Mills (almost entirely) excluding Merton from attack amidst his general critique of sociology while Alvin Gouldner being rent by ambivalence. Collins (1977) accords Merton a leadership role in the 1940s and 1950s, while arguing that "it seems apparent that his eminence in [sociology of science] is not due to his having organized a workable paradigm". Instead, Collins feels that the resonances of Merton's work sat well with the domestically complacent Cold War period, and that it is limited in its long-term significance because it was not grounded in key explanatory factors of class and conflict and thus fails to gain explanatory purchase. However, Sztompka (1986) has advanced a conflict reading of Merton, which is moving the pendulum too far in the opposite direction. A reasonable interpretation of Merton's position, including later writings on opportunity-structure would be that it can encompass any point on the conflict–competition–consensus continuum.

Merton as a 'cautious rebel'

Taylor et al. (1973) characterise Merton as a cautious rebel in moral terms because they feel that he is prepared to make definite, if limited, social judgements. A similar intellectual position with respect to his theory has been advanced by the group of writers from the late 1960s (e.g. Blau, 1990) that saw Merton as centred in a structural perspective adjacent to Parsonian functional analysis.

Merton as an unintended general theorist

A fourth line of interpretation is that most seriously advanced by Stinchcombe (1975) in which he argues that Merton's influence has been won by his implicit 'general theory'. In this book I have attempted to develop a stronger version of this by showing that Merton's general model incorporated rather more of Merton's work than Stinchcombe had supposed, and that a closer textual analysis could more closely support *his* line of argument. Sztompka (1986) also develops this line of argument, although in less appropriate 'systems' terms (see Crothers, 1989).

Merton as 'archaic'

While providing a sympathetic account, Sica (2007) argues that Merton's writing is anachronistic, particularly in portraying a social world which is stable and more unified than fast-changing contemporary reality allows. Clearly, Merton's examples are increasingly out of date and certainly his vocabulary in the 1930s seems old-fashioned (e.g. "deviate behaviour", "Opinionnaires"), and even Merton himself found looking back at his earlier writing that it was "Veblensque" (1994). Although Simonson echoes Sica's comments, he says of *Mass Persuasion*, "Many of the book's themes remain current" and belong in the study of the contemporary mediascape, particularly throwing light on its earlier years" (2004: xi). I personally find Merton's analyses still fresh and relevant, so perhaps this sort of judgement is a matter of personal taste.

Merton as a classic period sociologist

Sztompka (1986), and others, have argued that Merton is the last of the classical grand theorists, although this works against Merton's self-image and the difficulties in establishing such a 'grand theory'. Rather, he spans both the ending of the classical period and the early stages of more modern sociology, actively linking the two.

Merton as 'obvious'

Once Merton pointed out analytical points, they could seem obvious. David Caplovitz (1977) who took Merton's Soc 213–214 around 1950, made the point that student auditors of his lectures were enthusiastic about what they had heard, but were often unable to clearly articulate to others the content of his analyses. Perhaps Merton was too successful in clarifying social reality.

Merton as excellent writer

It may be the form as much as the content which empowers Merton's writings. Merton's love of words and exemplary writing style are widely recognised, and are a 'value-added' aspect of his work which is more based on advancing substantive concepts. A further contribution was Merton's intermediate medium-length preferred genre of writing: essay-style articles, or chapters loosely organised into a book. While Merton was one of the first sociologists to mainly publish through articles, these were far from 'report-style' research reports and allowed succinct but comprehensive advancement of arguments.

Sources

In exploring the questions raised by these various images, a large body of writing needs to be accessed. According to Garfield's listing (http://garfield.library.upenn. edu/histcomp/merton-rk_auth/index-tl.html), Merton's production included some 19 books, six chapters, 78 articles, 35 reviews and a considerable volume of research reports and unpublished material. See also Poros & Needham, 2004. Garfield records some 15,000 citations in the academic literature up to 2012, although this figure is just one of many possible measures which might be possible (see Chapter 7).

Almost all the significant earlier writings by Merton have been assembled in four volumes (with a very slight overlap in content). *Social Theory and Social Structure* (*STSS*) was first published in 1949 with subsequent enlarged and revised editions in 1957 and 1968. Each edition retains a four-part structure:

- on theoretical sociology (on relations between theory and research, and functional analysis);
- studies in social and cultural structure (anomie, bureaucracy and reference groups);
- sociology of knowledge and mass communications;
- sociology of science.

The 1957 edition includes four extra essays (two of which are 'continuities' that attempt to update analyses included in the first edition) which expand its volume by one-third, and it also incorporates some revisions. The 1968 edition differs from its predecessor only in a very considerable expansion of its introduction into two chapters, which were also published with Part 1 of *STSS* as a volume, *On Theoretical Sociology*, published in 1967.

Another 13 essays are gathered from symposia and journal articles into the 1976 collection, *Sociological Ambivalence*. Several of these essays provide analyses of sociological ambivalence (which involves examining the stresses arising for individuals out of contrasting aspects of the social structures they are embedded in), while other essays deal with a wide variety of theoretical issues, and a final set on ethnic relations.

In 1973 most of Merton's work in the *Sociology of Science* was assembled by Norman Storer into a volume with the same title. Much of Merton's work in the sociology of knowledge is also included. Storer provides a useful introduction and prefatory notes for each part that sketch the background of, and develop themes within, Merton's sociology of science. The volume has five parts:

- The Sociology of Knowledge;
- The Sociology of Scientific Knowledge;
- The Normative Structure of Science;
- The Reward Structure of Science;
- Processes of Evaluation in Science.

A further selection is reproduced in *Social Research and the Practising Professions* (1982) edited by Aaron Rosenblatt and Thomas F. Gieryn, who also provide a useful introduction. This volume seeks to relate Merton's analysis of the social organisation of (social) science, to his analysis of professions, and also to reprint some of his essays on the interaction between the two, and thus is organised into three parts:

- Sociology of Social Research;
- Sociology of the Practising Professions;
- Social Research Applied to Public Policy.

An interesting feature is the construction by the editors of a "composite form" of Merton's essay on 'Social Problems and Sociological Theory' from the 1961, 1966, 1971 and 1976 editions of *Contemporary Social Problems*.

Sztompka's compilation of key writings for the University of Chicago Press's The Heritage of Sociology series (series editor Donald N. Levine) is particularly useful. This is organised into:

- theoretical work in sociology (varieties of the theoretical work & analytical frameworks for sociology);
- social structure and its vicissitudes (structural complexities and contradictions, paradoxes of social process);
- science as social structure (sociology of science and the social institution of science).

Where possible references are made to the Sztompka collection as it is more likely to be at hand and all references to material from *STSS* are to the 1968 edition (although the date when an essay was first published is also indicated when this is important in establishing a chronological sequence). Similarly, where this is possible, reference is always made to the version of any article which is available in one or other of the four volumes, and this is indicated by square brackets in the citation.

The secondary literature is scattered but growing, with books including:

- Clinard (1964) provides a collection debating the success of Merton's 'anomie theory' to that point in time;
- Much material is available through the *Festschrift* edited by Lewis Coser (1975) and through reviews of this. This was timed to honour Merton's 65th birthday, and is wide-ranging, including important essays analysing the structure of Merton's argumentation. It also provides case studies of the influences on, and the reception of his work, as well as including a range of other essays that bear on themes he has worked on;
- A second rather more slight and much less useful *Festschrift* (in Merton's 70th year) edited by Gieryn (1980) addresses implications of Merton's work on the sociology of science This collection comes from a more remote set of commentators (American sociologists were excluded) and is somewhat disconnected from the main thrusts of Merton's work;
- Mongardini and Tabboni have published the original papers of a conference held in Amalfi, Italy, to celebrate Merton being awarded the Amalfi Prize sponsored by the Italian Sociological Association (1987: fully in English, 1998 by Transaction Publishers);
- Clark (1990) assembled a sparkling roster of authors to debate various aspects of Merton's work, published in his 80th year. For each of the main areas of Merton's work a supporter and a protagonist have been cast in argumentative mode against each other, together with opportunities for reprise;
- Cohen (1990) is a compilation of Merton's and others' writings around 'Puritanism and the Rise of Modern Science';
- Adler & Laufer's (1998) volume discusses the contemporary relevance of Merton's perspective for the understanding of crime and delinquency. This topic is projected into the future by a complementary 1997 volume edited by Nikos Passas & Robert Agnew;
- Calhoun's (2010) collection arises from a workshop hosted at Columbia University and particularly the Institute for Social Economic Research & Policy (heir institute to the earlier BASR): "[The book] is an examination of Merton's legacy by active sociological researchers seeking to advance knowledge through renewed engagement with the work of one of Sociology's pioneers as an effort to engage enduring and merging intellectual agendas" (viii);
- Elkana, Szigeti & Lissauer (2011) is loosely based on a concern about Merton's continuing influence which surfaced at the 2008 World Congress of the International Institute of Sociology. The book has essays on Merton's ideas

which have influenced authors' work and studies of reception first presented at
a workshop at the Central European University;

- Mica et al. (2011) launch a broad consideration of 'Sociology and the
Unintended' (based in part on a workshop held in 2011 at the Institute of
Philosophy, Sociology and Journalism at the University of Gdansk) and on the
75th anniversary of the publication of Merton's paper on 'Sociology and the
Unintended'.

Journal special issues include a 2004 special issue of *Social Studies of Science*
34 (5) edited by Michael Lynch, and also Stephen Turner et al. (2009) on the
'Columbia School of theory-construction' in *Philosophy of Social Science*, and a 2007
collection in *Journal of Classical Sociology* 7(2).

There are two intellectual biographies on Merton (both produced somewhat
simultaneously in the late 1980s and from the opposite ends of the earth: Poland
(Sztompka 1986) and New Zealand (Crothers, 1987). More recently primers on
Merton have been produced in French and German. Published interviews include
Cohen, 1998; Persell, 1984; & Schultz, 1995.

Overview: a formal biography

Merton was born on 4 July 1910 in Philadelphia. He attended Penn Southern High
School. In 1927 he won a scholarship to Temple College and in 1931 a fellowship
to Harvard University for graduate work in sociology. In 1932 he gained a Harvard
MA, and began his doctoral dissertation, completing this in 1935; becoming an
instructor and tutor at Harvard. In 1939 he was appointed as associate professor and,
a year later, a full professor at Tulane University, New Orleans – serving as chairman
of the department. In 1941 he became assistant professor at Columbia University,
New York; being subsequently promoted to associate professor (1944) and full professor (1947), and succeeding Lazarsfeld as Chairman of the Department in 1961
for several years (albeit with several previous stints as Chair/Executive Officer). In
1963 he was appointed Franklin Henry Giddings Professor of Sociology, in 1974
acquired the rank (shared then by only three others at Columbia) of 'University
Professor', and from 1979 on had been 'Special Service Professor' and 'University
Professor Emeritus'. From 1942 to 1971 he served as Associate Director in the
Bureau of Applied Social Research (sometimes as Acting Director).

Professional activities included the Presidencies of the American Sociological
Association (1956–1957), the Eastern Sociological Society (1968–1969), the
Sociological Research Association (1968) and the Society for Social Studies of
Science (1975–1976). Honorary degrees were given by some 20 universities
including Temple, Emory, Leyden, Western Reserve, Colgate, Yale, Wales,
Chicago, Pennsylvania, Harvard, Jerusalem, Maryland, Brandeis, State University
of New York, Columbia and Oxford. (It is significant that Merton's honour from
Oxford is a Doctorate of Letters rather than Philosophy.) In 1994, Merton was
awarded the US National Medal of Science by President Clinton, for "founding

the sociology of science and for his pioneering contributions to the study of social life, especially the self-fulfilling prophecy and the unintended consequences of social action". He was the first sociologist to receive the prize. Merton was a Fellow of the Guggenheim Foundation (1962–1963), the Center for Advanced Studies in Behavioral Science (1973–1974), and was Resident Scholar at both the Russell Sage Foundation and Adjunct Professor at the Rockefeller University since 1979. Prizes were awarded him by the American Council of Learned Societies, the National Institute of Medicine, the American Academy of Arts and Sciences (Talcott Parsons Prize for Social Science), the Memorial Sloan-Kettering Cancer Center, Society for Social Studies of Science (Bernal Award), American Sociological Association (Commonwealth award and Career Distinguished Scholarship award), Amalfi Prize sponsored by the Italian Sociological Association (1987), the 1995 Derek de Solla Prize awarded by the journal *Scientometrics*, the Social Psychology section of the American Sociological Association (the Cooley-Mead award, 1997), the Sutherland award of the American Society of Criminology (1997), and, perhaps most prestigious of all, he was a MacArthur Prize Fellow (1983–1988). He was one of the first sociologists elected to the National Academy of Sciences and the first American sociologist to be elected a foreign member of the Royal Swedish Academy of Sciences and a Corresponding Fellow of the British Academy. He was also a member of the American Philosophical Society, the National Academy of Education and Academica Europea. He has also held numerous advisory posts across a range of social science, humanities and scientific areas, in particular to the American Nursing Association. Several honours are in his name: The Robert K. Merton Professorship at Columbia; Merton Fellowship at the The Institute for Analytical Sociology (IAS), Linköping University, Sweden; Merton Fellow at Russell Sage Foundation; the Robert K. Merton Award for the best paper in analytical sociology (an annual award announced at the annual INAS – International Network of Analytical Sociologists) conference; and The Robert Merton Award for Distinguished Contribution to the Sociology of Science and Technology, International Sociological Association (2018). The University of Mannheim recently launched a Robert K. Merton Center for Science Studies. Several writers have suggested that had there been a Nobel Prize in Sociology this would likely have been awarded to Merton.

Merton married Suzanne M. Carhart, a social worker, whom he met when she was a student at Temple University, on 8 September 1934. They separated in 1968. At his death Merton had a son and two daughters, nine grandchildren, and nine great-grandchildren. From the 1970s, Merton's companion, colleague and wife (from 1993) was Harriet Zuckerman. He died on 23 February 2003 in New York after endless assaults by various cancers which had affected much of his career. He enumerates sprue, Ménière's syndrome, Dupuytren's contracture, a gangrened appendix, pneumonias and cancer (Merton, 1982: 924).

Merton's daughters are Stephanie Merton Tombrello (prominent for car safety advocacy) and Vanessa Merton (professor of law at Pace University). Merton was close to his son and they spoke most days ("at 90, Merton the father would call on his son for help learning enough new mathematics to read exciting work by younger colleagues like Duncan Watts": Calhoun et al., 2003). With Myron Scholes (see www.econlib.org/library/Enc/bios/Merton.html), Robert C. Merton received the 1997 Nobel Prize in economics "for a new method to determine the value of derivatives"). This led Merton to occasionally subsequently refer to himself as 'father of the economist'. In 1993, R.C. Merton had cofounded a hedge fund, Long-Term Capital Management, which earned high returns for four years but later lost $4.6 billion in 1998, blindsided by a hard-to-predict ('black swan') Russian bond default and was bailed out by a consortium of banks under the coordination the Federal Reserve and closed out in early 2000.

Sources on personal life

Details of Merton's personal biography are sparse, as this has received direct attention mainly in his own recollections in a *Life of Learning* (1994), with a few published interviews (see following chapters) and some biographical research adding more material. Simonson (especially 2010) has unearthed many details about Merton's earlier decades including from interviews. However, Merton published some attempts to document the 'career' of some of his projects (see subsequent chapters). He also wrote accounts of his working relationships with several teachers, colleagues and students (see Chapter 5). These reveal that often such relationships were deep and warm as well as intellectual. Moreover, later versions of material on a topic often recited their earlier history. Merton felt there were the barriers that militated against self-study: a poor memory of personal events and without the backup of recourse to any diary. However (Simonson, 2010: 125), "Merton kept abundant typewritten notes of his thoughts and reading, which he stored in notebooks in his office". The well documented resource of Merton's papers filed with Columbia University, www.columbia.edu/cu/lweb/archival/collections/ldpd_6911309/index.html also overcomes some limitations. Indeed, the richness of this source has led to it not just throwing light on Merton's own career, but also becoming, fittingly, a more general 'research site' for studies exploring patterns of interaction-at-a-distance (e.g. see DuBois, 2014).

Early years

Robert King Merton was born Meyer Schkolnick in his family home on 4 July 1910 (although recorded as 5 July) in Philadelphia, Pennsylvania. (*Schk* means 'schoolboy' in Russian.) Since this was Independence Day, he was a 'Yankee-doodle' baby. To reinforce this coincidental patriotic timing, his birthplace was a few city blocks from Independence Square. Robert was the second of two children, with Emma 11 years older. His parents were Jewish immigrants from Eastern Europe arriving in 1904, possibly from Lviv in the Ukrainian–Polish border region. His parents' migration was part of several million migrating to the USA in that period, hastened by pogroms. This area was part of the 'Pale of Settlement' of

25 provinces in central Europe where Jews could settle. The Pale was a cultural mix of traditional and modern. His mother was Ida Rasovskaya and father Aaron Schkolnickoff (named as Hebrew tailor Harrie Skolnic at port of entry). His father scraped a living variously as a carpenter, truck driver and shop proprietor in the respectable slums of South Philadelphia. They lived above a milk-butter-and-egg shop in ample six-room quarters. However, it burned down some years later and, without insurance, family living standards deteriorated while his father obtained a carpenter's job in the naval yard. The area was an ethnic mix of Irish, Italians and Russians. Being close to the centre of the city, major cultural and political institutions were within easy reach: a Carnegie library, orchestral concerts etc.

Merton's parents were Yiddish-speaking and kept Jewish dietary restrictions, but spoke in English with their son, who never had a bar mitzvah. His mother was an avid reader and held anarchist political views. She was solidly Americanising, attending night school regularly but not so much the synagogue (as with many Jewish women). His father was distant. In his youth, Merton built radio sets and often thereafter kept in touch with world news by radio. He extensively used the nearby Carnegie library from an early age when he was able to walk there, was 'adopted' by women librarians, and took advantage of the better lighting provided there than the gas illumination in his home. His boyhood interests lay in literature, social criticism and history, especially biographies and autobiographies. A favourite was Laurence Sterne's *Tristram Shandy* [*The Life and Opinions of Tristram Shandy, Gentleman*] – which was also resorted to in later life in order to repair bouts of melancholy. (Sterne is famous for his 'nonlinear divagating' writing style.) Other favourites were Ibsen, G.B. Shaw, Baudelaire and Flaubert. This immersion in books included consultation with dictionaries driven by a lifelong fascination with words. He attended orchestra performances and otherwise participated in local intellectual life. Merton sold papers outside Town Hall and took part in the street fights of his neighbourhood as a member of a juvenile gang. At Philadelphia High school Merton studied Latin, French, physics, chemistry and mathematics. He did well in secondary school, delivering the valedictory address 'Appreciation of school endeavour' when he and his class graduated.

Hop (Charles Hopkins) lived in the attached dwelling on the other side of Merton's home and in marrying Emma also became a proxy father to Merton. He also mediated Merton's way toward "scepticism, typewriting, speed and travel", each of which were constants in his life (Simpson, 2010: 131). Hop had mice and rabbits and was a juggler who coached Merton. At 12 he became an amateur magician performing for money at neighbourhood social functions. By 14 he had become adept enough to earn the financial support needed while studying. Learning that the names of performers were often Americanised, he became 'Robert K. Merlin' (not legally) and then (since that was seen as rather hackneyed) legally 'Robert King Merton' with his parents' assent. Arguably, Merton also refashioned his identity as a WASP over this period (Cullen & Messner, 2007).

Merton attended local Temple College which was a school founded for "the poor boys and girls of Philadelphia" which although not yet fully accredited, provided high-quality education. In his freshman year Merton majored in philosophy and became a protégé of James Dunham, the dean of Temple and a professor of philosophy. But he switched to sociology in his sophomore year, after he had taken an introductory course from a young and enthusiastic instructor, George E. Simpson (not to be confused with Brooklyn College's George Simpson, translator of Weber and later co-author with Adorno). Merton had wandered into a sociology class and was hooked. Simpson became a close friend. Temple provided Merton with a good sociological grounding, including in social psychology. Merton was the research assistant on Simpson's *The Negro in Philadelphia Press* (1936), providing a content analysis of references to Negroes over several decades to gauge changes in public imagery, together with some contributions towards the text. He later recalled that his dedication to sociology intensified when he experienced "the joy of discovering that it was possible to examine human behaviour objectively and without using loaded moral preconceptions". Under Simpson's auspices Merton also was linked into networks with black Philadelphia professionals such as political scientist and diplomat Ralph Bunche and sociologist (of families) E. Franklin Frazier. As founder and chair of the Sociology club Merton engaged with various invitees.

One of Merton's excursions (with Simpson) was to the annual meetings of the American Sociological Society (ASS) where he met Pitirim Sorokin (then newly appointed to Harvard), and as a result he applied for graduate study there. Sorokin's erudition was the hook. "I knew just about everything American sociology had to offer in the late 1920s", but only a superficial knowledge of European sociology. He saw the 1921 textbook treatise *Introduction to The Science of Sociology* by Park and Burgess as consolidating concepts about social processes, and in so doing incorporating much material from European sociology (1964: 214). But Sorokin was to expand Merton's knowledge of sociology.

Merton's early years in Philadelphia provided a solid platform for many strands of his later work. As he later recalled, his "Philadelphia slum provided a youngster with every sort of capital: social capital, cultural capital, human capital, and, above all, what we may call public capital that is, with every sort of capital except the personally financial" (1994). Onto this Merton had built a workable identity, particularly as a sociologist, and with research and writing skills. There were deeper learnings as well. The central puzzle of the relationship between order on the one hand and chance and chaos on the other pressed itself on him, perhaps somewhat unconsciously. The intrigue of *Tristram Shandy* was its presentation of the flurries of contingencies and diversions which complicated any underlying patterns. His experience as a prestidigitator led to lifelong presentational skills in summoning appearances which hid the underlying complexities in producing them. These two learnings constantly recurred through his career.

Various adventures punctuated his youth (Simonson, 2010). There was a trip with Hop to Massachusetts one summer to sell a new kind of phone directory, and a hitchhiking trip west when aged 14 staying for free in jails or with accommodating strangers. There were romantic liaisons as well. Merton met with Suzanne Carhart from a nearby fishing village, but from higher status ancestry: they were to marry in 1934. As a young adult Merton then abandoned Philadelphia for the wider field of Cambridge.

Phases of intellectual career: guide to chapters

Merton's research and writing programme can, at least for the purpose of exposition, be divided into some five phases, which *approximate* to the various decades of his academic working life – the 1930s, 1940s/1950s, 1950s–1970s, 1980-plus (and to his own age periods – his 20s, 30s/40s, 40s–60s and 70-plus). The periods cover Merton's youth, Harvard studies, and three periods of work while at Columbia University or as emeritus. However, as with any such schema, this is approximate, undermined by much work falling across several periods, and is used only to provide a general framework for understanding the progression of his interests, and the relationships amongst its various phases. Indeed, Merton's lifelong habit of returning to topics and reworking aspects militates against any sharply demarcated periodisation schema.

Merton's main interests have lain in social theory and the sociology of science and knowledge, but subsidiary interests also covered the sociological areas of deviance, ethnic relations, social research methodology, urban sociology, mass communications, professions, medical sociology, complex organisations, and the

TABLE 1.1 Phases of Merton's intellectual biography

Field of study	Phase				
	I	*II*	*III*	*IV*	*V*
	(1930s)	*(1940s)*	*(1950s/60s)*	*(1960s/80s)*	*(1980s–)*
Theory	xx	xx	xx	xx	xx
Science	xx	x	x	xx	xx
S. semantics			xx		xx
Knowledge	x	xx		x	x
Methods	x	xx	x		
Deviance	xx	x	x	x	
Ethnic relations	x	x			
Urban		x			
Mass communications		x			
Professions		xx	x	x	
Medical			xx	x	
Organisations		x	x		
S. of social research		x	x	x	

Key:
xx = major concentration
x = some work

sociology of (applied) social research, including relationships with policymakers. The summative diagram (see Table 1.1) indicates periods of concentration across this array. The next few chapters each covers one of these periods.

Conclusion

This chapter has briefly introduced Merton and this book, toured some of the rationale for developing a reintroduction to his work, and the key sources needed to accomplish this. The more formal parameters of Merton's career are presented, followed by discussions of sources of information on his life and his early days. The final section provides a brief overview of how some of the research areas in Merton's career map out onto the periods of his life and hence the chapters. Most of the following chapters describe and comment on a 'decade' or so of Merton's work across his long career, and the final two chapters pull together the lessons learned that are the core of reintroducing his work.

References

Adler, Freda & William S. Laufer (eds) (1998) *The Legacy of Anomie Theory*. New Brunswick, NJ: Transaction Publishers.

Bierstedt, Robert (1981) Robert K. Merton. *American Sociological Theory: A Critical History*. New York: Academic Press: 443–489.

Blau, Peter (1990) Structural Constraints and Opportunities: Merton's Contributions to General Theory. In J. Clark, C. Modgil & S. Modgil (eds) *Robert K. Merton: Consensus and Controversy*. London, New York & Philadelphia, PA: Falmer Press: 141–155.

Calhoun, Craig (ed.) (2010) *Robert K. Merton Sociology of Science and Sociology as Science*. New York: Columbia University Press.

Calhoun, Craig et al. (2003) Robert K. Merton Remembered. ASA Footnotes: www.asanet.org)sites)default)files)savvy)footnotes)mar03)indextwo.html

Caplovitz, David (1977) Robert K. Merton as Editor: Review Essay. *Contemporary Sociology*, 6: 142–150.

Clark, Jon (ed.) (1990) *Robert K. Merton: Consensus and Controversy*. London, New York & Philadelphia, PA: The Falmer Press, Taylor & Francis.

Clinard, Marshall B. (ed.) (1964) *Anomie and Deviant Behavior: A Discussion and Critique*. New York: The Free Press.

Cohen, I. Bernard (ed.) (1990) *Puritanism and the Rise of Modern Science: The Merton Thesis*. New Brunswick, NJ: Rutgers University Press.

Cohen, Patricia (1998) An Eye for Patterns in the Social Fabric; Patriarch of Sociology Sees His Insights Become Just What Everyone Knows. *The New York Times*, Section B: 9.

Collins, Randall (1997) Review of *On Social Structure and Science* by Robert K. Merton. Piotr Sztompka (ed.). *American Journal of Sociology*, 103 (1): 275–278.

Collins, Randall (1977) Reviewed Work: The Idea of Social Structure: Papers in Honor of Robert K. Merton. Lewis A. Coser (ed.) *Contemporary Sociology*, 6 (2): 150–154.

Coser, Lewis A. (ed.) (1975) *The Idea of Social Structure*. New York: Harcourt Brace Jovanovich.

Crothers, Charles (2019) Recent Writings on Robert K. Merton: A Listing and Some Observations. *The American Sociologist*, 50 (1): 121–135.

Crothers, Charles (2011) Robert K. Merton. In George Ritzer & Jeffrey Stepnisky (eds) *The Wiley-Blackwell Companion to Major Social Theorists*. Malden, MA: Wiley-Blackwell.

Crothers, Charles (1989[1997]) Sztompka's Analysis of Merton's Writings: A Description and Some Criticisms. In Carlo Mongardini & Simonetta Tabboni (eds): 299–306.

Crothers, Charles (1987) *Robert K. Merton: A Key Sociologist*. London & New York: Tavistock Publications.

Cullen, Francis & Steven Messner (2007) The Making of Criminology Revisited. *Theoretical Criminology*, 11 (1): 5–37.

Dubois, Michel (2014) From Discovery to Invention: Sociological Study of Academic Correspondence. *Revue européenne des sciences sociales*, 2 (2): 7–42.

Elkana, Yehuda; András Szigeti & György Lissauer (eds) (2011) *Concepts and the Social Order: Robert K. Merton and the Future of Sociology*. Budapest & New York: Central European University Press.

Epstein, Cynthia; William J. Goode, Melvin Kohn, David Sills, Neil Smelser, Charles Tilly, Duncan Watts, Harrison White, & J. Milton Yinger (2010) Robert K. Merton at 100: Reflections and Recollections: www.youtube.com)watch?v=XBpI_xrWsTQ

Garfield, Eugene (nd) www.garfield.library.upenn.edu/merton/list.html

Gieryn, Thomas F. (ed.) (1980) *Science and Social Structure: A Festschrift for Robert K. Merton*. New York: The New York Academy of Sciences.

Merton, R.K. (1994) A Life of Learning: Charles Homer Haskins Lecture. *American Council of Learned Societies*. Occasional Paper 25.

Merton, R.K. (1982) *Social Research and the Practicing Professions*. Cambridge: Abt Books.

Merton, R.K. (1976) *Sociological Ambivalence and Other Essays*. New York: Free Press.

Merton, R.K. (1973) *The Sociology of Science: Theoretical and Empirical Investigations*. Norman Storer (ed.). Chicago, IL: The University of Chicago Press.

Merton, R.K. (1964) Anomie, Anomia and Social Interaction: Contexts of Deviant Behavior. In Marshall Clinard (ed.) *Anomie and Deviant Behavior*. New York: The Free Press: 213–242.

Merton, R.K. (1949[1957/1968]) *Social Theory and Social Structure*. New York: Free Press.

Mica, Adriana; Arkadiusz Peisert & Jan Winczorek (eds) (2011) *Sociology and the Unintended*. Frankfurt am Main: Peter Lang.

Mongardini, Carlo & Simonetta Tabboni (eds) (1989/1998) *L'Opera di Robert K. Merton e la sociologia contemporanea*. Genoa: ECIG [English translation: *Merton and Contemporary Sociology*. New Brunswick, NJ: Transaction Publishers].

Passas, Nikos & Robert Agnew (eds) (1997) *The Future of Anomie Theory*. Boston, MA: Northeastern University Press.

Persell, Caroline (1984) An Interview with Robert K. Merton. *Teaching Sociology*, 11: 355–386.

Poros, Maritsa & Elizabeth Needham (2004) Writings of Robert K. Merton. *Social Studies of Science*, 34 (6): 863–878.

Schultz, Ruth (1995) The Improbable Adventures of an American Scholar: Robert K. Merton. *American Sociologist*, 26 (3): 68–77.

Sica, Alan (2007) Robert K Merton. in Rob Stones (ed.) *Key Sociological Thinkers*. London: MacMillan.

Simonson, Peter (2010) Merton's Skeptical Faith. *Refiguring Mass Communication: A History*. Urbana, IL: University of Illinois Press: 123–162.

Simonson, Peter (2006) Celebrity, Public Image, and American Political Life: Rereading Robert K. Merton's Mass Persuasion. *Political Communication*, 23 (3): 271–284.

Simonson, Peter (2004) Introduction. In R.K. Merton (ed.) *Mass Persuasion: The Social Psychology of a War Bond Drive*. New York: Howard Fertig.

Stinchcombe, Arthur (1975) Merton's Theory of Social Structure. In L. Coser (ed.) *The Idea of Social Structure*. New York: Harcourt Brace Jovanovich: 11–34.

Stinchcombe, Arthur (1968) *Constructing Social Theories*. New York: Harcourt Brace Jovanovich.

Sztompka, Piotr (2017) Robert K. Merton. In Bob Stones (ed.) *Key Thinkers in Sociological Theory* (3rd edn). Basingstoke & New York: Palgrave Macmillan.

Sztompka, Piotr (1986) *Robert K. Merton: An Intellectual Profile*. London & New York: Macmillan & St. Martin's Press.

Taylor, Bryan; Paul Walton, Jock Young (1973) *The New Criminology For a Social Theory of Deviance*. London: Routledge

Zuckerman, Harriet (2011) The Matthew Effect Writ Large and Larger: A Study in Sociological Semantics in Elkana et al. (eds) *Concepts and the Social Order: Robert K. Merton and the Future of Sociology*. Budapest & New York: Central European University Press: 121–164.

Zuckerman, Harriet et al. (2010) Robert K. Merton at 100: Reflections and Recollections: www.youtube.com)watch?v=XBpI_xrWsTQ

2

'1930S: THE HARVARD YEARS' (*JUGENDSCHRIFTEN*)

Personal

After Merton received his BA degree from Temple College in 1931, he was awarded a fellowship for graduate work at Harvard to work with Sorokin (at that stage Talcott Parsons was an unknown junior staff member). The array of distinguished Harvard professors there who influenced his work included Talcott Parsons, George Sarton, Pitirim Sorokin, L.J. Henderson and several outside of Sociology. The campus provided a rich environment for learning sociology. Merton worked at Harvard as a student, tutor and lecturer before completing the decade with a two-year stint in New Orleans at Tulane University, when hiring at Harvard ceased. While there is much written material on Merton's period at Harvard, Nichols (2010) correctly portrays this as Merton's 'less noticed' decade, compared to the extensiveness of treatments on other periods of Merton's career.

The Harvard environment at that time was anti-Semitic (e.g. Karabel, 2006), with quotas being imposed against 'too many' Jews applying: Merton's name change largely shielded him from such concerns. Even so, life was not easy. His stipend was low, leading to a need to subsist on a diet of sandwiches, milkshakes and his own manufactured whiskey. Later, more university money was forthcoming which enabled him to stay on. On the other hand, he had enough money to be able to snare a copy of the entire 1933 13-volume *Oxford English Dictionary* (*OED*) offered at Depression-era bargain prices (see Merton & Barber, 2004: 242). This provided a privately owned tool (together with an expanding array of dictionaries) often employed by Merton through the years.

The fortunate side of the necessity for obtaining summer work was the extension of Merton's research skills. In 1935, under the auspices of the Harvard Professors' Committee on Unemployment, an analysis of follow-up records on the graduates of Boston high schools was begun. The purpose was to study relationships between selected background factors and the graduates' economic status during the first year after graduation, with approximately 25,000 students studied ... from 1916 for boys and 1920 for girls to 1934, from 14 Boston High Schools.

(Merton, 1944a, 1944b)

Grants were obtained from the National Youth Administration and the Harvard Committee on Research in the Social Sciences. Merton also carried out Harvard fieldwork amongst the homeless of Boston, and several laborious library projects for Sorokin developing long-term quantitative indicators of changes in science, technology and medicine (Merton et al., 1977: 24, 25), which were then included as a chapter in Sorokin's book that Merton co-authored (1937b).

Harvard experience: student and thesis student

Harvard offered various learning opportunities, both within sociology and outside. Merton saw this period at Harvard as a 'golden age' for sociology. The University President (Abbott Lawrence Lowell) had dissolved a famous Department of Social Ethics (although the teachers remained) and set up a new Sociology department, although with only four tenured members it was supplemented by other authorities ('interdepartmental staff') on the campus who had appropriate knowledge (Persell, 1984).

Nichols (2010) summarises several paradigms as locally dominant:

• the 'integralistic' perspective of Sorokin and Zimmerman;
• the 'social action' approach of Parsons;
• the behavioristic, social-psychological functionalism articulated by Henderson;
• the melioristic 'social problems and social policy' approach of the former Department of Social Ethics (carried on by Cabot, Ford, and Sheldon and Eleanor Glueck).

Merton drew on all, although each was not equally important. The preface to *STSS* notes the varying effects of several in this group:

> Before he became absorbed in the study of historical movements on the grand scale as represented in his *Social and Cultural Dynamics*, Pitirim A. Sorokin helped me escape from the provincialism of thinking that effective studies of society were confined within American borders and from the slum en-couraged provincialism of thinking that the primary subject-matter of sociology was centred in such peripheral problems of social life as divorce and juvenile delinquency.

(1968: xiii)

Both Sorokin and Zimmerman were members of Merton's thesis committee, and he thanked them in his thesis preface:

> I am grateful to Professor Carle C. Zimmerman for suggesting improvements in presentation and expression … Above all, my thanks are due to Professor Pitirim A. Sorokin, who, considerately placing at my disposal his as yet unpublished researches, did most to direct my studies toward salient problems. It is to the stimulation of his writings and to his unfailing assistance throughout four years that I owe whatever is of merit in this study.
>
> *(Merton, 1936b, cited by Nichols, 2010)*

Sarton's assistance included providing the practicalities of a desk in his outer office (Harvard Library 189), with access to its multiple research resources as well as providing guidance, support and friendship (See Merton, 1985). He also offered Merton publishing experiences as an editor and reviewer. Merton worked with Sorokin for several years, in various capacities as teaching assistant, research assistant and co-author.

An on-campus scholarly group was the conservatively inclined 'Pareto Circle' (see Heyl, 1968) led by Lawrence Henderson. The three major positions in the circle's common reading of Pareto were:

(1) all social sciences needed a top-down methodology;
(2) the Paretan notion of general equilibrium had to be given a central role in any analysis of complex systems;
(3) the Paretan notion of general equilibrium had to be used to combat 'cause-and-effect' reasoning.

Merton attended, but apparently did not present material in, this seminar but this interest in Pareto's thought is undoubtedly reflected in his career-long interest in the theme of 'non-logical' or non-rational aspects of human action and his concerns with conceptual schema and functionalism. Moreover, he wrote publicly in reviews to welcome (with some nonchalance) books produced from members of the circle on Pareto's thought (such as Homans and Curtis' book on Pareto), rebutting the hagiographic tone of some of this writing.

Merton also belonged to "Talcott Parsons's sociological group" (Simonson, 2005) which explored theoretical issues. Clearly some of the ideas raised in this group affected its members. (For example, Merton and Kingsley Davis corresponded off and on during the late 1930s and after on a possible functional analysis collaboration: e.g. see Merton, 1976: 245.) Indeed, Merton went to Penn State in 1938 for a summer session (during which he taught) in order to explore this with Davis who had just been hired there as chair of the department of sociology, whose interest in functionalism had developed under the influence of W. Lloyd Warner. Merton provided extensive comments on drafts of Parsons's soon-to-be-famous *The Structure of Social Action* (1937).

Merton later recollected (1994) that most of his graduate education was out-side the field of sociology, narrowly conceived: auditing courses in economic history (with Edwin Gay), history of science (with George Sarton), philosophy (A.N. Whitehead), economics (Joseph Schumpeter), constitutionalism (Charles McIlwain), biology (William Wheeler), comparative religion (Arthur Nock), anthropology (Earnest Hooton and Alfred Tozer), and English Literature (George Kittredge). Influences were further extended through a roster of summer lecturers (some full-year), who would teach one or two courses. These included Robert Park and William Thomas (of 'Thomas theorem' fame), from whom Merton obtained the concept of the 'definition of the situation'.

Finally, although it was a one-off event, the 1936 Harvard Tercentenary was truly international (Elliott, 1999), with delegates sent by some 160 foreign universities and learned societies worldwide, together with over 3,200 from the USA. Merton was assigned the task of escorting Italian economist and sociologist Corrado Gini, learning written Italian very rapidly, and translating classroom material for Gini's teaching. This led to an ongoing correspondence after the conference (Santoro, 2017), although Merton seemed little affected by Gini's ideas.

Teaching at Harvard

Merton was Sorokin's teaching (and research) assistant for several years and also taught several classes in the period 1937–1939 as an instructor, which were seedbeds for later publications.

> The first major course I gave, as a youngish instructor at Harvard back in 1937, was entitled 'Social Organization'. … what became the 'Analysis of Social Structure' … In the first year or two of teaching, I had remark-able students. Harvard had intermediate courses wisely arranged to include undergraduates and graduates.
>
> *(from Nichols, 2010)*

This was taught by Merton to 33 students with the prospectus reading:

> This course will deal with social status, roles, relationships, differentiation and stratification and with the patterns of their integration into the total struc-ture of society. Particular attention will be paid to the relations of leadership, social norms, sentiments and interests to organized systems of social action, including social planning. Variations in the type and extent of organized social control during periods of social disturbance and stability as well as the bases of compatibility and conflict between various phases of the social structure will be studied. Finally, a series of concrete social structures will be systematically analyzed in terms of the conceptual framework developed in the course. As a whole the course attempts to constitute a morphology of human society.
>
> *(from Nichols, 2010)*

In 1939 Merton taught 17 students (including two graduate students) a course on racial relations:

> This course deals with the socio-psychological background of minority racial groups, particularly in the United States. The chief aim is to analyze the descriptive materials in terms of sociological theory. The development of the social attitudes sustaining the caste and class structure and the interplay of economic and social forces in successive patterns of race relations will be traced in detail. Special attention will be paid to problems of social control and organization which arise when groups with different racial and cultural backgrounds come into continued contact. Finally, the processes of conflict, competition and accommodation and their connections with the institutional life of minority groups will also be considered.
>
> *(from Nichols, 2010)*

He also began to teach two undergraduate offerings, Sociology 4, 'Social Organization and Structure', and Sociology 17, 'Race Relations and Culture Contact'.

The first-mentioned course shows clearly themes developed in later work, while the second illuminates an area of Merton's work not otherwise made explicit through more than a few publications (e.g. Merton 1940, 1941).

Research at Harvard

During the 1930s Merton produced three powerful research contributions on:

- the historical sociology of science;
- anomie;
- unintended effects.

Another essay on cultural patterning of Time (1937a) was co-written with Sorokin, and an essay on Sociology of Knowledge (see Chapter 3) was penned. Merton also wrote many book reviews, many as sociology associate editor to Sarton's journal *Isis*. Merton's position against "biological determinism" (still rife in public discourse at that period) was made clear in Merton and Montague (1940) – a detailed, critical and methodological analysis of two books authored by the Harvard criminologist E.A. Hooton on racial characteristics. Merton also wrote (1936b) a comparison of Albert Weber's notion of the two sides of development – civilisation (intellectual and technological) compared with culture (art, religion and philosophy) – each with its own dynamics.

Merton's earliest papers, and some later work in this period involved commentary (Explications de Texte) on existing literature. Sorokin provided an early publishing opportunity by inviting Merton to give a conference paper at the Eastern Sociological Society (since he had committed to presenting a paper he then couldn't provide) on French sociology. So, Merton became involved in intensive reading of European sociology, including the systematic scouring of the literature of French sociology which he wrote up in his first publication (Merton, 1934a). This review covered 46 books and 16 articles with the discussion organised around the various schools in French sociology and their concerns with primitive versus modern mentalities and between individual and social levels of explanation. This essay led to the editor of the *American Journal of Sociology* asking Merton to comment on the recently published translation of Durkheim's *Division of Labor* (1933). Coming to grips with Durkheim's work (1934b) was a valuable lesson as his perspective became vital for Merton. The review comments particularly on the positivist approach and applauded Durkheim's use of indexes to link theory and empirical reality, but deplores the quality of the translation.

Merton's contributions to (historical) sociology of science

Merton's main work, particularly for his dissertation, in the earlier part of his time in Harvard was in what was to become the historical sociology of science, looking particularly at the various interactions between society and the development of scientific work. His interest in sociology of science developed in a Harvard intellectual atmosphere in which a variety of scholars (including E.F. Gay, economic historian; George Sarton, historian of science; L.J. Henderson, biochemist, historian of science and social systems analyst; Alfred North Whitehead, philosopher of science; William Morton Wheeler, comparative animal sociologist; and E.B. Wilson, polymath) were concerned with interconnections between science, its history and intellectual linkages with the social sciences. In particular, Pitirim Sorokin was working up his *Social and Cultural Dynamics* assisted by Merton's research work looking at the development patterns of various sciences. Sarton was single-handedly building the sub-discipline of the history of science. Merton's involvement in his thesis on the rise of science in seventeenth-century England was so intense he talked after of living for some years in seventeenth-century England. The abstract (below) describes the thesis:

> *Dissertation Abstracts*: The rate and direction of scientific development are influenced by sociological factors as well as by the immanent logic of science … [T]his inquiry is oriented toward a threefold objective: the determination of the social factors which influence (1) the degree of interest in science generally, (2) shifts of interest between the several sciences and (3) the foci of interest within each science.
>
> *(Harvard University, 1932–1941: 445–446; from Nichols, 2010)*

Merton engaged several locally dominant paradigms (see above) to produce his own synthesis of selected elements. The dissertation's *problem statement* clearly reflects the social change emphasis of the integralistic Sorokin–Zimmerman approach, as well as the focus of Sorokin's major work, *Social and Cultural Dynamics*, on historical fluctuations of culture mentalities.

Merton is at pains to point out that the two thrusts of his argument are held together with an overall concern to analyse the interdependence between science as a social institution and other areas of society. He endeavours to overcome the myths that scientists operate as creative individuals unaffected by collectivities and that religion and science are at extreme odds. He also differentiates amongst social processes active in each of several different stages in scientific inquiry – problem selection, discovery, confirmation. The first line of argument was an 'outrageous hypothesis' garnered from the data, but subsequently supported in Weber's writings (there was one sentence Weber wrote on this: 365), that not only was the impetus to the development of science generated from outside scholarly institutions but was in fact located in the religious sphere – that erstwhile enemy of science. Moreover, within the religious spectrum of the time, Merton sought to show that it was from the otherwise unlikely dour and theologically encumbered Puritan/Pietist sects that this impetus had specifically sprung See Merton, 1936c).

The second line of analysis is rather more straightforward, although of equally high sociological relevance: it is an attempt to empirically specify the extent to which Marxian analyses of the dependence of science on dominant social and economic interests – at least in terms of foci of interest – seemed to be correct (in fact, Merton was able to document a major impact) although distancing himself from "vulgar materialist" interpretations. The practical topics of interest to English scientists in carrying out their experiments included (Merton, in Cohen, 1990: 315):

- enabling mines to be workable at increasing depths;
- supporting Mariners to sail safely to ever more far-off places;
- developing ever more efficient and inexpensive ways of killing the enemy;
- providing a form of mental discipline;
- enlarging and deepening the collective self-esteem of Englishmen [sic] as they advanced their claims to priority.

A further concern about the internal social organisation of science was barely emergent at this point. On the methods side, Merton's doctoral work involved quantitative analyses of shifts in the foci of scientific interests coding a couple of thousand articles in the *Royal Society* journal, and shifts in the occupational interests of the English elite which involved hand-tabulating 6,000 biographies, and the several hundreds of experiments recorded in the *Transactions of the Royal Society*. These studies involved content analysis and what became 'prosopography' (i.e. collective biography), both research procedures that Merton usefully helped transfer into the sociology of science.

Merton's PhD. was written during 1933–1935. Cohen (1990) has a long account of the vicissitudes in publishing the thesis. Sarton offered to publish it in his monograph series *Osiris*, and the reworked doctoral work was published soon after (1938a). The print run being held up in war-tossed Europe had a disruptive effect. But, it remained trapped in the specialist history of science literature where the impact was (eventually) great (cf. Cohen, 1990) – but not even obtaining a review in the *American Journal of Sociology* until some 30 years later and having almost no general impact within sociology, let alone historical sociology when it revived from the 1970s.

By the late 1930s, Merton began to add to his analyses of the impacts of non-science institutions on scientific work and scientists' motivation, an appreciation of science as a social institution in its own right. This began as part of an essay reacting to the threatening loss of autonomy of German science in the Nazi era by attempting to analyse the cultural conditions which support scientific work (1938b). In this analysis it was pointed out that the norms stressing the purity of science have the functional consequence of the furnishing of an ideological defence useful to protect science from incursions of other interests. On the other hand, given the economic and social consequences of scientific inventions, claims of scientific autonomy can be seen as overreaching. Another value of science is 'organised scepticism' which, when directed at values held in other institutional spheres, can seem a threat. In 1942 this conceptualisation of science as a social institution was extended with a fuller statement of the 'ethos of science' – the *moral norms* of universalism, communism, organised scepticism and disinterestedness that were seen to shape the social practice of science, alongside such socially supported *technical norms* as the need to provide both adequate, valid and reliable empirical evidence and the need for logical consistency. These norms were seen to be the social integument which allowed the implementation of the technical methods needed to achieve the institutional goal of the extension of certified knowledge. With this analysis, Merton had shifted his attention from the external social conditions which influence the development of science, to an analysis of the internal structure of science. Storer (1973) argues that this conceptualisation of science was theoretically significant, although not widely recognised as such at the time, and that it informed Merton's later theoretical work on the social organisation of science.

The ethos of science is that affectively toned complex of values and norms which is held to be binding on the man of science. The norms are expressed in the form of prescriptions, proscription and permissions. These are legitimatized in terms of institutional values. These *imperatives*, transmitted by precept and example and reenforced [sic] by sanctions, are in varying degrees internalized by the scientist. … Although the ethos of science has not been codified, it can be inferred from the moral consensus of scientists as expressed in use and wont, in countless writings on the 'scientific spirit' and in moral indignation directed toward contraventions of the ethos.

(Merton, 1942: 116–117)

From the mid-1930s Merton was also concerned to establish the foundations of a systematic sociology of science by securing the properly couched problematics of the area and by attention to its methodology: thus his 1938 essay on 'science and the social order' raises questions on a particularly sociological plane, while (as Storer in Merton, 1973, xviii notes) "his early (1935) paper with Sorokin, 'The Course of Arabian Intellectual Development, 700–1300 A.D.' is subtitled 'A Study in Method'".

Merton's work on the historical flowering of science in the seventeenth century has led to a complicated and vigorous debate within the history and historical sociology of science. This long debate has been marred by much misunderstanding arising over the specification of the concepts and terms involved (see Abraham, 1983) and has also involved much inch-by-inch trench warfare (see Becker's several re-examinations of data and the compilation in the appendix of Merton, 1984). Since the significance of the debate is very largely about matters of fact rather than forms of explanation, a detailed tour of the distant site over which the din of subsequent battles has been raised is unnecessary here. It may be sufficient to take haven in the magisterial re-specification of the 'Merton thesis' offered by Thomas Kuhn. Kuhn reconceptualises the 'Puritan/Pietist' label by substituting a broader, and more internalist term, 'Baconian ideology', which refers to an approach in science which stresses empirical research.

He then distinguishes between the transformation in conceptual development during the sixteenth and seventeenth centuries of the university-based classic branches of science (astronomy, mathematics, mechanics and optics) and the craft-based, experimentally orientated new branches of science (electricity and magnetism, chemistry, thermal phenomena) which were "pursued by amateurs loosely clustered around the new scientific societies that were the institutional manifestation of the Scientific Revolution" (Kuhn, 1977: 118). This second grouping was strongly influenced by the Baconian programme, and although of minor scientific impact during the seventeenth century, this grouping of scientific fields was, in subsequent centuries, of critical importance in the development of science. Another possible specification that assists in rescuing Merton's thesis is to suggest that the type of settlement location had a considerable influence on the development of science (Ben-David, 1971: 71–74).

Merton's contributions to the sociology of deviance (SSOA)

Merton's contributions to the sociology of deviance are sparse, episodic but highly impactful. Indeed, it consists of one article published in the late 1930s (1936c), reworked in the late 1940s, together with a few elaborations and comments added in the late 1950s and early 1960s, reprised finally in 1997. (The issue of deviance is also bruited in his sociology of science.) The almost-full weight is borne by this one early article, as his later extensions very usefully round out the perspective, and reach out to other perspectives, but the main structure of the argument is retained. Cole (1975: 185) suggests:

It would be an error to see the theory of SSOA as a single paper. The theory is in fact a research program which Merton developed over a thirty-year period. If one compares the initial 1938 paper with a more recent statement such as the Merton essay in the Clinard collection, one can easily see that the theory has been added to and modified. It has been a dynamic rather than a static theory, developing in response to its environment.

It should be noted that Merton draws attention to the extended version by referring to it as "anomie-and-opportunity-structure theory". Perhaps what is most surprising is that although 'Social Structure and Anomie' is arguably the most cited article in sociology, its empirical backing is sketchy, and has never been flanked by empirical work from Merton himself (although he proposed an extensive 'design of inquiry' in his 1964 essay). As a theorist Merton saw that this contribution sufficed.

The theory has two parts, as recent commentators (e.g. Deflem, 2018) emphasise. More generally, there is a comparativist argument that there are some societies in which particular goals are emphasised. In his case study, the USA is seen as a society in which monetary or material success is given a major cultural value. (It is arguable whether 'success' precisely means income, wealth, educational or career success: all are interrelated.) This value directs Americans' attention to seeking *individual* success. In many other societies long-term social sustainability seems sufficient and the difficulties of the American situation therefore don't arise, or arises to a lesser extent. But of course, many modern societies include some drive to economic success, making Merton's theory widely potentially applicable. In such societies there is an imbalance between the (great) emphasis on outcomes and the (lesser) emphasis on the means for (legitimately) achieving them and also lesser emphasis on alternative non-materialistic values. There is less approbation of illicit means for gaining success and less support for those who are disadvantaged.

The second part of Merton's theory concerns the explanation of different rates of deviance by the differential location of people in relation to their (their position's) particular 'opportunity-structure'. Because of socially structured gaps between aspirations (shared goals) and capacity for achievement (access to the social means for achieving) of those goals, the power of the dominant social norms (which operationalise the cultural goals) to control some key areas of social behaviour breaks down and 'anomie' ('normless-ness') irrupts into the social system.

Although this is intended as a general theory, applicable across a range of historical conditions, it is dressed in the form of concrete analysis of the consequences of the 'American Dream' success goal. This is seen as providing the commonly held aspirations which are held out as appropriate and realistic for all participants in the system. It is held that the very overall material success of American life ironically, and cruelly, creates despair and deviance for many within it. Indeed, it is argued that when the social conditions underlying anomie are examined, that the particular emphasis in America on propagating goals without similar attention to ensuring the means of obtaining those goals means that American society is historically and cross-culturally one of the sites most ripe for producing structural strain. "A cardinal American virtue, 'ambition,' promotes a cardinal American vice, 'deviant behavior'" (Merton, 1968: 200). Merton documents the prevalence of the dominant American cultural goals, and then provides an acerbic and penetrating critique. He points out:

- the extent to which money is fetishized as a sign of success, and
- the way in which the dominant ideology deflects any criticism of the social structure back into blaming the unsuccessful victims.

Differential rates of deviance between people in different social locations are seen to be the results of different motivations and access to means, with these in turn being generated by these locations. The opportunity-structure relates to several alternative social positions which vary in terms of their access to the means for achieving these goals. These positions are organised in three groupings – conforming, aberrant and nonconforming – which in detail (see Table 2.1) involves:

- conformists (accepting both goals and means);
- innovators (accepting the goal but rejecting – or not having access to the socially approved means);
- ritualists (rejecting the goal but continuing adherence to the means)
- retreatists (rejecting both goals and means); and
- rebels (rejecting both goals and means and substituting new versions of both).

Rebels are clearly separated from the other forms of deviant behaviour as nonconforming rather than merely aberrant. Using this framework, Merton then is able to portray many Americans as plodding conformists, hollow ritualists, desolate retreatists, desperate innovators or creative rebels. A major form of innovation is criminal activity. A further development of the theory asserts linkages between particular social strata and rates (probabilities) of one or other of the five likely outcomes. Only two linkages are indicated: ritualism *is* seen as more frequent amongst the lower-middle class, whereas innovation *is* seen as more frequent amongst the working class.

TABLE 2.1 Modes of adaptation

Type	Modes of adaptation	Cultural goals	Institutionalized means
1	Conformity	+	+
2	Innovation	+	−
3	Ritualism	−	+
4	Retreatism	−	−
5	Rebellion	±	±

Note: ± = reject and replace.

The provenance of Merton's interest in deviance is largely unknown. In later comments (1964: 215: see also Cullen & Messner, 2007), Merton *is* content to laconically observe that "It was in this local climate of sociological theory, induced by Sorokin and Parsons, that I found myself focusing on the theoretical problems of the master sources of *anomie*". Given the focus on conformity of the functional analysis he was beginning to adopt, this was an attempt to also explore its flip side of change and deviance, while still retaining the explanation of conformity. The provenance of the basic idea involved is rather more obvious. As Cole points out (1975: 187), that although "perhaps the most significant influence on Merton's work was Durkheim's development of the concept of anomie", yet this source is only briefly mentioned, and in the original article the single, forlorn reference to Durkheim cites *The Rules of Sociological Method* rather than the more obviously related *Suicide*. As Merton later makes clear (1964: 213, 214) this idea is so well known that it hardly needed detailed citation.

There have been several major extensions and reformulations of Merton's anomie theory. Talcott Parsons (1951) uses three variables to develop a typology of eight types of deviant behaviour, and generalises deviance beyond that arising from the stress generated when cultural goals do not mesh with means. Dubin (1959) also attempts to extend Merton's typology of types of deviant, in his case by adding a variable of 'attitude to norms' between goals and means, and then by distinguishing between behavioural and value innovation and ritualism. Cloward (1959) suggests extending the concept of opportunity-structure by adding to Merton's variable of 'access to legitimate means', a further variable of 'access to illegitimate means' and points out that the access to learning and opportunity components of either type of means is socially structured. Cloward's extension suggests that "different strata provide varying opportunities for the acquisition of deviant roles, largely through access to deviant subcultures and the opportunity for carrying out such deviant social roles once they have been acquired" (as summarised by Clinard, 1964: 27). Cloward and Ohlin (1960) later developed this further in studying the formation of delinquent subcultures. Depending on whether the social surrounds of a group are integrated or not: either criminal, conflict or retreatist group responses are likely. 'Retreatist' gangs are seen as 'double failures' – unsuccessful in employing either legitimate or illegitimate means to success. With this extension of Merton's framework, Cloward and Ohlin claim to be linking anomie theory to the earlier idea of E.H. Sutherland that deviance is spread through cultural transmission and differential association.

Cohen (1959), while critical of much of Merton's framework, and seeking to enlarge it, adds a more explicit interactionist aspect, and to bring in reference-group theory. In a summary to that date on deviance, Merton (1964) absorbs many of these extensions into his own schema. In his final discussion on this topic, Merton focuses on his earlier addition of 'opportunity-structures' (1995) as the ensemble of means available to particular social positions. In particular, Merton shows how various complementary theories fit within a paradigmatic frame: some are better at answering particular questions than others (e.g. originating, continuing; see also Chapter 6).

Anomie theory has also attracted a long and complex series of critiques and empirical testings. Much of this material was assembled for an ASA conference session in 1962 attended by 1,000 sociologists and later published under Clinard's editorship (1964). However, this collection hardly stilled the continuing attention. It did, though, mark a high tide of interest in anomie theory (cf. Cole, 1975). It is difficult to do more than indicate the broad lines of criticism (cf. Clinard, 1964: 55–56):

(1) From an interactionist perspective, anomie theory is seen as too individual-istic (whereas adaptations are often shaped by group contexts) and suggests too abrupt a switch from strain to deviancy (whereas deviance may more often be built up gradually within an interactional framework);
(2) Many deviant acts arise out of role expectations rather than disjunctions between goals and means;
(3) Since they are so linked, the analytical separation of cultural goals and social means may be too artificial;
(4) Given the pluralist nature of complex modern societies it may be difficult to identify a set of universal cultural goals shared by all;
(5) The societal conditions generating anomie may be limited to societies stressing achieved rather than ascribed statuses;
(6) It is possible that the empirical foundations are incorrect, given methodo-logical difficulties with official data on deviance;
(7) It is not explained why most of the lower class is prepared to conform;
(8) Support for the cultural goals may not be uniform over all social classes;
(9) Societal reaction in actively defining deviance is ignored;
(10) The social conditions influencing different forms of adaptation especially retreatism – are not specified.

Several of these points seem relatively unimportant, and some seem, to me, to be adequately covered in at least the later versions of the theory, which include elements of the associational and deviant–opportunity–structure approaches. However, at least two empirical areas of criticism are important. There is some evidence that while there is widespread sharing of important social goals – such as the value of educational credentials – that there are sharp class differentials (see Merton, 1968: 224–228; Thio, 1975). The problem is whether to read the evi-dence as supporting the view of consensus or dissensus in terms of overarching goals (such as the culturally induced drive for material success). This is clearly a complex question in which the type of goals involved (e.g. their degree of abstractness), the level of support and the necessary methodology to research this, are all problematic. But, this question is really most affected by alternative theor-etical stances. Those working out from an 'interpretative' position are unlikely to perceive cultural uniformities, whereas few Marxists are likely to disagree with a view that capitalist societies are dominated by an ideological hegemony that covers a wide range of materialistic cultural goals and values including individual success motives. From a Marxist viewpoint this hegemony is in large part imposed, and works to the benefit of the 'ruling classes', but nevertheless has deep impacts on people from all classes.

The second crucial question is the extent to which there are class differentials in deviance. Thio (1975) has provided the sharpest critique, and suggests that by continuing to use what he regards as class-biased data, Merton is stigmatising the lower class. Thio draws an analogy with the fierce controversy over the apparent social class distribution of intelligence. Instead, he suggests deviance may be more prevalent amongst the upper class. However, Matza (1969: 99) suggests that if anything, the official statistics point to the high prevalence of official deviance amongst the *lumpenproleteriat* rather than throughout the working class as a whole, and he castigates the anomie theorists for their lack of attention to relevant empirical data (especially on patterns of working-class mobility). The empirical debate has continued since without clear-cut certainty arising.

A theoretical problem remains about the relationship between Mertonian anomie theory and Durkheim's analysis of anomie and also its relationship to Marx's analysis of alienation. Thio argues that Durkheim developed two conceptions of anomie:

- as a sudden break in life events;
- as a chronic condition generated by highly developed division of labour.

In both types of anomie, the upper classes are more likely to be affected than the lower class.

> Poverty protects against (anomie) because it is a restraint in itself. … Wealth, on the other hand, by the power it bestows, deceives *us* into believing that we are dependent on ourselves only … The less limited one feels, the more intolerable all *limitation* appears.
>
> *(Durkheim, 1951[1893]: 253–254)*

However, Merton had included discussion of the 'anomia of success' in his penultimate statement of his theory (1964), so that this aspect may have already been attended to. He also thought his theory could accommodate explanation of white-collar crime.

Anomie theory has seldom been explicitly related to the wider and complex concept of alienation. Indeed, Clinard (1964) suggests using the term to refer to the subjective aspect of anomie, and the term anomia has been used to express the individual level of experience of the condition. It seems better to see anomie as an aspect of alienation, and to be careful when investigating at the individual level where a wider range of explanatory factors, other than structural, may pertain.

Another theoretical problem is that neither the provenance of the goals nor the inegalitarian social structure are explained:

> It is as though individuals in society are playing a gigantic *fruit* machine, but the machine is rigged and only some players are consistently rewarded. The deprived ones then either resort to using foreign coins or magnets to increase their chances of winning (innovation) or play on mindlessly (ritualism), give up the game (retreatism) or propose a new game altogether (rebellion). But in the analysis, nobody appeared to ask who put the machine there in the first place and who takes the profits. Criticism of the game is confined to changing the pay-out sequences so that the deprived can get a better deal.
>
> *(Taylor, 1971: 148)*

It is interesting, from the perspective argued in this book, to note that the 'anomie' theory of deviance is seldom labelled as a functional theory. For example, in the Clinard collection 'function' does not seem to be used except in the strict sense of the functional consequences of deviance, and is not included in the index.

There is actually some explicit attention to a functional analysis of deviance within Merton's theory of deviance. In the main version of his essay, Merton notes, amongst other limitations, that his essay "has only briefly considered the social functions fulfilled by deviant behaviour" (1968: 214) which is an interesting indication that Merton saw his analysis as mainly other than a functional one. However, in the introduction to the reprinting of this essay in *STSS* Merton reworks the presentation of the framework of his anomie theory to stress that it involves an analytical concern with social and cultural change (1968: 176).

> The key concept bridging the gap between statics and dynamics in functional theory is that of strain, tension, contradiction or discrepancy between the component elements of social and cultural structure. Such strains may be dysfunctional for the social system in its then existing form; they may also be instrumental in leading to changes in that system.

It is clearly possible to develop a functional analysis of non-conformity which spells out its consequences for wider social systems, and Merton is alert to the need to distinguish short-term and long-term effects of deviance.

However, the main overwhelming thrust of anomie theory is clearly structural and causal: social structure causes differential behaviour, mediated by 'strain'. As the anomie theory formulation is refracted widely throughout other parts of Merton's work, the importance of this essentially 'structural' formulation is particularly strategic.

There is a long tail of continuing work in this area, although Merton's contributions are less frequently directly referred to. Instead, revisionist theories have become instituted:

- General strain theory (e.g. see Agnew 2006) which continues the micro aspects of Merton's approach but widens the range of factors considered to create strain, resulting in some suffering such strains engaging in criminal activities;
- Institutional anomie theory (e.g. see Messner & Rosenfeld, 2008) which continues the macro aspects of Merton's approach by examining the relative strengths of the effects of the economy on social life as opposed to other institutional areas.

The empirical success of the theory has also been doubted, although it clearly has considerable intuitive appeal. There has been some doubt that empirical tests have often failed to properly and fully operationalise the theory. The reformulated successor approaches seem to have provided better empirical support.

Maybe we have been too cautious in restricting anomie theory to analyse contemporary conditions. A recent vivid attempt to provide an acute analysis of the contemporary condition provided by Young (2008) refers to 'Global Merton' since the mass poor of the world including the outcasts of modern societies are subject to ever more massive doses of cultural consumerism etc. (in part delivered through newer mechanisms) while being denied opportunities to meet such goals.

In conclusion, it can be readily shown that Merton's work on anomie has not only shaped much work in criminology but has also fructified more general understandings of the darker side of society. Over time, some of the lurking complexities have been identified and the whole approach plumped out so that it can more adequately understand deviance as well as conformity (let alone the other modes of adaptation).

Unanticipated consequences of action (UCA)

Despite the central place of the actor and action in Merton's system of theorising, UCA has been widely used but relatively unexplicated component. ('The best-laid schemes o' *Mice* an' *Men* Gang aft agley, An' lea'e us nought but grief an' pain, For promis'd joy'. *To a Mouse* (1785), Robert Burns). His early treatment was provided in the essay 'The unanticipated consequences of purposive social action' (1936a). Oddly, this important area of analysis did not make the cut of being included in *STSS*, perhaps because it didn't fit the increasingly functionalist cast of that volume. Subsequently, a recapitulation by Stinchcombe (1975) which in turn has been confirmed by Merton (1976: 124) has partially restored its centrality.

This early work was based on the analysis of the Chicago economist Frank Knight (1921) who helped found the important 'Chicago/Friedmanite' school of Economics and is concerned to show how objective (and often collective) consequences can arise unbidden from purposive action. Purposive action is defined as "'conduct' as distinct from 'behaviour', that is, with action that involves motives and consequently a choice between alternatives" (1976: 147). This is not to be assumed to be reducible to psychological reflexes, nor involving a clear-cut explicit purpose nor even involving a rational model. One of the major ways in which unanticipated consequences may arise is through limitations to the 'existing state of knowledge' on which social action is based. These limitations are barriers to the correct anticipating of consequences, and include (1936a [1976: 149–155]):

- ignorance (not only is knowledge of human affairs limited, but even more difficult is organizing means to achieve an aim);
- error (especially in applying knowledge to a particular situation);
- 'imperious immediacy of interest' (a sharp focus on one set of consequences may exclude consideration of other consequences);
- basic values (consequences are not considered because of the overriding importance accorded the action by cultural values);
- self-defeating (suicidal) prediction (the very awareness of a social prediction may itself lead to action to put into effect behaviour that will negate the original aim of the social action).

Stinchcombe depicts Merton's conceptualisation of the core process as the:

> choice between socially structured alternatives … [which] differs from the choice process of economic theory, in which the alternatives are conceived to have inherent utilities. It differs from the choice process of learning theory in which the alternatives are conceived to emit reinforcing or extinguishing stimuli. It differs from both of these in that … the utility or reinforcement of a particular alternative choice is thought of as socially established, as part of the institutional order.
>
> *(Stinchcombe, 1975: 12; quoted approvingly by Merton, 1976: 124)*

A later passage in the same essay contrasts Merton's model of choice with symbolic interactionism ("the choice determined by definitions of the situation") and Parsonian theory ("choices about inherent value dilemmas determined by cultural values": Stinchcombe, 1975: 14). Criticising symbolic interactionism, Stinchcombe points out that because of wider social frameworks which impinge on people they cannot define situations as they please (1975: 15). Criticising Parsonian theory, Stinchcombe argues that value dilemmas are pitched at too general an analytical level for the theory to be able to show how they affect people's choices.

It is not too clear there are explicit paths of further take-up of this concern, although it has received steady attention (e.g. Mica et al., 2011). Merton, reflecting on this line of his work, points out that the conception arose during his doctoral studies, and his later essay on SFP complements the suicidal prophecies the earlier paper ended with. Commentary by de Zwart (2015) analyses the difference between unanticipated and unpurposed, noting a slide towards conflating the two (including Merton's own later 1968 definition which equates them) and unfortunately emphasising the latter. He draws attention to the role of side consequences of planning in that literature and the obscuring of an interesting and real category of phenomena – consequences that are both unintended and anticipated – that warrant separate attention. A possible extra type is unanticipated effects which arise accidentally. Some commentary draws attention to the social conditions which lead to one or other of the limitations on more effective choice-making, and the actor's intention which lies at the heart of this model is bracketed not just by conditions but by outcomes. Also, more individualistic outcomes are contrasted with more collective ones. Work in this area was increased by Portes's (2000) presidential address to the ASA which drew attention to barriers which inhibit achievement of choices. The complexities of the notion have increasingly been exposed, but defy easy summary.

The Tulane interlude

In 1939 Merton took up a two-year stint at the Sociology Department of Tulane University in New Orleans, becoming its chair. The choice was in part cultural, given the attraction of living in the 'South'. He taught Race Relations and Social Psychology and otherwise extended some of his Harvard teaching material. He recounted in Persell (1984) a tactic he adopted during his

> first session in an introductory course at Sophie Newcomb, then the women's adjunct of Tulane. As I entered the room, fully equipped with notes for a more-or-less standard overview of the course, I was startled to find that at least half the class were busily knitting away. In the time I took to reach the podium I made an instant decision: I would see to it that they stopped knitting and not because I would tell them to cease and desist. And so, I scrapped my planned lecture and having introduced myself, announced the subject for this first session: a report on some research I was doing at the time designed to give them an idea of how some sociologists went about their research. The research subject: patterns of Negro-white intermarriage in the United States. This, mind you, was 1939 and the place was New Orleans. The knitting stopped. A collective sense of numbed disbelief took over.

The interlude furthered work towards his publications 'Intermarriage and the Social Structure' (which related rates of intermarriage to stratification and other social factors) and 'Fact and Factitiousness in Ethnic Opinionnaires' (in which Merton challenged some assumptions underlying the Thurstone mode of attitude measurement). The former article developed a status exchange theory of inter-marriage in which the lower status race might have their lower marital value offset by their economic success. The opinionnaires article critiqued the linear claims of scales, based on analysis of a survey concerning race relations given students at Tulane, Newcomb and Louisiana State, all representing the South, and Harvard, Radcliffe, and Penn State representing the North.

In the summer of 1937 Merton (Simonson, 2010) had travelled to Europe to study German in Austria, staying in picturesque Gründlsee (between Salzburg and Wien), and slipping across to Heidelberg (where Talcott Parsons had earlier studied) to collect Nazi anti-science propaganda material (pamphlets). This led to a public lecture on his arrival at Tulane in September 1939 on the role of propaganda amongst combatant nations. Closer access to Mexico led to a summer expedition, staying at the village where Trotsky had lived, and he linked up with later colleague William Goode in Mexico City. Merton began to learn Spanish and considered research with local tribal groups. However, largely because of personal and family illness, this did not happen.

Overview

Beyond completing a Harvard PhD and establishing himself as an academic teacher and expanding his repertoire of research skills, between 1934 and 1939, Merton published 13 sole-authored works (12 journal articles and one monograph), two articles co-authored with Sorokin, and over 40 book reviews (Nichols, 2010). In sum, although Merton accomplished major contributions to sociology during his time at Harvard, several of these were 'sleepers' requiring a considerable passage of time before their impact became clear. He also married and explored regions of North America and Europe beyond his hometown. The stage was now set for his longer-term career.

References

Abraham, Gary A. (1983) Misunderstanding the Merton Thesis: A Boundary Dispute Between History and Sociology. *Isis*, 74: 368–387.

Agnew, R. (2006). General strain theory: Current status and directions for further research. In F.T. Cullen, J.P. Wright, and K.R. Blevins (eds) *Taking Stock: The Status of Criminological Theory: Advances in Criminological Theory*. New Brunswick, NJ: Transaction Publishers: vol. 15: 101–123.

Ben-David, Joseph (1971) *The Scientists' Role in Society*. Englewood Cliffs, NJ: Prentice-Hall.

Clinard, Marshall (1964) The Theoretical Implications of Anomie and Deviant Behaviour. In Clinard (ed.) *Anomie & Deviant Behaviour*. New York: Free Press.

Cloward, Richard (1959) Illegitimate Means, Anomie and Deviant Behaviour. *American Sociological Review*, 24: 165–176.

Cloward, Richard & Lloyd Ohlin (1960) *Delinquency and Opportunity*. New York: Free Press.

Cohen, I. Bernard (1990) Robert K. Merton and the 'Merton Thesis'. Part One of *Puritanism and the Rise of Modern Science: The Merton Thesis*. New Brunswick, NJ: Rutgers University Press.

Cohen, A.K. (1959) Social Disorganization and Deviant Behaviour. In Robert K. Merton, Leonard Broom, and Leonard S. Cottrell, Jr (eds) *Sociology Today*. New York: Basic Books: 461–484.

Cole, S. (1975) The Growth of Scientific Knowledge: Theories of Deviance as a Case Study. In Lewis A. Coser (ed.) *The Idea of Social Structure, Papers in Honor of Robert K. Merton*. New York: Harcourt Brace Jovanovich: 175–220.

Cullen, Francis & Steven Messner (2007) The Making of Criminology Revisited. *Theoretical Criminology*, 11 (1): 5–37.

Deflem, Mathieu (2018) Anomie, Strain, and Opportunity Structure: Robert K. Merton's Paradigm of Deviant Behavior. In Ruth A. Triplett (ed.) *The Handbook of the History and Philosophy of Criminology*. Malden, MA: Wiley-Blackwell: 140–155.

de Zwart F. (2015). Unintended but not unanticipated consequences. *Theory and Society*, 44 (3): 283–297.

Dubin, Robert (1959) Deviant Behaviour and Social Structure: Continuities in Social Theory. *American Sociological Review*, 24: 147–164.

Durkheim, Emile (1951[1893]) *Division of Labour in Society*. New York: Free Press.

Elliott, Clark (1999) The Tercentenary of Harvard University in 1936: The Scientific Dimension. *Osiris*, 14: 153–175.

Heyl, B.S. (1968) The Harvard "Pareto Circle." *Journal of the History of the Behavioral Sciences*, 4: 316–334.

Karabel, Jerome (2006) *The Chosen: The Hidden History of Admission and Exclusion at Harvard, Yale, and Princeton*. Boston, MA: Houghton Mifflin.

Knight, Frank (1921) *Risk, Uncertainty and Profit*. Cambridge, MA: Houghton Mifflin.

Kuhn, Thomas (1977) *The Essential Tension*. Chicago, IL: The University of Chicago Press.

Matza, David (1969) *Becoming Deviant*. Englewood Cliffs, NJ: Prentice-Hall.

Merton, R.K. (1997) On the Evolving Synthesis of Differential Association and Anomie Theory: A Perspective from the Sociology of Science. *Criminology*, 35 (3): 517–525.

Merton, R.K. (1995) Opportunity Structure: The Emergence, Diffusion, and Differentiation of a Sociological Concept, 1930–1950. In Freda Adler and William S. Laufer (eds) *Advances in Criminological Theory: The Legacy of Anomie Theory*. New Brunswick, NJ: Transaction Publishers: vol. 6: 3–78.

Merton, R.K. (1985) George Sarton: Episodic Recollections by an Unruly Apprentice. *Isis*, 76: 477–486.

Merton, R.K. (1984) The Fallacy of the Latest Word: The Case of Pietism and Science. *American Journal of Sociology*, 89: 1091–1121.

Merton, R.K. (1976) *Sociological Ambivalence*. New York: The Free Press.

Merton, R.K. (1973) *The Sociology of Science: Theoretical and Empirical Investigations*. Norman Storer (ed.). Chicago, IL: The University of Chicago Press.

Merton, R.K. (1964) Anomie, Anomia and Social Interaction: Contexts of Deviant Behavior. In Marshall Clinard (ed.) *Anomie and Deviant Behavior*. New York: The Free Press: 213–242.

Merton, R.K. (1949[1957/1968]) *Social Theory and Social Structure*. New York: Free Press.

Merton, R.K. (1942) A Note on Science and Democracy. *Journal of Legal and Political Sociology*, 1: 115–126.

Merton, R.K. (1941) Intermarriage and the Social Structure: Fact and Theory. *Psychiatry*, 4: 361–374.

Merton, R.K. (1940) Fact and Factitiousness in Ethnic Opinionnaires. *American Sociological Review*, 5 (1): 13–28.

Merton, R.K. (1938a) *Science, Technology and Society in Seventeenth Century England* in *Osiris: Studies on the History and Philosophy of Science and on the History of Learning and Culture*. George Sarton (ed.). Bruges: The St Catherine Press: 362–632.

Merton, R.K. (1938b) Science and the Social Order. *Philosophy of Science*, 5: 321–337.

Merton, R.K. (1938c) Social Structure and Anomie. *American Sociological Review*, 3: 672–682.

Merton, R.K. (1936a) The Unanticipated Consequences of Purposive Social Action. *American Sociological Review*, 1: 894–904.

Merton, R.K. (1936b) Civilization and Culture. *Sociology and Social Research*, 21: 103–113.

Merton, R.K. (1936c) Puritanism, Pietism and Science. *Sociological Review*, 28: 1–30.

Merton, R.K. (1934a) Recent French Sociology. *Social Forces*, 12: 537–545.

Merton, R.K. (1934b) Durkheim's Division of Labor in Society. *American Journal of Sociology*, 40: 319–328.

Merton, R.K. & Elinor Barber (2004) *The Travels and Adventures of Serendipity: A Study in Sociological Semantics and the Sociology of Science*. Princeton, NJ: Princeton University Press.

Merton, R.K.; Jerry Gaston & Adam Podgorecki (eds) (1977) *The Sociology of Science in Europe*. Carbondale, IL: University of Southern Illinois Press.

Merton, R.K. & M.F. Ashley Montagu (1940) *Crime and the American Anthropologist*, 42: 384–408.

Merton, R.K. with Bryce Ryan (1964) Anomie, Anomia and Social Interaction: Contexts of Deviant Behavior. In Marshall Clinard (ed.) *Anomie and Deviant Behavior*. New York: The Free Press: 213–242.

Merton, R.K. with Bryce Ryan (1944a) Paternal Status and Economic Adjustment of High School Graduates. *Social Forces*, 22: 302–306.

Merton, R.K. with Bryce Ryan (1944b) The Value of High School Scholarship on the Labor Market. *Journal of Educational Sociology*, 17: 524–534.

Merton, R.K. & Pitirim A. Sorokin (1937a) Social Time: A Methodological and Functional Analysis. *American Journal of Sociology*, 42: 615–629.

Merton, R.K. with Pitirim A. Sorokin (1937b) Sociological Aspects of Invention, Discovery and Scientific Theories. In Pitirim A. Sorokin, *Social and Cultural Dynamics*. New York: American Book Co., vol. 2: 125–180, 439–476.

Merton, R.K. & Pitirim Sorokin (1935) The Course of Arabian Intellectual Development, 700–1300 A.D. *Isis*, 22: 516–524.

Messner, Steven F; Rosenfeld, Richard (2006) The Present and Future of Institutional-Anomie Theory in Francis Cullen (ed.) *Taking Stock New Jersey*: Transaction: 127–154.

Mica, Adriana; Arkadiusz Peisert & Jan Winczorek (eds) (2011) *Sociology and the Unintended: Robert Merton Revisited*. Frankfurt am Main & New York: Peter Lang.

Nichols, L. (2010) Merton as Harvard Sociologist: Engagement, Thematic Continuities, and Institutional Linkages. *Journal of the History of the Behavioral Sciences*, 46 (1): 72–95.

Parsons, Talcott (1937) *The structure of social action*. New York: McGraw-Hill Book Company.

Parsons, Talcott (1951) *The Social System*. New York: Free Press.

Persell, Caroline H. (1984) An Interview with Robert K. Merton. *Teaching Sociology*, 11: 355–386.

Portes, Alejando (2000) The Hidden Abode: Sociology as Analysis of the Unexpected. *American Sociological Review*, 65 (1): 1–18.

Santoro, Marco (2017) The Gini-Merton Connection. An Episode in the History of Sociology and Its International Circulation. *Sociologica: Italian Journal of Sociology*, 3: 1–33.

Simonson, Peter (2010) Merton's Skeptical Faith in *Refiguring Mass Communication: A History*. Urbana, IL: University of Illinois Press: 123–162.

Simonson. (2005) The Serendipity of Merton's Communication Research. *International Journal of Public Opinion Research*, 17 (3): 277–297.

Stinchcombe, Arthur (1975) Merton's Theory of Social Structure. In L. Coser (ed.) *The Idea of Social Structure*. New York: Harcourt Brace Jovanovich: 11–34.

Taylor, Laurie (1971) *Deviance and Society*. London: Michael Joseph.

Thio, A (1975) A Critical Look at Merton's Anomie Theory. *Pacific Sociological Review*, 18: 139–158.

Young, Jack (2008) Vertigo and the Global Merton. *Theoretical Criminology*, 12 (4): 523–527.

3

EARLY YEARS AT COLUMBIA

Overview: the setting

The 1940s was the period when Merton solidly established himself on the sociological landscape, securing a highly strategic institutional base at prestigious Columbia University in New York, linking up there with colleagues who would actively support his work, and pulling together his work to date in the then-definitive volume *Social Theory and Social Structure* (*STSS*). The Bureau of Applied Social Research (BASR) established by Paul Lazarsfeld was an organisational base for much of this work, with the topics investigated also influenced by their funders.

When a full professorship fell vacant in 1940, the Columbia University Sociology Department was split between (empirically orientated) Robert Lynd and (theoretically orientated) Robert MacIver and could not agree on a nomination. A Solomonic compromise was effected by the University President (Nicholas Murray Butler) who split the position into two assistant professorships – one emphasising social theory and the other empirical research, although teaching urban sociology was to be covered. Merton was appointed to one (as an Assistant Professor), and Paul Lazarsfeld to the other (as an Associate Professor). For a while the two had little contact, but then followed an intellectual seduction. Lazarsfeld invited Merton and his wife to dinner, but after receiving an urgent call from the Office of Facts and Figures (predecessor of the IWA) diverted him to his research enterprise on audience-testing a government pre-war morale-building radio programme.

> After the program, when an assistant of Lazarsfeld's questioned the audience on the reasons for its recorded likes and dislikes, Merton perked up; he detected theoretical shortcomings in the way questions were being put. He started passing scribbled notes to Lazarsfeld ... As a second batch of listeners

entered the studio, Lazarsfeld asked Merton if he would do the post-program questioning. Merton did …

(Lazarsfeld, 1975: 36, quoting Hunt's, 1961 account)

Thereafter, Merton became engaged in work with the emerging BASR, supervising projects and becoming an Associate Director (and sometime Director in Lazarsfeld's absence). Both worked at the Bureau, and Lazarsfeld would knobble Merton in the late afternoon and early evening for discussions often lasting two to three hours (in Bureau idiom "scheming sessions") in which ways for improving studies and developing the Bureau were explored. Later, Merton was to estimate this interaction at 18,000 hours over a 35-year stretch. More generally, too, the Columbia Sociology microenvironment built up over time as demand for sociology education increased, and included several staff who actively engaged with Merton (and Lazarsfeld). Some were ex-students although to continue on at Columbia would have been overshadowing for some and indeed the preference for any Columbia hires was to appoint only after they had served a period elsewhere. The earlier Columbia senior professors (Robert MacIver and Robert Lynd) continued to hold departmental power for some time, but fairly quickly ceded leadership to the increasingly confident Merton and Lazarsfeld combination, who dominated the department for several decades. Terry Clark (1998) has provided an interesting vignette on later departmental staff meetings which he described as merely dealing with minor administrative teaching matters, whereas he had expected forceful projection of leadership.

The departmental context at Columbia included the undergraduate programme (where C. Wright Mills served) and Barnard College (where Mirra Komarovsky and Bernard Barber served), while there were several distinguished professors in cognate departments such as Lionel Trilling in literature and Richard Hofstadter and Jacques Barzun in history. One way in which these towering figures related to each other was through university seminars (see Katznelson, 2002). Merton participated in the Columbia Seminar of the State from 1945 and the Seminar on Bureaucracy the year before that. This was a gathering of Columbia social science notables who presented (empirically orientated) papers on a wide swath of topics concerning the operation of democracy in the US, on the way forging a more systemic stance within the social sciences, against the backdrop of the desolation spawned by the development of totalitarianism, World war and the Holocaust. McCaughey (2003) also suggests that the residential and institutional ecology (office but also residential propinquity) of Columbia reinforced the linkages amongst these campus elite intellectuals.

The broader New York intellectual ecology included the frequently Jewish 'school' of New York Intellectuals, including some local sociologists (e.g. Lewis Coser, Marty Lipset, Daniel Bell, Nathan Glazer), which were a left-leaning intellectual force – although in later years many swung to the right as their intellectual movement faded. Merton was not particularly engaged with the New York intellectuals (e.g. Bloom, 2018), but they were part of the 'intellectual field' in which he was placed. So too was the Frankfurt school-in-exile who were accommodated on campus for their years in New York, but these scholars too seemed to have limited interaction with Merton, apart from Leo Lowenthal who carried out empirical studies of the media – to Merton's intellectual appreciation. Lowenthal respected Merton's work, writing an appreciative review (years later) of Merton et al.'s *Freedom to Read*. Merton was a paid consultant on the Advisory Council to the Scientific Department (headed by Max Horkheimer) of the American Jewish Committee from 1945. Projects the Advisory Council focused upon were creating a script for a movie to combat prejudicial attitudes, and a series of studies of prejudice culminating in the *Authoritarian Personality* (1950).

Merton lived in the village of Hastings-on-Hudson village (population 7,000–8,000) 15 miles north of New York with Merton commuting by snappy sports car down to Columbia on the Parkway. The Mertons lived in a superbly equipped Tudor-style house with views of Hudson River. His wife and mother-in-law looked after the house and children, and their many cats. Simpson (2010: 141) reports that there "were 6 rooms, 30 kinds of birds, 6 squirrels, a 4-minute walk to the woods, & views of the Hudson river", together with a BBQ pit, fishpond and several bathrooms. The neighbourhood was mixed, although Merton participated in a campaign to stop white flight as black families moved in. Kenneth Clark (a black academic psychologist) was a neighbour and Merton contributed to Clark's work on the desegregation brief for the famous case leading to the 1954 federal ruling in *Brown v. Board of Education*.

Shortly after arrival at Columbia, Merton was struck down with exhaustion, finding it difficult to get out of bed, and Charles Page was brought in to cover his teaching. However, he recovered fairly quickly. He went on leave the next semester to carry out radio and film analysis for the army, initially at the Pentagon and later at the BASR offices.

Teaching at Columbia

While earlier teaching spells had set Merton up to develop his teaching practices, they hit full stride in his Columbia days. Some of his earliest teaching at Columbia, when he took over Robert Lynd's graduate seminar and lecture course in urban sociology (ancient cities) did not pan out, largely as his interest did not become engaged. His teaching became famous, attracting repeat attendances at classes, outsiders dropping in, and leading to several published accounts of his teaching success. Such was Merton's prowess as a lecturer that when Stephen Cole carried out a survey, the student respondents overstated his height! Except for a few occasional undergraduate students admitted to his classes, these were all graduate level.

Over time student numbers varied. When the GI boom came after WW2, Merton was lecturing to classes of 100 students from several disciplines, although interaction was still possible and some superb students came through. Lectures continued to fuel Merton's publishing programme. Working through classroom material which would be elaborated over one or two semesters can allow the establishing of a wider perspective and rounding out. He estimated that the modal range was some ten to 12 years before a concept nurtured in 'oral publication' in the classroom surfaced in a formal publication. Merton arranged for a teaching assistant to take and then type up notes of each lecture (even where they were broadly similar from year to year) and examination of this stockpile can reveal aspects of his work that did not surface in formal publications. Studies of two of his courses have been published – Marsh (2010) on his analysis of social structures and Swedberg (2019) on his theorising course, both focusing on the courses as depicted by class notes in the early/mid-1950s. As Fox (2020) documents, Merton also taught a course in urban sociology, which included a theory of the ecological dynamics of fertility. Given the importance Merton placed on 'oral publication' of ideas promulgated in class, it is important to have a closer look at these.

The recruitment net was cast wide because of Columbia's very high reputation, but many were local students, with a stream at one point comprising socialist students recruited from the City College of New York. (Famously, there were two groupings in the student lunchroom heavily involved in highly energetic internecine verbal warfare: Trotskyites in Alcove 1 and Stalinists in Alcove 2: see www.pbs.org/arguing/about_essays.html)

In 1943 Merton offered a one semester course – 'Analysis of Social Structures' (Sociology 113). By the 1950s this was taught as a year–long graduate course (215–216) in Fayerweather 313 mornings from 11 till noon. Students learned that there should always be an interplay between theory and empirical research, and therefore, their recommended career choice was to be *both* theorists and empirical researchers. They learned to critically examine theoretical work; to respecify and reconceptualise earlier theory and empirical findings, so as to cumulate these efforts. The sociological enterprise was held out to be the most important calling in the world!

> Apart from the [50] odd students registered in these courses, the classroom would be packed with auditors. Many of the auditors would return year after year. The reason that auditors would return year after year was because these courses were living things, continuously evolving. Before each lecture, Merton would spend several hours preparing his presentation for the day. He always managed to evolve new ideas and insights that gave his lectures freshness in spite of his many years of lecturing on the same topics. Because he was so deeply involved with his own insights and developing thought, Merton managed to convey his intellectual excitement to his students.
>
> *(Caplovitz, 1977: 142)*

The essay on 'Manifest and Latent Functions' (published in *STSS*, 1949) was the foundation of the course. In addition, it was shown that problems investigated by non-functionalists could also be fruitfully re-examined from the standpoint of the functionalist paradigm: non-functionalists included symbolic interactionism and the (almost obsolete) culture-and-personality school, while earlier "factor" theories, based on a single independent variable were seen as completely obsolete. Texts were Merton's own *STSS* and Parsons' *The Social System* (1951), supplemented by his *The Structure of Social Action* (1937). (Parsons gave a guest lecture in the course.) While Merton did not use Talcott Parsons or action theory in his published work, in lectures he declared that the frame of reference of action is presupposed in every one of the analyses he presented. During the 1952 academic year, just after Parsons' *The Social System* (1951) had appeared, James Coleman describes how Merton "asked us [students] to go through the early chapters and to note each theoretical sentence, labelling it according to type: was it a definition, an empirical generalization, a reconceptualization, a respecification of a lower level empirical generalization?" (Coleman 1990b: 29, 1990c: 83). In carrying out this assignment Coleman quickly came to realize that Parsons' work "was full of definitions but contained nearly no empirical generalizations".

This content course was supplemented by a less famous and less frequently taught course on theory building methods. Richard Swedberg (2019) has excavated from records in the Merton archive the content of Merton's course on theorising (Soc 213–214) which he taught from 1942–1954, undoubtedly the first such course in sociology. While this material received negligible attention in Merton's own subsequent writings, it was to some extent taken up in the 'theory construction' movement in sociology some decades later – the link was through several Columbia associates (especially Hans Zetterberg), students or Stinchcombe's book (1968) which Merton commented on as one of its editors. Swedberg establishes that Merton uses the term "theoretic work" (e.g. Merton 1945c: 465); but later introduced the term "theory work" in sociology (Levine, 2006: 239).

Merton saw his approach as a new kind of theorising in sociology, centred around the use of systematic empirical data (Swedberg, 2019). Often this data was produced by sociological fieldwork and not just inherited from official statistics. The course included specifying the tools for theorising that he devised, such as respecification, reconceptualisation and levels analysis. Theorising was not seen as consisting merely of a set of labels that could be attached to some phenomenon, but a special way of interaction with data. In teaching "[The] emphasis will be on direct examination of researches to ascertain the content and operation of theory".

In the second half of the course, Merton's goal was teaching the acquisition of a general knowledge of theory, so that once students were involved in a concrete research project, they would have some theoretical knowledge to fall back on. Re-analysis allowed past sociological studies to be linked to new sociological studies. The texts that Merton chose to re-analyse in his class on theorising included *The Protestant Ethic* by Weber and *Suicide* by Durkheim, exemplary books but differing in the systemacity of the data on which they were based, and also the sociological essays by Georg Simmel, who had an uncanny talent for detecting "strategic new variables" which could lead to new and interesting insights. Another exhibit was *The American Soldier* by Samuel Stouffer et al. (1949–1950) whose 1,500 pages contained an enormous amount of data, but very little theory, although the concept of 'relative deprivation' was advanced.

Another topic discussed in the course at this time was levels analysis. The recommended goal was to cover all four: individuals (Level 1), positions (Level 2), social structure (Level 3) and the 'definition of the situation' (Level 4). Merton showed how a full body of theory had gradually emerged following Durkheim's initial formulation of the problem, while subsequent theorists had provided answers to further issues so that theories were often complementary. Durkheim, for example, had paid no attention to individual psychology, and this work could be complemented by that of Freud.

For the times, Columbia was enlightened concerning women, who were encouraged although they were still required to take on lower-status jobs and withdraw from active paid work while child-rearing. Merton co-authored, for example, a series of studies with female sociologists (e.g. Merton and Kitt, 1950; Merton, West and Jahoda, 1951; Merton, Fiske and Kendall, 1956). Merton was also the thesis adviser and/or teacher of several well-known female sociologists, including Alice Rossi, Patricia Kendall, Rose Laub Coser and later Cynthia Epstein and Harriet Zuckerman.

Simonson (2010) argues that the gendered division of labour assigned the basic task of field interviewing to women while males tended to step in for the analysis and writing, garnering credit.

Intellectual themes of the early Columbia years

Merton's retrospective intellectual description of himself when he arrived at Columbia University in 1941 was as

> 'a confirmed social theorist albeit with something of an empirical bent' insisting on the importance of sociological paradigms (in a pre-Kuhnian sense of 'paradigm') … engrossed in developing the paradigms of functional analysis and deviant behaviour while trying to bring a nascent sociology of science into fuller being by exploring sciences as a social institution with a distinctive historically evolving ethos, normative structure and reward system … the inveterate loner working chiefly in libraries and in my study at home … something of a doubting Thomas who, in my very first published paper had dared satirize the 'enlightened Bojum [mythical animal imagined by Lewis Carroll] of Positivism'.
>
> *(1994: 16/1995: 154)*

This mind-set was to continue in part, but also to be violently (albeit willingly) wrenched towards team research carried out in a social research institute environment. Thus, much of Merton's work in the 1940s was sourced on material from several empirically based studies arising from research projects carried out in the Bureau of Applied Social Research – many at the behest of wartime authorities. The development of theoretical and methodological stances continued from his work of the previous decade. Through much of this period, Merton saw his work as contributing to 'social psychology' and was much focused on the analysis of 'propaganda' and communication. But his work also began to build up a wide-ranging analysis of the key institutions of then-contemporary US society which had not been particularly highly placed on the agenda of US sociology. I will some-what artificially package Merton's work over this period into three broad topics:

- ideas concerning middle-range theory and functional analysis;
- the melange of empirical and methodological work, particularly concerned with media and with morale during the war and immediate post-war years, together with urban/housing studies;
- an ensemble of studies of features of 'Modernity': Communications, Bureaucracy, Knowledge and Applied Social Research organisations.

Complementing these was the assemblage of a dozen essays into *STSS* which had its own 'value-added' effect as the volume became very popular.

Empirical and methodological studies

Merton's work at Columbia included a backlog of material from the Harvard and Tulane periods consisting of reviewing work, together with a minor range of essays. Znaniecki reported that he was enthused about Merton's analytical review of his *Social Role of the Man of Knowledge*. Several chapters from Merton's dissertation were compiled into articles (including one sent to nascent Marxisant journal *Science and Society* edited by senior Columbia colleague Bernhard Stern). Merton's published work included work on the social background factors affecting educational success (with Ryan, 1944). (Although this latter work was competent, if not particularly evocative, it could have been seen as an interesting precursor to the later work on social mobility developed particularly by Blau and Duncan: and could have linked the interest in the American Dream of social mobility he exhibited in his 'anomie theory'.)

The Columbia years witnessed a major commitment to empirical work, and codification of methodological developments forged in the fire of war-related urgency, with Merton one half of an 'odd couple' with Paul Lazarsfeld. The various projects intertwined and everything was grist for the mill of developing an effective sociology as suggested in the following passage (from the foreword to *STSS*):

> In recent years, while we have worked in double harness in the Columbia University Bureau of Applied Social Research, I have learned most from Paul F. Lazarsfeld. ... Not least valuable to me has been his sceptical curiosity which has compelled me to articulate more fully than I might otherwise have done my reasons for considering functional analysis the presently most promising, though not the only, theoretical orientation to a wide range of problems of human society. And above all, he has, through his own example, reinforced in myself the conviction that the great difference between social science and social dilettantism resides in the systematic and *serious*, that

is to say, the intellectually responsible and austere, pursuit of what is first entertained as an interesting idea.

(1968: xiv)

Some methodological and social critical work also flowed out of these early 1940s research experiences. Merton's methodological interests during this period included running a test of statistical significance (reputedly the first published by a sociologist), several aspects of the fieldwork involved in community/housing studies (1947b), the development of the methodology of 'the focused interview' (1946: with a more extensive treatment available as a full mimeod report and later published in book form in 1956) and more general issues concerning fieldwork. The focus interview (sometimes spelled focussed!) combined concern with both objective and subjective factors, with the former mainly ascertained by content analysis of stimuli (e.g. analysis of components of a film or audience reactions as measured by the Lazarsfeld–Stanton programme analyser – where audience members recorded their ongoing reactions to a film being recorded by pens onto a rolling paper). The manual provided a range of suggested procedures for eliciting respondents' subjective experiences and reactions to these established stimuli. The manual has one chapter on focus *group* interviewing and this later became a widely used research technique by market and then sociological researchers (see Merton, 1987a). This chapter is based on a practical understanding of small-group dynamics and a variety of factors likely to lead to research success are recommended. There is a small literature on the evolution of the focus group as a research technique (e.g. Lee, 2010). Spread and development of the technique gathered pace in its market research context but then it reverberated back into academic social research as qualitative work became again more popular. There are theoretical issues too: the techniques illustrated Merton's concern to cover both objective (quantitative) and subjective (qualitative) information and the interaction between the two, and the need for better codification of the latter. Merton was also concerned to research the generalisability of findings by carrying out quantitative survey research: later termed 'triangulation'.

Merton also participated in a group evaluation of the monograph *Family Meets the Depression* organised by the SSRC along several other such methodological exercises (Platt, 1992). A group of scholars (including Merton) was fed data produced by Angell and asked to develop a predictive model. This exercise shows that there was some predictive success from delving into the case studies.

Several of the earlier of these Bureau projects arose out of war-related work as the BASR probed various facets of civilian and military morale at the behest of the Psychological Division of the Office of Strategic Services (OSS) including a several-months' spell when Merton worked in the Pentagon. Research was also carried out for the Office of War Information (OWI). Schweber (2002) is one of many writers pointing to the importance of morale studies in the conduct of WW2 and the importance of statistical work within the widespread studies which were carried out.

Between war-related and then subsequent work Merton worked on many projects across his early years at Columbia. But as the war-related efforts began to wind down, other topics emerged. During 1943, Merton worked on a study of magazine reader-ship in Dover, NJ, sponsored by *Time* magazine, in which he developed the concepts of 'local and cosmopolitan influentials'. In late 1944, Merton was approached to become director of a study of planned housing communities (the Hilltown-Craftown study) commissioned and funded by the Fred L. Lavanburg Foundation (Fox, 2020). This was linked to a contemporary trend for large-scale 'planned commu-nity' housing developments, and a resultant set of 'evaluation' studies. This study involved a survey of two planned communities of similar size – about 700 households each – but different racial composition and economic settings. Craftown was a fed-eral project that was designed to provide housing for workers in the shipbuilding industry, for which Newark, NJ, and surrounding areas was a major national focus. With the relocation of populations attendant on WW2 growth of manufacturing and growth of cities, and the continuing northward streams of black labour force, housing, and especially housing in planned communities, became a significant policy and research topic. The study was to examine how planned communities could facili-tate the desires of residents and how local democracy could be strengthened at a community level, especially interracial housing on which this was one of the first studies. The study involved a household survey (one adult per household) of all the workers and their families in each of the two communities. The plan was to asso-ciate social characteristics – class, race, family size – with community participation. The study team consisted of three to four full-time researchers and more than 70 part-time interviewers when the families were being canvassed. Merton spent much effort on the study over much of the time until the final report was prepared in 1955. A long manuscript entitled 'Patterns of Social Life' was prepared part-way through the study and was reworked, but never formally published, although some methodological spin-off articles were, together with an analysis of friendship patterns (Merton & Lazarsfeld, 1954). In this analysis friendship relations were described as either exhibiting 'homophily' (based on social similarities) or 'heterophily'.

The study showed (1) that the layout of dwelling units strongly shaped the day-to-day interactions of residents, which in turn influenced relationship patterns, particularly the formation of friendships; and (2) the persistence of long-standing, cooperative relationships in the two communities suggested that the often-documented absence of "neighborly" relationships in densely populated cities was not insurmountable. Earlier analyses explored the effects of length of time respondents had lived in the community and the extent to which characteristics of prior residence affected their engagement, but later analysis seized on the informa-tion yielded by asking for the names of three closest most intimate friends which led to analyses of friendship patterns. Results from the study were included in 'To Secure These Rights', *The Report of the President's Committee on Civil Rights* in 1947 and in the *Social Science Statement* drafted by Kenneth Clark – and edited by Merton – that was submitted during the litigation in the Supreme Court of *Brown v. Board of Education* (1954).

Merton developed theoretical material from some of these studies, and indeed those not yielding theoretical fruit were often delayed in publication (if they ever appeared). With Lazarsfeld, several reflective workshops on important books were assembled including *The Authoritarian Personality* (1950) and *The Lonely Crowd* (1950) (Schweber, 2002). That most visible was Merton's co-editorship of a volume of restudies based on the array of empirical findings produced in wartime surveys sponsored by the American army. An essay on 'Contributions to the Theory of Reference Group Behavior' eventuated. The authors (Merton and Kitt [later Rossi], 1950) proceed as follows: they first locate a number of statements by soldiers in *The American Soldier* that show that what each soldier individually felt was based not only on their own individual reactions, but also on their view of what others feel. Soldiers who were married, for example, would often compare themselves to soldiers who were not married, and who had not had to give up as much when they joined the army. This type of phenomenon was given the name 'relative deprivation' by Samuel Stouffer and his co-authors. Merton and Rossi then suggest that you can go one step further in the analysis, by better specifying the relevant variable which was a reworking of the concept of 'reference groups' developed by Herbert Hyman. (This analytical framework was developed much further in the 1950s, and is dealt with in the next chapter.) More precisely, the groups with which soldiers compared themselves divided into two different kinds. On the one hand, there are the kind of groups to which the soldiers themselves belong (in-groups); and on the other, the kind of groups to which they do not belong (out-groups). This was Merton's early foray into status-and-role analysis which he developed very considerably through lectures and publications in the mid- and late 1950s (see next chapter).

The BASR was a 'greedy organisation' sucking in any available surplus of ideas and energy, but Lazarsfeld in particular, supported by Merton saw it as insufficient. A much larger enterprise that would carry out advanced training was required, perhaps located at Columbia. Over time, the proposal for such a centre to be funded by the Ford Foundation evolved and eventually the Center for the Advanced Study of the Behavioral Sciences (CASBS) was established adjacent to Stanford, resulting from their advocacy efforts. While developing their proposal, Merton and Lazarsfeld disagreed on the format each cohort of fellows might comprise: Merton suggested teams of colleagues while Lazarsfeld, drawing on his European experience, saw a more hierarchical structure.

Merton's immediate interests lay as much in in teasing out significant methodological or theoretical aspects as carrying through practical study reports. Some of the studies were never completed beyond in-house reports although several are rich albeit currently under-appreciated gems.

Studies of features of modernity

There is no indication that Merton saw himself developing a set of analyses of the different components of modern societies, as they were largely separate ventures, nevertheless Merton helped to put on the sociological agenda study of several of the key institutions or more generally features of modernity – communications, knowledge and beliefs, applied social research and bureaucracies. (The second generation of studies of science and the *Student Physician* study of professions were carried out in the 1950s and so discussed in the next chapter.) This is in some contrast to the Chicago School which had mainly concentrated on social problems, often at the periphery of society.

Communications

Although Merton's several works on propaganda/communication studies over a decade (last study published in 1948) were delivered separately, Simonson (2006: 271) indicates that there was a wider picture. This work exemplified a concern for understanding (and critiquing) the emergent multiplex and changing cultural order of then-contemporary society. He writes:

> In the 1940s, Robert K. Merton charted a world that became our own. Operating at the highest levels of intellectual and social scientific culture, Merton … explored the new modes of popular communication of that century: radio, motion pictures, mass circulation newspapers, public relations, propaganda, advertising, and public opinion polling.

Moreover, there were methodological innovations with Merton's mode of carrying out such studies being able to be characterised as "combining content analysis, focused interviews, and survey research with an eclectic variety of social theory and classical humanist thought" (272). (Simonson also points to an even more general theme about a concern with communication running through Merton's sociology overall. Whereas in this period his concern was with *mass* media, in his later (and also earlier) work on *scientific* communication, he was also studying communication – the *elite* version.)

Of those studies which Merton carried out the most well developed was a multimethod study of the effectiveness of a campaign in which the radio star Kate Smith hosted a marathon all-day war-bond radio drive (1946). With a $5,000 grant, Merton led a nine-person research team, deploying a mix of content analysis, focused interviews and a survey.

> Merton writes about cynicism and public distrust. He explores the cultural contradictions of celebrity and image carefully cultivated through public relations technique. He outlines the emotional contours of fans who feel personal closeness with distant stars more widely than presidential candidates. … Merton shows us how popular nationalism can gain collective expression through mass media and cultures of commercialized entertainment.
>
> *(Simonson, 2004: xi)*

The population studied was mainly working-class women who were 'fans' of Kate Smith.

> *Mass Persuasion* charts these women's affections and wartime anxieties, sketches working class Americans' uneasy encounter with the national creed of material success, and shows the symbolic work Smith does in both easing her listener's social tensions and reinforcing dominant ideologies.
>
> *(xii)*

A key concept in the book is pseudo-Gemeinschaft ('the feigning of personal concern with the other fellow in order to manipulate him the better' (1946 [1971: 142]). Merton's last publication in this field (1948a) is a critical overview of the media and its role in society, written with Lazarsfeld. He argues that the media (radio, press and picture theatres) may have 'limited effects', compared to other change such as cars. He enumerates and then discusses three functions:

- the status-conferral function: appearing in the media validates a person, organisation etc.
- the enforcement of social norms, including bringing to bear the 'glare of publicity';
- the narcotising function of keeping the population preoccupied and politically inert through the broadcasting of trivia.

Expanding on the second point, Merton writes a commentary on 'crusades' which might be shepherded by an active media, and suggests that the third is a dysfunction, as a politically apathetic population is not in the interest of modern complex society. Capitalist ownership of the media and the selling of its services primarily to big advertisers sharply circumscribes possibilities for the media to educate. Finally, it is argued that campaigns to effect social change will only work under particular conditions, including supplementary face-to-face contact. Other important points Merton drew attention to include the media-propelled role of celebrities, the importance of 'public images' (especially given limited objective measures of agency performances) in relation to the exigencies of people's (audience members') lives.

Later research engagements included a limited involvement in the famous Columbia election studies in 1948. Another study arose when General Eisenhower was President of Columbia University 1948–1952. Many letters were written to him urging him to run for President (which he later did, being elected in 1952). Merton and a team analysed this material and prepared a manuscript 'Mass Pressure', but Eisenhower refused permission to publish (see Goldhamer, 1997 and Merton's preface to Sussmann, 1963).

Sociology of knowledge

Although societies were not at the time Merton was writing referred to as 'knowledge societies', their highly developed stocks of knowledge were clearly a major characteristic. In a set of three essays stretching from the 1930s, Merton sought to come to some terms with the European 'discipline' (an indicator of how it was seen as a somewhat autonomous development) of sociology of knowledge (*Wissenssoziologie*). The sociology of knowledge has tended to retain something of an aura of mystery, delving into philosophical issues more than most sociology. It was developed in the first part of the century by German and French writers (Scheler, but above all Mannheim and also Durkheim). This, of course, is the 'parent field' of the sociology of science, which Merton recognises, although he doesn't draw the two together in substantive terms. Instead, the main contrast he makes is with the field of the sociology of communications. (Looking far forward there would be a potential link with his sociological semantics.) So, Merton's attempt at reckoning is also broader, drawing a relationship with the inherited 'European' mode of sociologising, and how an optimum approach might be built by adding to it an 'American' mode of sociologising.

The extensive introduction to the three essays in part 3 of *STSS* contrasts the two modes of sociologising (European and American) along several dimensions summarised in the famous aphorism that whereas Europeans might say, "We don't know that what we say is true, but it is at least significant" (1949 [1968: 494]), the American might retort, "We don't know that what we say is particularly significant, but at least it's true". In terms of subject matter and problem definition, Europeans excavate the social roots of *knowledge* and *esoteric doctrines*, whereas the US is focused on *opinion* and popular culture, whereas Europeans study knowledge and ideology; other differences include empirical data v. speculative reading, contemporary v. historical timeframes, formal v. informal research techniques, team research v. individual scholarship. The introduction ends with a (not too convincing) plea for the joining of the two approaches with Lowenthal's work on *magazine biographies* being put forward as superior to work located solely in either mode. Unmoored from its comparative task, this essay could be seen as providing an interesting typology of different types of knowledge/opinion structures.

In his substantive essay on the sociology of knowledge Merton develops an analytic paradigm which is then used as a framework for discussing much of the material then available on the sociology of knowledge. The paradigm involves (1968: 494ff):

- where is the existential basis of mental productions located? Social (e.g. class) v. cultural bases (e.g. ethos)?;
- what mental productions are being sociologically analysed? Spheres of moral beliefs etc. or aspects analysed (e.g. foci of attention)?;
- how are mental productions related to the existential basis? Causal/functional (e.g. determined)/symbolic/organismic/meaningful relations (e.g. consistency)?; and
- why do the imputed relations of the existential base and knowledge obtain? Historicist v. universal?

The next essay in this trio on sociology of knowledge is a thorough description and critique of Mannheim's work (cf. Sica, 2010). The final essay reports on some studies of domestic propaganda in radio and motion pictures. 'Propaganda' is seen as communication defined by the receiving community as controversial. Moreover, it is a term used neutrally and not suggesting truth/untruth. The role of content analysis is described and illustrated, followed by an examination of the role of focused interviewing and the programme analyser in exploring audiences' responses to a propaganda item. Some concepts are also mentioned such as the 'boomerang response' where people respond to propaganda in the opposite way than that intended.

In 1942, Merton laid out the "ethos of science'", building on his 1930s work to begin an analysis of the internal structure of science, and thereby single-handedly founding a new field of sociology of science (see next chapter). An extension of the sociology of knowledge theme (see also later chapters) was his 1961c address on social conflict over styles of sociological work and his 1971 address on 'Insiders and Outsiders: A Chapter in the Sociology of Knowledge' (and indeed these all link up with his much later development of "Sociological Semantics").

Prejudice

The post-war period in the USA continued to roil with issues of race relations, and sociologists became more aware that ethnic differences are a continuing feature of most modern societies. The official creed called for equality, but this was far from automatically ensuing. A significant contribution was an essay on the social structural arrangements affecting prejudice that Merton produced in an attempt to clarify some of the conceptual issues involved. Rather than merely contrast *cultural* ideals and actual practices, Merton suggested inserting belief as an intervening variable. By this move: (1948c[1973: 192])

> the entire formulation of the problem becomes changed. We escape from the virtuous but ineffectual impasse of deploring the alleged hypocrisy of many Americans into the more difficult but potentially effectual realm of analyzing the problem actually in hand.

Merton develops a typology of combinations:

> Individuals may recognize the creed as part of a cultural tradition, without having any private conviction of its moral validity or its binding quality. Thus, so far as the beliefs of individuals are concerned, we can identify two types: those who genuinely believe in the creed and those who do not (although some of these may, on public or ceremonial occasions, profess adherence to its principles). Similarly, with respect to actual practices: conduct may or may not conform to the creed. And further, this being the salient consideration: conduct may or may not conform with individuals' own beliefs concerning the moral claims of all people to equal opportunity.

TABLE 3.1 Typology of ethnic prejudice and discrimination

Type	Attitude dimension	Behaviour dimension
1 All-weather liberal	+	+
2 Fair-weather liberal	+	−
3 Fair-weather illiberal	−	+
4 All-weather illiberal	−	−

Having developed his typology of ethnic prejudice (Merton, 1948c) by the cross-tabulating of attitudes to ethnic groups (prejudice v. non-prejudice) against behaviour towards them (discrimination v. non- discrimination), four types of mixes of prejudice and discrimination are yielded (see Table 3.1) (1948c [1976: 192]).

Merton then analyses the likely positioning in the overall social structure of those holding various of these views and then suggests quite differentiated recommended ways of relating to each particular combination of community mixes.

Self-fulfilling prophecy (SFP)

A particularly acute observation was the way in which social beliefs through which we understand (and to some extent experience) the social world can feed back to affect social reality. Merton deliberately published the SFP essay in a more general publishing outlet (as well as in his *STSS* compilation), as he considered the message vital to the public's understanding ongoing social reality, particularly *race relations*. To fine-tune appropriate writing for addressing a public audience Merton enlisted (1989) the drafting help of his friends James Reid and John McCallum (senior editors at Harcourt) although it was an academically aligned magazine (*Antioch Review*) which published the essay. This careful writing effort bore fruit in the widespread public adoption of Merton's term.

Merton defines a self-fulfilling prophecy as "a false definition of the situation evoking a new behaviour which makes the originally false conception come true" (1948d [1968: 477]). The examples he offers include the collapse of banks under 'runs' and the way in which people in minority groups have not been allowed access to institutions and then been damned because they pursued alternatives. The suicidal prophecy (ftnt on 185) involves changing the course of behaviour such that the prophecy fails to be brought about. Merton is careful to point out that there are social mechanisms that can intervene in such vicious cycles and that institutional controls are often able to quell rumours and panics that feed at the informal interactional level of operation.

Focusing on instances of racial discrimination and pointing out their self-fulfilling character, Merton intended to show how "ethnic prejudice dies" once the actors become aware of the spiral that they themselves have triggered (1948b: 210). Although it was often also necessary to cut "off their sustenance provided by certain institutions of our society", so Merton's concern to draw attention to self-fulfilling prophecies was to attempt to falsify them, in order to break the vicious spiral of self-fulfilling-ness.

To count as an SFP, a belief must have particular consequences that make reality conform to the initial belief. Moreover, at least some of the actors within the process fail to understand how their own belief has helped to construct that reality and because their belief is eventually validated, they assume that it had been true at the outset. His examples are social pathologies, but not merely in the sense that they are socially undesirable. They are "pathological" for being predicated on misunderstanding. Depositors fail to realise that their own panicked withdrawals cause the bank to collapse; whites fail to realise that their own racial discrimination makes African Americans seem intellectually inferior.

Local and cosmopolitan influentials

A community-based exploratory study, primarily based on interviews with 86 men and women drawn from diverse social and economic strata in 'Rovere' (Dover, New Jersey), a town of 11,000 on the Eastern seaboard, focused upon the place of mass communications in patterns of interpersonal influence. The study was originally carried out on readership of *Time* magazine. Merton found (after close consideration) that it was useful to conceptualise 'influentials' into those orientated to local issues (locals) and those orientated to national and international issues ('cosmopolitans'). Locals are more deeply rooted in the community as they'd been there longer, were more committed to remaining, had a wider range of local contacts and a more extensive involvement in local voluntary groups. This distinction about different orientations (sometimes conceptualised as 'latent social roles') has usefully since been taken up in many studies.

Bureaucracies

An overpowering feature of modern societies, and especially in wartime, are bureaucracies. Weber's ideal type model of bureaucracies was the received wisdom. Merton tackled this topic with a few essays, although with more impact he encouraged the fieldwork in organisations of several Columbia doctoral candidates:

> One of the most memorable seminars I ever ran (memorable to me at least) was on bureaucracy. It derived from my earlier work condensed into the papers, 'Bureaucratic Structure and Personality', and 'Role of the Intellectual in Public Bureaucracy'. The inter-action between the students and myself was so intense that sessions would often run on and on, long after the appointed time. We could not distinguish teaching from research. As I recall, the series of Columbia dissertations on bureaucracy did not grow directly out of that seminar. For the most part, they came later. Alvin Gouldner's dissertation

work was reported into monographs. *Wildcat Strike* and *Patterns of Industrial Bureaucracy*, both published in 1953. Peter Blau's *Dynamics of Bureaucracy* appeared a year later.

(Persell, 1984: 367)

Merton's essay (1940) swiftly summarises Weber's arguments, adding on a coating of more social analysis, noting that the organisational rules may limit friction and that sentiments are built into the operation of organisations. He then turns to the dysfunctions of bureaucracies, which arose from the 'trained incapacity' as people remain settled in their grooves, and organisational goal displacement as the focus remains on locking-in preferred means (e.g. self-preservation) rather than achieving the original goals: that is, they are "ritualists" in Merton's anomie schema. He also points out the dependence of workers on their workplace in order to access the tools of their trade.

Drawing on other passages in *STSS*, Jaworski (1998) points to the concern of the Columbia writers about the relationship of bureaucracy and democracy. Other Columbia writers had suggested democratic control from the top whereas he described Merton's approach as seeing bureaucracies as inherently democratic since leaders depend on the legitimacy accorded them by the rank and file, and their activities are mutually observable.

Merton added another essay/chapter on the 'intellectual' (i.e. 'policy adviser': 1945) in the bureaucracy to his earlier analysis. The intellectual is seen as varyingly circumscribed by their organisational context, with a trade-off between short-term effectiveness versus maintaining long-term relative autonomy. The 'Machine, the Worker and the Engineer' (1947a) is a tour de force centred on an analysis of engineers as key personnel in an industrial society and how the social effects of technology might best be lived with, including as mediated through social research. In the early 1950s, Merton et al. (1952) produced an eclectic reader on bureaucracy that pulls together existing material, without an active direction. (For lengthy analysis of the 'Columbia Organisations' study group see Crothers, 1990, also Haveman, 2009.) Mertonian organisational analyses were a powerful set of early studies which brought out the dysfunctions of organisations, but were largely eclipsed by other research programmes so that their longer-term effect was muted.

Applied social research

Applied social research, including polling studies, are one of modernity's feedback mechanisms, assisting in the setting and resetting of policy. Interests in bureaucracy as well as reflection on applied research methodology led to research on AT&T's programme of applied social research – with the preliminaries presented in an essay on the intellectual (social scientists) in public bureaucracies (1949). He also studied the 'public image' of polling, which was attracting public attention for its presumed methodological inadequacies.

Merton's methodological doctrines

Working out the best recipe for developing sociology was a preoccupation of many sociologists. Getting this right would make or break the success of the discipline. Given his familiarity with the development of natural science, Merton was in a good position to make recommendations. The major players of the time were positivists, even empiricists, and on the other hand the grand theory of Talcott Parsons (and earlier grand systems theorists). Merton wanted to develop an 'end run' around each of these.

Towards a 'scientific' methodological stance for sociology

Merton was concerned – through lectures and publications – to sculpt an appropriate scientific status for sociology. He saw sociology as settled by the two disconnected camps of theorists and empiricists and was concerned to chart out a course for sociology to extricate itself from the difficulties of the disconnection between these. Merton's detachment from grand systems of social theory (which had often arisen in earlier times when each writer felt a need to justify an entire approach to studying mankind) was driven home dramatically by his use, as a masthead citation to *STSS*, of Whitehead's aphorism that "a science which hesitates to forget its founders is lost". This was a criticism of history of sociological thought as potted summaries of previous thinkers without placing these in their social and intellectual context, and was to draw a contrast with 'systematics' of theory work which focuses on the logic of the ideas. Both types of work are necessary, but one should not subsume the other, with Merton in other writings discussing how the two might relate (see 1968: 26ff).

The key image he puts forward is of sociology as an advancing, accumulative ('evolving') science broadly based on a 'natural science' model and sharply demarcated from 'common-sense' social knowledge. This systematic sociology is to be achieved mainly through theoretical activity, working up new theories and consolidating smaller-scope theories into wider theoretical structures. As well, he saw theories as progressively accumulating (or not) supportive empirical evidence, with the success of testing sorting out the wheat from the chaff. But the theories are to be of a particular type, theories of the middle range located between broad-scale theoretical orientations on the one hand and small-scale empirical generalisations on the other.

This theme of the cumulation of sociology through middle-range theory is constantly repeated in many of Merton's essays, as well as being centrally located as a main theme of his *STSS*. The foundation of this stance was laid in the introduction to the first edition of this book, together with the pair of short essays, written at about the same time, that deal with each side of the interplay between theory and research ('The bearing of sociological theory on empirical research' and 'The bearing of empirical research on sociological theory': 1945c, and 1948b). Merton's subsequent writing only slightly extended or modified the methodological stance laid out in the mid- and late 1940s.

This basic methodological doctrine was extended over the whole of his career in his essays on applied sociology (1949c, 1963), formalisation of theory (1954), the relationship between sociology and psychology (1957a[1982]), problem selection (1959[1982]), the anti-sociologist's canon (1961b), the role of the sociologist in relation to social problems (1961a), the role of theory classics (1968), the role of values in social science (1971) and the conception of 'theoretical pluralism' (1975, 1981). In the later stages of his career Merton provided a more extensive version of his then writing agenda covering such issues (see table Merton produced in 1987b and below Chapter 6). (It also should be noted that Merton has drawn attention to methodological concerns in a wide variety of his more general writings.

Merton's methodological stance was later modified in two significant aspects. His apparently sharp demarcation between the history of sociology and its presently advancing research front is relaxed in a 1967 essay on the 'History and Systematics of Social Theory' (1968: chapter 1) which brings his 'methodological ideology' into line with his own practice by enumerating the useful ways in which the classical tradition can feed into contemporary sociology. He also points up that contact with the legacy of social thought stresses the 'humanistic' aspects of sociology.

In several later essays (1961c, 1972a) on conflicting and competing approaches in sociology, Merton explicitly relaxes his image of the future of sociology lying primarily with functional analysis, to point up a conception of sociology as a multiparadigm or theoretically pluralist science, in which theories derived from different theoretical approaches can shed complementary, rather than incommensurate, combined insights into social phenomena. But his practice had always been to draw on any appropriate theoretical formulation – as in his links to Thomas's 'definition of the situation' or Sutherland's differential association approach to the generation of deviance.

Merton's methodological stance carried weight not so much because it was original, but because of its careful, detailed and well-written presentation. Certainly, it is far less crude than some alternative contemporary images, such as Lundberg's social physics, and more concrete than many other stances. Nor am I arguing that Merton's published methodological stance had a causal impact, such that its exposition alone had a strong impact in setting sociology on its scientific feet. Rather, his methodological doctrine suited an emerging climate of opinion in sociology and helped to shape and justify this. This was no mean achievement, as some of the praise for the successful development of American sociology in the post-war period can be given to Merton's methodological writings, although some sociologists unfortunately retained an empiricism (the doctrine that theory unproblematically flows from social facts) that it unintentionally seemed to support.

Merton was instrumental, not only in helping to build a cumulative sociology from its earlier 'social problems' and 'history of ideas' components, but also in building into the core of this cumulative sociological enterprise various emerging components (such as social survey research). So, Merton both distanced his vision of sociology from some narrowing earlier American work and also knitted together newer aspects into a workable coalition of approaches. As might be expected, Merton's attempt to stitch together the methodological frameworks necessary for a cumulating sociology, did not nicely and neatly flow from the published doctrine, but was rather more complex. The doctrines themselves had unintended consequences, and took sociology into directions not contemplated. One example of this can be that supposed middle-range theories are but slightly dressed up empirical generalisations.

One outcome of his work (see Turner special issue, 2009) was the development of a 'theory-construction school' within sociology which stressed the importance of the more formal statement of theories. Foundational to this enterprise was Merton's formalised casting of Durkheim's theory of suicide:

1. Social cohesion provides psychic support to group members subjected to acute stresses and anxieties;
2. Suicide rates are functions of unrelieved anxieties and stresses to which persons are subjected;
3. Catholics have greater cohesion than Protestants;
4. Therefore, lower suicide rates should be anticipated among Catholics than among Protestants.

(1949[1968: 151])

The development of a 'theory-building school' began in the early 1950s with Zetterberg (1965[1954]) and flourished into the early 1970s. A signal concern in the dozen or so theory-construction texts which were written over this period was the continued development of Merton's formalisation of Durkheim's theory of suicide. While this 'school' may have helped clarify sociological thinking about the nature of formal theories, there was also a tendency to value both the informal and formal 'means' of theorising over the 'content' of the theories, and thus too often these books became ground down in technicalities.

Merton's image of science

Merton drew on the cognitive authority accorded natural science to bolster his methodological views. He compared a public image of science at present, built on a long history (several centuries), with the neophyte social sciences. Just because sociology coexists at the same time as the natural sciences did not mean that it has a similar degree of maturity. He portrayed the need, if the social sciences were to advance, for huge inputs of person power over extended periods, the need for careful accumulation of empirical studies which extend and develop lines of investigation, the necessity of a modest stance which stresses the tentativeness of scientific statements and the requirement of some aloofness (detached concern) from both the common sense of public views and policymaker demands for immediate application and relevance. Above the dull patient mass of scientific workers there is a role for scientific geniuses (Newton, Einstein, etc.), but Merton made it clear that he saw their role as one of consolidation of an accumulation of findings into pithy summative perspectives, rather than that of revolutionary thinkers opening up cognitive realms for the regiment of empirical research workers to invade. The image corresponds to Kuhn's image of the 'normal' phase of science, without any hint of any revolutionary irruptions to an essentially linear growth of progress over the long run. Merton is, however, very sensitive to discontinuities and change (1965, 1967c). The role of empirical research is seen very largely to extend a research programme rather than to carry out any strategic tests to overthrow it (as Popper might counsel). He pessimistically draws the analogy that "Perhaps sociology is not yet ready for its Einstein because it has not yet found its Kepler – to say nothing of its Newton, Laplace, Gibbs, Maxwell or Planck" (1968: 147).

His later doctrine (1968 [1967c]) is rather more sensitive to differences between the natural and social sciences (and the humanities), and these differences are seen to lie both in the historical stage of development of the discipline and in features inherent to social phenomena. This means that the social sciences must adopt a mix of historical erudition and contemporary intellectual enterprise in their approaches to study.

The image of science is presented without any fanfare. No particular appeal to the writings or behaviour of scientists is made, nor is his doctrine backed by citing philosophers of science. (Later, he does claim assent to this policy from Plato, Bacon, John Stuart Mill and George Cornewall Lewis [1968: 56–64] and also a number of then-contemporary writers, especially T.H. Marshall.) Yet, his account of science is rather more plausible and complex than other doctrines circulating at the time (for example, Lundberg's ideal of a 'social physics') and it must be remembered that by the mid-1940s there was little readily available useful writing in the philosophy of science to be drawn upon, although developments quickly occurred. Indeed, when discussing the implications of the multiparadigm/pluralistic theory situation of sociology, Merton extensively draws on the philosophical literature which reacted to Kuhn's image of science (1977).

To some, Merton might well appear to be a 'positivist' or even an 'empiricist'. Indeed, Merton would seem to accept at least to a considerable degree the various assumptions that positivists are considered to cleave to (cf. Wilson, 1983: 11–17). However, his positivism is always of a nuanced and sophisticated variety which stresses the centrality of theoretical work and the importance of qualitative sensitivities and the limitations to generalisability, and indeed the context-sensitivity, of findings. Moreover, Merton has recorded his distaste for cruder versions of these doctrines he was exposed to in his early years as a scholar (1934, 1985).

A useful rendition of Merton's methodology is provided by Sztompka (1986: 11) who enumerates its five Cs: consolidation, codification, clarification, continuity and cumulation.

The doctrine of middle-range theory

The central methodological precept for which Merton is undoubtedly most famous is his advocacy of 'theories of the middle range'. This directly addresses the two deficiencies Merton had identified in then-contemporary sociology, and suggests avoiding the pitfalls of either by driving in between them. The key passage was indicated in an address in 1947 and published in 1949d (1968: 39):

> Middle-range theory is principally used in sociology to guide empirical inquiry. It is intermediate to general theories of social systems which are too remote from particular classes of social behaviour, organization and change to account for what is observed and to those detailed orderly descriptions of particulars that are not generalized at all. Middle-range theory involves abstractions, of course, but they are close enough to observed data to be incorporated in propositions that permit empirical testing. Middle-range theories deal with delimited aspects of social phenomena, as is indicated by their labels. One speaks of a theory of reference groups, of social mobility, or role-conflict and of the formation of social norms just as one speaks of a theory of prices, a germ theory of disease, or a kinetic theory of gases.

Middle-range theories are distinguished from general sociological orientations ("Such orientations involve broad postulates which indicate types of variables which are somehow to be taken into account." 1968: 41–42) and empirical generalisations ("an isolated proposition summarizing observed uniformities of relationships between two or more variables" 1968: 149).

Some of the characteristics of middle-range theory noted are:

- "the seminal ideas in such theories are characteristically simple" (1968: 40);
- "the idea itself is tested for its fruitfulness by noting the range of theoretical problems and hypotheses that allow one to identify new characteristics of [the phenomenon pointed up by the imagery of the theory]" (1968: 40);
- it is not just an image for thinking about an aspect of a phenomenon, but it "generate(s) distinctive problems for sociological inquiry" ... and "points directly to relevant empirical research" (1968: 42, 43);
- it provides understanding of a phenomenon by, for example "identifying the social mechanisms" which generate it, and then "discovering how those mechanisms came into being, so that we can explain why the mechanisms do not operate effectively or fail to emerge at all in some social systems" (1968: 42, 43);
- "they are frequently consistent with a variety of so-called systems of sociological theory" (1968: 43);
- "these theories do not remain separate but are consolidated into wider networks of theory" (1968: 68); and
- "this type of theory cuts across the distinction between microsociological problems ... and macrosociological problems" (1968: 68).

The examples he gives are: the theories of social mobility, reference groups, relative deprivation, social stratification, authority, change, institutional interdependence, anomie, role conflict, and formation of social norms (1968: 40, 41), dissonance and social differentiation (1968: 64) and theories of racial, class and international conflict (1968: 68). (This listing is a significant pointer to those areas of his work that Merton considers theoretically significant.)

The middle-range approach was aggressively deployed as an alternative to Parsons' proposal that sociology should concentrate on developing general theory. Drawing on his general image of how scientific knowledge advances, Merton considered Parsons' call premature, and hence doomed to failure. The explication of the middle-range approach was a useful outcome of the debate. Nevertheless, Merton closed his extended debate with Parsons over the most appropriate theory-building strategy on a conciliatory note (or more precisely, footnote) in the third edition of *STSS* (1968: 52) in which Merton stresses that their differences particularly lay over the most appropriate means for gaining the same scientific end. However, Merton never provides pointers to what an achieved grand theory would look like.

A key characteristic of middle-order theories is that they should cut across different institutional areas of sociological investigation, and that they apply across different historical societies. As Kolb (1958) suggested in reviewing the second edition of *STSS* "'Middle-range theory', then, must mean not a middle level of abstraction but rather theory at the highest level of abstraction in dealing with social systems but concerned only with selected aspects of those systems" (545).

In practice, there has been something of a slewing away from this doctrine. It is often taken as a justification for merely tacking a few explicit theorems onto the beginning of the presentation of an empirical study. In the apparent absence of exercises which sweep up a range of middle-order theories into consolidated wider frameworks, it is possible that, in practice, this doctrine has not assisted in the cumulation of sociological knowledge. If the achievements from this doctrine have not met up to the standards it attempted to set, nevertheless, it has provoked much more attention to theory in the everyday practise of sociology.

A difficulty with the middle-range theory strategy lies in the art of couching theories at the optimal pitch of abstractness and degree of empirical connectedness. Few can pitch social theory in a way that captures essentially human features of the operation of social structures while avoiding too much historical specificity or retention of the particular flavour of some institutional area. It is not entirely accidental that almost all the examples Merton uses (apart from those drawn from the natural sciences) are his own. The right mix of abstractness is often more easily developed in studies on small groups, or perhaps formal organisations, and so it is not surprising that many of Merton's middle-range theories have been developed in his microsociology. A much later formulation, Merton indicates some alternatives in his 'Fallacy of the Latest Word' (1984: 1095, 1096) where he posits three levels of abstractness:

1. *Least abstract level*: the socio-historical hypothesis: Ascetic Protestantism helped [n.b.] motivate and canalize the activities of men in the direction of experimental science;

2. *Middle-range level*: dynamic interdependence of the social institutions of religion and science: science like all other social institutions, must be supported by values of the group if it is to develop. There is, consequently, not the least paradox in finding that even so rational an activity as scientific research is grounded on non-rational values;

3. *Most general and abstract level*: the dynamic interdependence of social institutions: a principal sociological idea governing this empirical inquiry holds that the socially patterned interests, motivations and behavior established in one institutional sphere – say, that of religion or economy – are inter-dependent with the socially patterned interests, motivations and behavior obtaining in other institutional spheres – say, that of science.

Merton also spelt out an active process of codifying (1968: 155) in which the abstract qualities of theories are encouraged by progressively stripping lower-order theories of their empirical limitations. Although this doctrine was introduced long ago, sociologists are still fine-tuning its effectiveness.

Social mechanisms

Merton provides a highly consequential glimpse of a concept of social 'mechanisms', which has since, of recent years, exploded into widespread sociological use. His approach has two prongs. He specifies 'social mechanisms' as elements in developing explanations of how structures and their environing social systems work, requiring that sociology "calls for a 'concrete and detailed' account of such mechanisms". They are element 6 in his paradigm of functional analysis where they are couched as "mechanisms through which functions are fulfilled" (1968: 106). He suggests the questions: "what is the presently available inventory of social mechanisms? What are the methodological problems entailed in discerning the operation of these social mechanisms?" He also provides examples: "role-segmentation, insulation of institutional demands, hierarchic ordering of values, social division of labor, ritual and ceremonial enactments etc."

In a further passage, he ties identification of mechanisms to structures. "The concept of role-set generates distinctive problems for sociological inquiry" (1968: 42).

> It raises the general but definite problem identifying the social mechanisms – that is the social processes having designated consequences for designated parts of the social structures – which articulate the expectations of those in the role-set sufficiently to reduce conflicts for the occupant of a status. It generates the further problem of discovering how these mechanisms came into being, so that we can also explain why the mechanisms do not operate effectively or fail to emerge at all in some social systems. Finally, [it] points directly to relevant empirical research.

(43)

I think these two passages relate to two levels:

- mechanisms that explain how a structure operates (through processes, activities, practices), and then
- mechanisms which are alternative structures that explain how a system works.

More person-level mechanisms are eschewed, although these are at the heart of the Analytical Sociology movement (see Hedstrom & Swedberg, 1996) which has so heartily adopted mechanisms as a more satisfactory alternative to covering-law explanations. Mechanism-analysis fits into middle-range theorising by providing concrete accounts of practices which mediate between a causal force and the consequential social arrangements.

Other aspects of Merton's methodology: practicalities

Merton's doctrine of 'middle-range' theory is embedded in a broader framework stressing the importance for sociology in developing testable theories of empirical data, while locating practical difficulties in doing so.

Much of the methodological impact of Merton's image of a scientific sociology was carried by the pair of essays (1949d [1968]) which examine the bearing of social theory on research, and of social research on theory. The first essay differentiates several conceptions of theory, especially contrasting theory proper with general sociological orientations on the one hand, and empirical generalisations and ad hoc explanations on the other. In the second essay of the pair, research is seen as initiating, reformulating, deflecting and clarifying theory. In particular, Merton urges alertness (having a prepared mind) to the possibility of 'serendipity': the unanticipated discovery of theoretically strategic facts. This concept and the general role of chance and accident is a lifetime theme in Merton's sociology, touched on in much of his work.

Merton is concerned that 'proper' (that is, middle-range) sociological theories should be 'explanatory' in form. Usually, this is taken to require specifying alternative behavioural outcomes which are specifically linked to particular different social structural situations. For example, in commenting on Cloward's extension to anomie theory, Merton (1959b) reproves him for providing no more than a typological exercise, however fruitful he considers the suggested extended typology to be. This concern with inductively locating the grain of social reality, so that its structure can be revealed through a clean, deep conceptual axe-cut, had the consequence of deflecting attention from philosophical issues about the nature of social reality. However, Merton recognises a role for general social theory in providing basic imagery from which more specific theories can be generated (1968: 141–143). For example, he suggests that: "to the extent that the general theoretical orientation provided by Marxism becomes a guide to systematic empirical research, it must do so by developing intermediate special [i.e. middle-range] theories" (1968: 66).

In cultivating the development of such theories Merton enumerates several functions of classical social theoretical writings:

> These range from the direct pleasure of coming upon an aesthetically pleasing and more cogent version of one's own ideas, through the satisfaction of independent confirmation of these ideas by a powerful mind, and the educative function of developing high standards of taste for sociological work to the interactive effect of developing new ideas by turning to older writings within the context of contemporary knowledge.
>
> *(1968: 37)*

Much of the appeal in Merton's sociology lies in its working within and against common sense. Merton utilised the dramatic potential for taking the common-sense stance and then sharply circumscribing its limits and exposing the unexpected 'rationality' of the more sociological viewpoint.

Paradigms as an analytical device

One methodological tool used by Merton to assist in codifying areas of study is what he termed a qualitative or analytical paradigm. That these are considered central tools in his vision of the progress of sociology is attested by his several references to them (1968: 69–72, 104–109 and 1976b: 209–216). As examples, he lists his paradigms for functional analysis in sociology and the sociology of knowledge, and as worked examples ("delimited paradigms") those relating to anomie, intermarriage and prejudice–discrimination.

Paradigms are seen as not just notational devices, but as 'logical designs for analysis' which "bring out into the open the array of assumptions, concepts and basic propositions employed in a sociological investigation" (1976b: 211) and also as "preliminary efforts to assemble propositional inventories of sociological knowledge" (1976: 211). They are seen as having five related functions:

- notational (by setting out concepts in a summary form);
- avoidance of inadvertent oversight (by providing a checklist of concepts);
- enhancement of accumulation (by providing a framework allowing extra theoretical interpretations to be added);
- promotion of the cross-tabulation of concepts;
- enhancing codification by providing a framework for assembling qualitative information.

Merton points out that while qualitative insights are valuable, they must also be codified into 'publicly certifiable procedures' for sociology to progress.

The methodological role of paradigms in Merton's sense has some distant similarity to Max Weber's tool of 'ideal types'. But Merton's device, unlike Weber's, has fortunately not generated a confusing and unproductive secondary literature. This is largely because the term was effectively 'kidnapped' by Kuhn (1962), and used rather differently as a tool to refer to the set of ideas and research practices actually shared by research communities.

In my interpretation, Merton's conception spans at least four types:

- the paradigm of functional analysis involves a listing of steps to be undertaken and issues to be confronted in carrying out a functional analysis;
- the paradigm of the sociology of knowledge sketches out a conceptual framework of the types of variables and the relationships between them, that allows alternative theories about particular linkages to be mapped out;
- the paradigms of anomie and prejudice–discrimination are typologies of 'modes of adaptation' or 'behavioural patterns';
- a paradigm is seen as providing a framework analogous to statistical handling of quantitative data, for analysing qualitative data (but no example is given of this).

Of these types, the third is more appropriately termed a typology. As such it can be found to be endemic to Merton's implicit theoretical model and thus more widely used in his own writings than Merton might suggest. The multipurpose character of a paradigm is surely being stretched too far by trying to enlist it as a framework in actual research studies, as in the fourth usage. (Indeed, Lazarsfeld's concept of an 'accounting scheme' (1975: 45–56) might be more appropriate for that purpose.)

The first and second usages blend together more if the methodological function of the first is downplayed and its review function emphasised. It is the second usage that is most important. Laying out the major conceptual units in a field of study is a useful approach to building up codifications of both theories and research findings in a problem area.

As Merton himself notes, more explicit and direct theories can be developed if the prevalent discursive essay format of the sociology of that time could be broken up into more graspable and workable argument structures in which the exact formulations of the theories are exposed. Merton, although himself a master of the essay form, is trying to validate a different style of discourse. This is emphasised in the awkward analogy he draws between paradigms and data analysis procedures for quantitative variables. A more recent term used to describe a similar type of analytically reviewing of a field is 'meta-analysis'.

Interestingly, the paradigm (analytical framework) is not seen by Merton as a device for cumulating general theory from an aggregation of middle-range theories. And yet surely this is a function of a paradigm, and could easily be developed to complement the doctrine of 'middle-range' theorising. There are examples which could be recruited for this purpose, such as his passages relating the different purposes of different sociologies of deviance (see Table 4.4 below). Developing the notion of paradigm in this direction has another payoff as it allows us to glimpse the essential commonality between the Mertonian and the Kuhnian versions of the concept: paradoxically, Merton gives the term a 'normative' usage to suggest what a cognitive framework in an area ought to be, whereas Kuhn uses the concept 'socio-logically' to indicate what the conceptual structure in an area actually is.

Merton as a functional analyst

Merton has somewhat studiously avoided too explicit a theoretical stance within the broad parameters set by the 'middle- range' approach discussed in the previous chapter. However, in *STSS* (1968) he explicitly stakes a claim to being a 'functional analyst' and this is claimed in the introduction to the first and second editions to be the framework which ties together the remainder of the book (the third edition does not include a general introduction as several passages in early versions are expanded into full-scale essays in their own right). The preface to the third edition does not attempt to provide a definition, let alone a programmatic statement of this position. Instead the reader is directed to the edition's Chapter 3, in which a para-digm for functional analysis is laid out. Here we do find a definition: "the practise of interpreting data by establishing their consequences for the larger structures in which they are implicated" (1968: 101).

In his essay, Merton is concerned to elucidate the key points of functional ana-lysis as a mode of sociological *interpretation*. To emphasise the *logic* of functional analysis Merton strips down the theoretical content involved. In some contrast, Parsons' 'structural-functional' analysis was developed as a general *theory* of how social integration was accomplished (through a basic consensus over values and norms and other social machinery) and had negligible stress on the methodology involved. The key feature of Mertonian functional analysis is that it sees social systems as collections of *parts*, and is concerned to analyse the complex relationships of interdependence among these parts. Functionalism was originally an approach fashioned by anthropologists to map regularities behind the cultural complexities of non-literate societies, rather than tracing the *evolution* of cultural forms. Merton is able to take this, and to convert it to an approach suited to the analysis of modern societies – he is concerned to take *anthropological* conceptual equipment and turn it to *sociological* use.

Merton begins his essay with some terminological notes setting out alternative usages of the term, with a concern to establish a technical definition. Following this definitional exercise, a formal programme (described as a 'paradigm') is laid out of the agenda of methodological issues that functional analyses must address (or it might be construed, the steps through which a functional analysis might advance: 1968: 104–108). This involves (in my reworked presentation):

1. identification and description of the item (social or cultural phenomena) to be analysed;
2. analysis of the motivation (or motives, purposes or subjective dispositions) of the individuals involved;
3. identification and description of the system within which the item is set;

4. analysis of the objective consequences of the item, especially for the system;
5. separation of the schedule of objective consequences into 'functions' ("those observed consequences which make for the adaptation or adjustment of a given system") 'dysfunctions' ("which lessen the adaptation or adjustment of the system"), 'nonfunctions' (which are functionally irrelevant) and a 'net balance of the aggregate of consequences';
6. separation of objective consequences (in relation to the previous analysis of motives) into those which are manifest functions ("intended and recognized by participants") and those which are latent functions ("neither intended nor recognized");
7. analysis of the 'functional requirements' (or needs or prerequisites) of the system;
8. identification and description of the (social) mechanisms through which functions are fulfilled;
9. analysis of functional alternatives (equivalents or substitutes) by specifying the range of possible variation amongst the items in the system capable of sub-serving a functional requirement;
10. analysis of the structural context or structural constraint on the range of variation in the items which can effectively satisfy functional requirements (especially, analysis of the inter-relationships which lock items into the system and ensure that their elimination would affect the rest of the system);
11. attention to the functional analysis of dynamics and change;
12. attention to the development of approaches to validate functional analyses (especially through comparative or quasi-experimental research designs);
13. attention to the ideological implications of functional analyses.

I think that this listing can be usefully grouped into three areas:

- steps involved with carrying out a *partial* functional analysis (steps 1 to 6) in which an item is analysed in relation to its context (but the context is not necessarily seen as a 'system');
- steps involved with carrying out a *full* systemic functional analysis of a system (steps 7 to 10);
- points of wider methodological concern to functional analyses generally (steps 11 to 13).

Merton points up the major methodological difficulties standing in the way of carrying out a full systemic functional analysis. He suggests that the idea of functional requisites "remains one of the cloudiest and empirically most debatable concepts in functional theory" and that "as utilized by sociologists the concept of functional requisites tends to be tautological or even *ex post facto*" (1968: 106).

In his portrayal of functional analysis Merton develops several points. He is at some pains to distance his version from the 'classical' mode of functional analysis as developed in anthropological writings of the 1920s and 1930s. (However, several commentators have suggested that Merton's reconstruction of classical functional analysis is 'forced': e.g. Davis, 1959.) To adapt functional analysis to the study of more complex societies, is seen to require a *rejection* of three postulates usually held to be 'essential' to classical functional analysis (1968: 79–91):

- the postulate of the *functional unity* of society (that is, that "every culturally standardized activity or belief is functional for the society as a whole and uniformly functional for [all] the people living in it": 1968: 81);
- the postulate of *universal functionalism* (which "holds that all standardized social or cultural forms have positive functions": 1968: 84);
- the postulate of *indispensability* (that there are certain functions which are indispensable in the sense that, unless they are performed, the society (or group or individual) will not persist [and] ... that certain cultural or social forms are indispensable for fulfilling each of these functions": 1968: 87).

This rejection of the trinity of classical functional postulates has several direct implications for a reformulated functional analysis: that the consequences of social units for other areas of social life be recognised as:

- multiple,
- specified as either functional or *dys*functional,
- and not inherently tied to a particular form (but rather, units may have alternatives).

Some attention in this essay is also devoted to laying out the descriptive material required in any research study (1968: 109–114), including:

- a description, in social structural terms of participation in the observed pattern;
- an indication of the principal alternatives to the observed pattern which are excluded (i.e. the boundaries of the pattern, especially in comparison with those pertaining cross-culturally);
- the meanings of the pattern to the actors;
- the array of motives associated with the pattern;
- those regularities of behaviour associated with the pattern, but not recognised by participants, as part of the pattern.

Another concern in his essay is his detailed rebuttal of the logical necessity of the conservative ideological freight often thought to be carried by functional analysis: by skilfully comparing ideological orientations *shared* by dialectical materialism *and* functional analysis Merton is able to claim that a radical impulse (as well as the admitted usual conservative patina) *can* be associated with functional analysis, and is able to conclude that "functional analysis may involve no *intrinsic* ideological commitment" (Merton, 1968: 93).

But perhaps the leading methodological argument in this crucial essay on functional analysis concerns the 'heuristic purposes' of the identification of latent functions (i.e. those not intended or recognised by participants: see above) for theoretical work in sociology. Merton argues that identification of latent functions (1968):

- "clarifies the analysis of seemingly irrational social patterns" (that may serve wide social functions while not achieving their ostensible purposes, especially in terms of Western physical science) (118);
- "directs attention to theoretically fruitful Fields of inquiry" (by bypassing the rather more obvious and restricted questions posed by only examining manifest functions) (119);
- "represents significant increments in socio close up logical knowledge" (because the uncovering of latent functions represents greater departures from 'commonsense' knowledge, by exposing an added level of complexity in social life) (122);
- "precludes the substitution of naive moral judgements for sociological analysis" (as moral judgements often only encompass manifest consequences) (126);
- "by imply[ing] the concept of strain, stress and tension on the structural level, provides an analytical approach to the study of dynamics and change" (107).

Merton's discussion of functional analysis is larded with a wide range of examples – religion in modern sociology, magic, the Chiricahua puberty ceremonial for girls, patterned responses to mirriri (hearing obscenity directed at one's sister), the 'romantic love complex' in American society, the cultural pattern of conspicuous consumption, taboo on out-marriage, hostility to deviants, Polish peasant cooperative institutions, Hopi rainfall ceremonies, the effect of the researcher in the Hawthorne studies, and the North American 'political machine'. Most are briefly referred to, but the functions of religion, the pattern of conspicuous consumption and especially the role of the political machine are addressed at greater length. This analysis of the political machine has been recognised as a particularly important contribution, apart from its usefulness as an illustration (Landau, 1968).

A summary may be useful in providing a more concrete specification of how he saw, at that stage in his writing, what was involved in carrying out a functional analysis (in my paraphrase):

American political machines were generally considered to be evils, allowed to continue only because of 'deficiencies' in the running of American local government, especially because of the insufficient exercise of political strength by 'responsible citizens' to secure reform. However, attention to latent functions points to other deficiencies in official local government structures which make it difficult for effective decisions and action to take place such that they do not seem to serve the 'human' needs and expectations of their 'clientele'. The political machine fulfils these needs of ordinary men and women more effectively, by providing aid suited to the diverse needs of different groups, in a manner that does not stigmatise its recipients. For those in groups that find it difficult to achieve upward mobility, in a society renowned for its cultural emphasis on 'getting ahead', the machine offers alternative channels of social mobility. For businesspeople, political machines expedite business efficiency by cutting through the red tape which surrounds the divided bureaucracies. For 'illegitimate business' (crime) engaged, as is legitimate business, in the provision of goods and services for which there is an economic demand, the political machine provides 'protection' from undue government inter-ference and a rationalisation of the organisation of the services. The deep-rooted needs that the structure (i.e. the political machine) fulfils means that it will be difficult to eradicate without complex social engineering. Merton completes his analysis by pointing out that the structure may come to quite transparently show up the functions, as when the social opposites – but functional similars – of the big businessman and the big racketeer both meet "in the smoke-filled room of the successful politician" (see 1968: 135).

Social Theory and Social Structure (STSS)

The publication of STSS was a cumulative 'added-value' through its packaging of the theoretical and empirical work Merton had already published. In the late 1940s, Merton, then in his late 30s, assembled much of his then-published material into STSS. Seen analytically, STSS is a tripartite book:

*   methodologically, it sketches a programme about how sociology might best advance;
*   theoretically, it provides a theoretical orientation and also a wealth of concepts which can be used in sociological explanations' and
*   substantively, it provides a glittering array of particular insights and specific studies which illuminate the approach and concepts.

Merton puts it slightly differently: STSS is claimed to be particularly concerned with developing, in a systematic unfolding, of two pervasive sociological concerns:

*   the interplay of social theory and social research, and
*   the concern with codifying both substantive theory and the procedures of sociological analysis, most particularly of qualitative analysis.

(1949[1968: vii])

Each of the three editions emphasises one or other of these three major contributions. The first edition indicates the approach and the theoretical orien-tation but places greatest weight on substantive applications. The second thickens very considerably the theoretical apparatus. The third revisits the broader meth-odological or meta-theoretical concerns.

Most of the chapters in STSS were published previously. However, the key essay on functional analysis was not previously published. Furthermore, considerable fresh editorial material was included in the book, not only in the introduction but also as introductions to each of the four parts. Later editions included more material which was previously unpublished: the two long essays on 'continuities', with some of the writing (e.g. the essays on the "self-fulfilling prophecy" and that on the "machine, the worker, and the engineer") aimed at a lay audience (Merton, 1949: 120). Co-authors of chapters include Paul Lazarsfeld (on media research) and Alice Rossi (on reference group theory; Merton, 1957). Interestingly, the chapters tend to be included in order from newest to oldest.

Not all of his previously published material was included. The most surprising omission is his essay on the "unanticipated consequences of purposive action" (Merton, 1936) which would have strengthened the theoretical core of the book. The exclusion of this essay is likely related to the shift in sociological thinking in this period away from the interests in the social psychology of "social action" which had been more influential over the previous decade, to a more systems-interest in functional analysis in which the place of social psychology was more problematic.

STSS famously begins with a masthead quotation culled from scattered (and unidentified) pages from Whitehead's (1917) *The Organisation of Thought* which leads to discussion in which Merton steers a complex path between natural sciences and humanities. Although the introduction eschews the task of integrating the book as a whole, the introduction to each part spells out the connections its material has to the remainder of the book. On page 11, Merton (1949) brings in the main character in his plot. The main thrust of *STSS* undoubtedly was seen by Merton as an enunciation of a programme of work to extend functional analysis. This task is seen as much methodological as theoretical, thus sitting easily alongside the two clearly methodological essays in *STSS* which address the mutual inter-relations of theory and research.

While Merton argues for a structural-and-functional analysis approach to understanding cultural and social structures, this approach is extended in the book by a more thorough structural treatment and the deployment of a considerable array of social structural concepts which are offered to his sociological colleagues to invite further conceptual development and empirical exploration. Finally, in the substantive material gathered in the book, Merton draws attention to the sociological need to study the various institutions and social forms of modern societies, including bureaucrats, scientists and social science experts.

Merton tended to eschew the classic "research report" format for his papers and he admits that his book is a compilation of essays, yet is "reluctant to believe that the book lacks altogether the logical, and not merely literary, graces of coherence, unity and emphasis" (Merton, 1949: 3).

Although in this period it was not always easy to get sociological books published, Merton (and some other sociologists) had the active interest of Jeremiah Kaplan who had recently founded the Free Press, and was keen to purvey sociological books (Lipset: 1993). Not that this was a straightforward offer: Kaplan needed

Merton's work more than Merton needed him. Indeed, to help launch Kaplan's enterprise *STSS* was published on faith and a prayer, and with no hard promise of royalties. "Merton, whose book sold well over 100,000 copies, never received more than a 10 percent royalty" (Lipset, 1993: 7).

The title is evocative, with a catchy symmetry: two two-word terms/phrases 'social theory' and 'social structure' are joined together, and with repetition of 'social'. The title broadly indicates Merton's concern with an approach and a subject matter. His purpose is further indicated by the subtitle. Interestingly he prefers 'social theory' to 'sociological theory', in part so that psychological variables might also be included. And of course, the titles of his other books also boast similar abstract titles, unencumbered by detail.

There have been as many as 20 translations. These were not all mere carbon copies of the American original, but several differed in content. Sztompka (1996: 265) notes that "for many of the multiple foreign translations of *STSS*, Merton adduces special introductions which relate to the sociological tradition of the given country". Indeed, some of the later translations have given rise to more debate than earlier versions – such as the review symposium on the German edition in the *Berliner Journal für Soziologie* (from 1996) which included the point, derived from Merton's own middle-range doctrine of the transitoriness of theories that the translation was decades late.

No review of the original volume appeared in the *American Journal of Sociology*, although *Social Forces*, the *British Journal of Sociology* and other journals reviewed the first issue and the *American Sociological Review* reviewed all editions. The book was clearly welcomed in these reviews, with fervour rising over time: but some critical comments are also included. Nor are Merton's own comments on his work much help in providing further context: as when *STSS* was declared a citation classic, Merton (1980) merely enumerates some of the areas of work it contains: reference groups, local and cosmopolitan influentials, the self-fulfilling prophecy, unanticipated consequences, the paradigm of the sociology of knowledge, and sociology of science – without reference to any underlying theme. *STSS* remained Merton's major publication, reinforced by the revised and extended further editions in 1957 and 1968.

Conclusion

Merton put his stamp on the sociological world in the 1940s and early 1950s through a flow of publications emanating from a new research-based, theoretically framed approach to sociology. Thrust into larger-scale empirical research by his involvement in BASR, Merton often struggled to wring theoretical material of sufficient sophistication out of these empirical studies, many lying unpublished. But some major attempts had been made yielding insightful books. In addition, Merton began to sketch out the contours of the key institutions of modern society: its communities, organisations, professions and especially its media. This was a platform on which launch more powerful impacts on sociology.

References

Bloom, Alexander (2018) Whatever Happened to the New York Intellectuals? *Society*, 55: 512–516.

Caplovitz, David (1977) Robert K. Merton as Editor: Review Essay. *Contemporary Sociology*, 6: 142–150.

Clark, Jon, et al. (ed.) (1990) *Robert K. Merton: Consensus and Controversy*. London, New York & Philadelphia, PA: The Falmer Press.

Clark, Terry (1998) Paul Lazarsfeld and the Columbia Sociology Machine. In Jacques Lautman & Bernard-Pierre Lecuyer (eds) *Paul Lazarsfeld: le sociologie de Vienne à New York*: Paris: L'Harmattan: 289–362.

Coleman, James (1990) Robert K. Merton as Teacher in Clark (ed.) *Robert K. Merton: Consensus and Controversy*. London, New York & Philadelphia: The Falmer Press: 25–34.

Coleman, James (1972) Paul Lazarsfeld's Work in Survey Research and Mathematical Sociology. In Paul Lazarsfeld (ed.) *Qualitative Analysis*. Boston, MA: Allyn & Bacon: 395–499.

Crothers, Charles (1990) The Dysfunctions of Bureaucracies: Merton's Work in Organizational Sociology in Clark (ed.) *Robert K. Merton: Consensus and Controversy*. London, New York & Philadelphia: The Falmer Press: 193–230.

Davis, K. (1959) The Myth of Functional Analysis as a Special Method in Sociology and Anthropology. *American Sociological Review*, 24: 757–772.

Fox, Kenneth (2020) Sociology Applied to Planning: Robert K. Merton and the Columbia–Lavanburg Housing Study. *Journal of Planning History*, 19 (4): 281–313.

Goldhamer, Joan (1997) General Eisenhower in Academe: A Clash of Perspectives and a Study Suppressed. *Journal of the History of the Behavioral Sciences*, 33 (3): 241–259.

Haveman, Heather (2009) The Columbia School and the Study of Bureaucracies: Why Organizations Have Lives of their Own. In Paul Adler (ed.) *The Oxford Handbook of Sociology and Organization Studies: Classical Foundations*. New York: Oxford University Press.

Hunt, Morton (1961) How Does It Come to Be So? Profile of Robert K. Merton. *New Yorker*, 28 January, 36: 39–63.

Jaworski, Gary D (1998) Contested Canon: Simmel Scholarship at Columbia and the New School. *The American Sociologist*, 29 (2): 4–18

Katznelson, Ira (2002) *Desolation and Enlightenment: Political Knowledge After Total War, Totalitarianism, and the Holocaust*. New York: Columbia University Press.

Kolb, William (1958) Review of Social Theory & Social Structure. *American Journal of Sociology*, 64: 115–127.

Kuhn, Thomas S. (1968) The History of Science. *International Encyclopedia of the Social Sciences*. New York: Macmillan: 14: 74–83 (also 'The Merton Thesis', 79–82).

Kuhn, Thomas (1962) *The Structure of Scientific Revolutions*. Chicago, IL: The University of Chicago Press.

Landau, Martin (1968) On the Use of Functional Analysis in American Science. *Social Research*, 35: 48–75.

Lazarsfeld, Paul F. (1975) Working with Merton. In L.A. Coser (ed.) *The Idea of Social Structure*. New York: Harcourt Brace Jovanovich: 35–66.

Lee, R. (2010) The Secret Life of Focus Groups: Robert Merton and the Diffusion of a Research Method. *American Sociologist*, 41 (2): 115–141.

Levine, Donald N. (2006) Ambivalence towards Autonomous Theory – and Ours. *Canadian Journal of Sociology/Cahiers canadiens de sociologie*, 31 (2): 235–243.

Lipset, S.M. (1993) Jeremiah Kaplan, The Free Press, and Post-War Sociology. *American Sociological Association Footnotes*, 7.

Marsh, Robert (2010) Merton's Sociology 215–216 Course. *The American Sociologist*, 41 (2): 99–114.

McCaughey, Robert (2003) *Stand, Columbia: A History of Columbia University*. New York: Columbia University Press.

Merton, R.K. (1994) A Life of Learning: Charles Homer Haskins Lecture. *American Council of Learned Societies*, Occasional Paper No. 25.

Merton, R.K. (1987a) The Focussed Interview & Focus Groups: Continuities and Discontinuities. *Public Opinion Quarterly*, 51: 550–566.

Merton, R.K. (1987b) Three Fragments from a Sociologist's Notebooks: Establishing the Phenomenon, Specified Ignorance and Strategic Research Materials. *Annual Review of Sociology*, 13: 1–28.

Merton, R.K. (1985) George Sarton: Episodic Recollections by an Unruly Apprentice. *Isis*, 76: 477–486.

Merton, R.K. (1984) The Fallacy of the Latest Word: The Case of Pietism and Science. *American Journal of Sociology*, 89: 1091–1121.

Merton, RK (1982) *Social Research and the Practicing Professions*. Cambridge: Abt Books.

Merton, R.K. (1981) Remarks on Theoretical Pluralism. In R.K. Merton and Peter M. Blau (eds) *Continuities in Structural Inquiry* (4th edn). London: Sage Publications: i–v.

Merton, R.K. (1977) *The Sociology of Science in Europe*. Robert K. Merton, Jerry Gaston and Adam Podgorecki (eds). Carbondale, IL: University of Southern Illinois Press.

Merton, R.K. (1961a[1976]) Social Problems and Sociological Theory. In Robert K. Merton and Robert Nisbet (eds) *Contemporary Social Problems* (4th edn). New York: Harcourt Brace Jovanovich: 1–43.

Merton, R.K. (1975) Structural Analysis in Sociology. In Peter M. Blau, ed. *Approaches to the Study of Social Structure*. New York: The Free Press: 21–52.

Merton, R.K. (1972a) Insiders and Outsiders: A Chapter in the Sociology of Knowledge. *American Journal of Sociology*, 77: 9–47.

Merton, R.K. (1971) The Precarious Foundations of Detachment in Sociology. In Edward A. Tiryakian (ed.) *The Phenomenon of Sociology*. New York: Appleton-Century-Crofts: 188–199.

Merton, R.K. (1968) *Social Theory and Social Structure*. Free Press.

Merton, R.K. (1963) Basic Research and Potentials of Relevance. *American Behavioral Scientist*, 6: 86–90.

Merton, R.K. (1961b) Now the Case for Sociology: The Canons of the Anti-Sociologist. *New York Times Magazine*, 16 July.

Merton, R.K. (1961c) Social Conflict in Styles of Sociological Work. *Transactions, Fourth World Congress of Sociology*, 3: 21–46.

Merton, R.K. (1959) Notes on Problem-Finding in Sociology. In Robert K. Merton, Leonard Broom, & Leonard S. Cottrell, Jr. (eds) *Sociology Today*. New York: Basic Books: ix–xxxiv.

Merton, R.K. (1949d) Patterns of Influence: A Study of Interpersonal Influence and Communications Behavior in a Local Community. In Paul F. Lazarsfeld & Frank Stanton (eds) *Communications Research, 1948–49*. New York: Harper & Brothers: 180–219.

Merton, R.K. (1948a) The Bearing of Sociological Theory on Empirical Research. *American Sociological Review*, 13: 505–515.

Merton, R.K. (1948b) The Self-Fulfilling Prophecy. *Antioch Review* (Summer): 193–210.

Merton, R.K. (1948c) Discrimination and the American Creed. In R.M. Maclver (ed.) *Discrimination and National Welfare*. New York: Harper & Brothers: 99–126.

Merton, R.K. (1947a) The Machine, the Worker, and the Engineer. *Science*, 105: 79–84.

Merton, R.K. (1947b) Selected Problems of Field Work in the Planned Community. *American Sociological Review*, 12, 304–12.

Merton, R.K. (1945a) Role of the Intellectual in Public Bureaucracy. *Social Forces*, 23: 405–415.

Merton, R.K. (1945b) Sociology of Knowledge. In Georges Gurvitch & Wilbert E. Moore (eds) *Twentieth Century Sociology*. New York: Philosophical Library: 366–405.

Merton, R.K. (1945c) Sociological theory. *American Journal of Sociology*, 50: 462–473.

Merton, R.K. (1940) Bureaucratic Structure and Personality. *Social Forces*, 18, 560–568.

Merton, R.K. with Marjorie Fiske & Patricia Kendall (1956) *The Focused Interview*. New York: The Free Press (1990 Second edition; 2004 with introduction by Peter Simonson).

Merton, R.K. with the assistance of Marjorie Fiske & Alberta Curtis (1946) *Mass Persuasion*. New York: Harper & Brothers

Merton, R.K. with Alisa P. Gray, Barbara Hockey & Hanan C. Selvin (eds) (1952) *Reader in Bureaucracy*. New York: The Free Press.

Merton, R.K. with Paul K. Hatt (1949c) Election Polling Forecasts and Public Images of Social Science. *Public Opinion Quarterly*, 13: 185–222

Merton, R.K. with Paul Lazarsfeld (1954) Friendship as a Social Process: A Substantive and Methodological Analysis. In Morroe Berger, Theodore Abel & Charles Page (eds) *Freedom and Control in Modern Society*. New York: Van Nostrand: 18–66.

Merton, R.K. with Daniel Lerner (1951) Social Scientists and Research Policy. In Daniel Lerner & H.D. Lasswell (eds) *The Policy Sciences*. Stanford, CA: Stanford University Press: 282–307.

Merton, R.K. with Alice Kitt Rossi (1950) Contributions to the Theory of Reference Group Behavior. In Robert K. Merton & Paul F. Lazarsfeld (eds) *Continuities in Social Research*. New York: The Free Press: 40–105.

Merton, R.K. with Bryce Ryan (1944) The Value of High School Scholarship on the Labor Market. *Journal of Educational Sociology*, 17: 524–534.

Merton, R.K. & Arnold Thackray (1972b) On Discipline Building: The Paradoxes of George Sarton. *Isis*, 63, 219: 473–495.

Merton, R.K. with Patricia S. West, Marie Jahoda & Hanan C. Selvin (1951) Social Policy and Social Research on Housing. *Journal of Social Issues*, 8 (1, 2).

Persell, Caroline H. (1984) An Interview with Robert K. Merton. *Teaching Sociology*, 11: 355–386.

Platt, Jennifer (1992) The Social Science Research Council's 1940s Restudy of Robert Angell's Cases from *The Family Encounters the Depression*. *Journal of the History of the Behavioral Sciences*, 28 (2): 143–157.

Schweber, Libby (2002) Wartime Research and the Quantification of American Sociology. The View from the *American Soldier*. *Revue d'Histoire des Sciences Humaines*, 2002/1 (6): 65–94.

Sica, Alan (2010) Merton, Mannheim, and the Sociology of Knowledge. In Craig J. Calhoun (ed.) *Robert K. Merton Sociology of Science and Sociology as Science*. New York: Columbia University Press: 164–181.

Sica, Alan (2007) Robert K. Merton. In Rob Stones (ed.) *Key Sociological Thinkers*. London: Macmillan.

Simonson, Peter (2010) Merton's Skeptical Faith. In *Refiguring Mass Communication: A History*. Urbana, IL: University of Illinois Press: 123–162.

Simonson, Peter (2006) Public Image, Celebrity, and American Political Life: Re-reading Robert Merton's *Mass Persuasion*. *Political Communication*, 23: 271–284.

Simonson, Peter (2005) The Serendipity of Merton's Communications Research. *International Journal of Public Opinion Research*, 17 (3): 277–297.

Simonson, Peter (2004) Introduction. In Robert K. Merton, Marjorie Fiske & Alberta Curtis (eds) *Mass Persuasion: The Social Psychology of a War Bond Drive* by Robert K. Merton, Marjorie Fiske, & Alberta Curtis. New York: Howard Fertig: xi–xlix.

Stinchcombe, Arthur (1968) *Constructing Social Theories*. New York: Harcourt, Brace & World.

Stouffer, Samuel (ed.) (1949–1950) *The American Soldier 4 vols. Studies in Social Psychology in World War II*. Princeton, NJ: Princeton University Press.

Sussmann, Leila A. (1963) *Dear FDR: A Study of Political Letter-Writing*. Totowa, NJ: The Bedminister Press. (Merton's preface xiii–xxv).

Swedberg, Richard (2019) How Do You Make Sociology out of Data? Robert K. Merton's Course in Theorizing (Soc 213–214). *The American Sociologist*, 50 (1): 1–36.

Sztompka, Piotr (ed.) (1996) *Robert K. Merton on Social Structure and Science. The Heritage of Sociology*, Donald N. Levine (ed.). Chicago, IL: The University of Chicago Press: 1–20.

Taylor, Bryan; Paul Walton, Jock Young (1973) *The New Criminology For a Social Theory of Deviance*. London: Routledge

Turner, Stephen (2009) Many Approaches, but Few Arrivals: Merton and the Columbia Model of Theory Construction. *Philosophy of Social Science*, special issue 39 (2).

Whitehead, Alfred (1917) *The Organisation of Thought*. London: Williams & Norgate.

Wilson, John (1983) *Social Theory*. Englewood Cliffs, NJ: Prentice-Hall.

Zetterberg, Hans (1965[1954]) *On Theory and Verification in Sociology* (3rd edn). Totawa, NJ: Bedminster Press.

4

MIDDLE YEARS AT COLUMBIA

What might be seen as Merton's 'third scholarly phase' began in the mid-1950s. It retains much of his broad programme, although one which had a higher theoretical emphasis and less explicit methodological concerns than his previous work. Merton also developed a broader 'structural analysis', in part building on more explicit attention to the work of Simmel which he facilitated through a course. He returns to his 'roots' or 'first love': sociology of science. This return was staged on the highly visible occasion of his presidential address to ASA (1957). A wider sponsorship for the sociology of science programme was sought, and there is a concern to gain resources and recognition for the continued development of sociology as a discipline. During this period Merton served a term as President of ASA and produced several volumes concerned with reviewing the state of sociology and applied sociology. This change of direction is not large.

A long article by Hunt (1961) revealed something of Merton's modus operandi during this period:

> What Merton does in his study after four-thirty every morning is to evaluate, classify, and abbreviate into notes the masses of material derived from his own readings and from surveys, interviews, and tabulations made under his direction by a dozen graduate students. Picking out some item … he studies it, pauses to puff on his pipe and stare meditatively at the ceiling, then turns to a battery of ten staggeringly cross-indexed filing cases containing the thousands of figures and millions of words he has compiled over the last twenty-five years and rummages through one of them for a document to compare with the paper before him. Having drawn some conclusion from the comparison, he jots a few notes on a pad, looks up a handful of obscure allusions, computes a quick mean deviation or chi-square analysis, and rattles off his findings on a typewriter, using paper of three different colors for extra-special cross-referencing.

Engagements

Merton gave radio talks from time to time, although he missed an immediate audience. From late 1962 through early 1963 he was the moderator for *Court of Reason* screening on independent New York 'educational channel' WDNT sponsored by the University of Chicago. In each weekly session on Wednesday evenings Merton moderated (Simonson, 2010: 158–160), endeavouring to steer the discussion amongst a panel of relevant experts to provide sound arguments on topics such as "Red China, censorship, the military industrial complex, *Webster's Dictionary*, birth control, the death penalty, automation, social revolution abroad, educational testing integration, religion". The programmes were well received by relevant intelligentsia. But Merton resigned to protest the dismissal of the station manager who had innovatively developed interesting educational and cultural programmes. Two years after, Merton interviewed Marshall McLuhan for the same station, subjecting McLuhan's rather untamed showmanship to sober analysis (Simonson, 2010).

Continuities (*STSS*)

In this period Merton continued his work on updating and extending various of the theoretical essays laid down in the previous period, in a series of 'continuities' and these were included in a much-expanded version of *Social Theory and Social Structure* published in 1957. Indeed, this was a period of considerable theoretical development. As he later commented:

> By the mid-50s my own research programme, as distinct from that of the local thought-collective of which I was a member, had shifted from a monographic focus on particular sets of empirical sociological questions to a renewed focus on *identifying* problems in structural sociology.
>
> *(1984: 279)*

Merton's development of 'role-set' theory was worked up in this period. Work on the properties of groups was facilitated by a 1955/56 post-graduate course on Selected Problems in the Theory of Organizations with a reading programme on Simmel's writings (Levine et al., 1976; Merton, 1968: 364, ftnt. 46).

During this period Merton also attempted to come to terms with broadening streams in the development of sociology – both through his sociological accounts of social theory (presaging the later sociology of sociology developed by Gouldner, 1970 and Friedrichs, 1970) and through theoretical restatements, in which he signalled the importance of recognising 'sociological ambivalence' that are generated by social structures (1963). With Paul Lazarsfeld he launched a programme on the history of social research which was to yield several books.

Alongside these two major foci of interest there continued a stream of tasks associated with being a prominent figure in American sociology, especially providing commentaries, forewords and updating previously published material.

In 1961 he was with a group extensively touring Russia, meeting with Russian sociologists, whom he criticised in his later report as overly empiricist. A third, and final, edition of *STSS* was produced in 1968. This included an extension of the introduction by two new chapters in Part 1 which had been published separately in 1967 as *On Theoretical Sociology*. The new Chapter 1 "states the case for the distinctive functions of histories of sociological theory and formulations of currently utilized theory". He distinguishes between several ways in which past ideas might be related to current – multiple simultaneous discoveries, rediscoveries (where an idea emerges again after a long interval), prediscoveries (precursor ideas), anticipations ("earlier formations overlap the later ones but do not focus upon and draw out the same set of implications") and adumbrations (mere vague foreshadowing). The chapter then illustrates these concepts. A final section brings out the several functions of classical theory,

> All apart from reading the Masters for the purposes of writing a history of sociological theory, then, acquaintance and re-acquaintance with the classics have a variety of functions. These range from the direct pleasure of coming upon an aesthetically pleasing and more cogent version of one's ideas, through the satisfaction of independent confirmation of these ideas by a powerful mind, and the educative function of developing high standards of taste for sociological work to the interactive effect of developing new ideas by turning to older writings within the context of contemporary knowledge.
>
> *(1968: 17)*

The new Chapter 2 was devoted to further development of the conception of 'middle-range theories'.

At this stage in his career Merton played an important role in developing two major texts that brought together much of then-contemporary American sociology. As with other presidential tenures, Merton contributed a presidential address but also presided over the preparation of a volume – *Sociology Today: Problems and Prospects* which sought to not just describe many of the 30 (25 were covered) or more sociological specialities but to

> sort out and critically examine problems for investigation that developments in the major branches of sociology have thrust into prominence. They deal, for the most part, with strategic problems, with those that must be solved before it becomes possible to work, to good effect, on other sociological problems in the offing.
>
> *(Merton et al., 1959)*

Fitting in with the volume's concern with problematics, Merton's introductory essay deals with 'problem-finding'. As well as editing the papers published in the book, he included in his essay examples from many. As a result, he provides an exploratory review of the types of research problems which occur at different stages of a research programme and the social conditions underlying these.

Another edited collection *Contemporary Social Problems* (1961[1976]), edited with Robert Nisbet, included 13 chapters on various areas of social problems (e.g. crime). The volume reviewed the relationship between social issues and sociological knowledge, across the whole field of social problems. Again, Merton's epilogue (in the first three editions) or introductory chapter (in the fourth edition) provided a framework for the whole volume, laying out ways sociologists might study social problems. This requires the following agenda, which provides an overview of his chapter:

> In examining the sociological notion of a social problem, we must treat at least eight connected questions: (1) the central criterion of a social problem: a significant discrepancy between social standards and social actuality; (2) the sense in which social problems have social origins; (3) the judges of social problems, those people who in fact principally define the great problems in a society; (4) manifest and latent social problems; (5) the social perception of social problems; (6) the ways in which belief in the corrigibility of unwanted social situations enters into the definition of social problems; (7) the hazards of 'subjectivism' as an orientation toward social problems; and finally, (8) the muddle surrounding the question of a 'value-free' sociology.
>
> *(48)*

These cooperative intellectual enterprises, under Merton's active coordination, might be seen as further mapping out a long-term programme for the systematic development of sociology. They perhaps, too, were an expression of his central role in the discipline, and the exercising of a responsibility which came with that position.

Professions

Professions, too, are major institutions in modern societies (see Chapter 3) and Merton contributed to their study over this period.

> Occupations in general and the professions in particular have come to be recognized as one of the more significant nuclei in the organization of society. A great share of people's waking hours is devoted to their occupational activities; the economic supports for group survival are provided through the pooled work of socially interrelated occupations; the aspirations, interests, and sentiments of men and women are largely organized and stamped with the mark of their occupations.
>
> *(1956: 156)*

His coverage of professions overlaps with and interpenetrates his writing on organisations, which is appropriate for studying modern societies. His broad essay is fairly orthodox, but an improvement on 'trait list' studies of professions. They are seen as strategic groups:

> Professionals are expected to apply their theoretically derived knowledge to the solution of paramount problems in life: disease, injustice, sin, and violation of human rights where stakes are high and uncertainty rife. To find ways of coping with the major troubles generally takes precedence over the routine demands of everyday life.
>
> *(1978[1982: 172])*

He sees a triad of characteristics as central to professions:

- systematically arranged knowledge (which it seeks to expand);
- trained capacity and technical skill;
- helping (i.e. altruistic behaviours).

Altruism is defined

> generically as behavior which benefits others at the expense of the benefactor. ... *Institutionalized altruism* is the special form of altruism in which structural arrangements, notably the distribution of rewards and penalties, promote behavior that is beneficial to others: especially as channeled by social structure.
>
> *(1982: 110)*

The main way Merton studied professions was through an invitation to study the training (i.e. in sociological terms 'professional socialisation') of doctors in a few innovative medical schools (Cornell, Western Reserve and Penn.), which at that period were considering major changes (e.g. 'comprehensive care') and wanted to bring social research to bear in assisting with that process. The work involved a multistage interview study, backed up by observations. Medical training involves socialisation into both technical and moral areas of skill, together with learning about working in tandem with other professions and paraprofessions. The study traced attitudes and relationship changes over the four-year college period. The analysis of the multiplex of values governing the physician's self-image was another useful contribution. In passages indicating the aspirations of young doctors Merton coined the (now extremely popular) term 'role model'.

Social structure (status-and-role analysis)

Merton extensively developed his analytical approach to social structure over this period. This is organised around the key concepts of status-set and role-set, but also includes attention to characteristics of membership groups, non-membership groups (e.g. reference groups), status-sequences and role-sequences and opportunity-structures. Social structure is defined as "that organized set of social relationships in which members of the society or group are variously implicated" (1968: 216).

However, the boundary between *cultural* and *social* structures is not entirely clear, and there is some ambiguity in Merton's various writings on this point. Cole (1979: 74–76) declares that norms belong in social structure whereas other aspects such as the meanings which people attach to social activities lie in culture. While it seems important to avoid reifying analytical distinctions, it may, however, be more useful to think of norms as spanning both culture and social structure, with culture providing an array of norms amongst which the social structure selects and then puts its selection into operation through frameworks of reward and constraints.

The central place of status-sets and role-sets is not entirely apparent in the architecture of Merton's published writings, although it was a major part of his lectures for more than a decade. These two key concepts were developed somewhat later in his intellectual career (from the mid-1950s through the 1970s in lectures) and are backed into his extended discussion of reference groups, and it is part of a discussion of the structural contexts of reference groups. (Indeed, whereas status-and-role theory is part of Merton's reference-group theory, I would prefer to reverse the emphasis and make reference-group theory a consequent set of ideas about how status-and-role structures actually work.) Moreover, Merton has otherwise signalled the importance of these analytical tools:

- by a separate article published in the *British Journal of Sociology* (Merton, 1957);
- by reasonably extended reference to them as examples of 'middle-range' theories in his introductory chapters of *STSS*; and
- using these two concepts in the title of an unpublished MS subtitled 'Structural Analysis is Sociology' (referred to in 1973: 501).

The concepts of status-set and role-set are developments of the general conceptions of 'status' and 'role' that were expounded by Linton. "By status Linton meant a position in a social system occupied by designated individuals; by role, the behavioural enacting of patterns of expectations attributed to that position" (Merton, 1968: 422). Essentially, a status involves a bundle of cultural expectations which guide the actual practice of social relationships amongst social positions which comprise any social structure.

The concept of a status-set refers to Linton's point that people occupy multiple statuses, or in Merton's definition it refers to "the complex of distinct positions assigned to individuals both within and among social systems" (1986b: 434) – for example, the distinct statuses of teacher, wife, mother, Catholic, Republican and so on (423).

Merton briefly develops one implication of his conception of status-sets – the problems they pose to the individual in articulating his/her status-set. The extent of the difficulty is seen to vary with the complexity of the status-set. Various mechanisms that may handle stress in status-sets include:

- perception by others in the status-set of competing obligations (e.g. employees are to a degree recognised to have families);
- shared agreement on the relative importance of conflicting status obligations;
- self-selection of successive statuses that lessen differences between the values learned in earlier-held statuses and those pertaining in later statuses;
- self-selection of statuses which are 'neutral' to one another.

Status-sets are seen as neither randomly sorted nor fully and tightly integrated, although the structural sources of the degree of integration are only briefly explored (see Cole, 1979: 204–206). Social structures are seen as likely to evolve norms and other mechanisms that will assist in articulating status-sets. This is related to the significance of status-sets as a mechanism through which different institutional areas of society are linked, in the person of individuals.

The related concept of status-sequence: a "succession of statuses through which an appreciable proportion of people move" (436) is also advanced (in part being pinpointed as a mechanism through which status-sets are articulated.) This allows a more precise translation of the distinction between achieved and ascribed statuses: these are different forms of status-sequence. Status-sets need to be ordered. Sztompka (1986: 288) cites from lecture notes the differences between particular statuses and the overall status-set of the person:

- Salient status: that status which is a focus of attention in interaction;
- Dominant status: in case of conflicting obligations between statuses in a status-set, that status to which other statuses are accommodated (or subordinated);
- Central status: that status which constrains the probability of acquiring or dropping other statuses during a person's life-course.

The conception of role-set is rather more innovative. Merton takes the widely used concept of role, and gives it a strong, useful social structural twist. Whereas Linton saw each status being matched by a single role, Merton suggests that it is analytically more fruitful to conceptualise each status as comprising an array of roles, which is *jointly* played out in relation to several types of complements to the status (and which he collectively termed the role-set). The concept of role-set is defined, and then described as:

> that complement of role relationships which persons have by virtue of occupying a particular social status. As one example, the single status of medical student entails not only the role of a student in relation to his teachers, but also an array of other roles relating the occupant of that status to other students, physicians, social workers, medical technicians, etc.
>
> *(1968: 423)*

The concept is rather more complicated than some analysts have realised since role-set refers not to the 'sub-statuses' constituting the status, but to the other positions/roles which the status occupant relates to. This relationship can be illustrated as Table 4.1 (cf. Cole, 1979: 58). Having indicated this complexity, Merton points to the structural sources of instability in role-sets, and the social mechanisms for the articulation of roles in a role-set.

Since the values and expectations of the role partners will differ, the individual occupying any status will face disparate, inconsistent and conflicting role expectations. Interestingly this inconsistency is seen as often welling up from the different social and economic strata within which various role partners are located (for example, in relation to a teacher, the social background of fellow teachers as opposed to school board members), and increasing with the diversity of strata locations from which various role partners are recruited. As he points out in his article (but does not then incorporate in *STSS*): "It is after all, one of the principal assumptions of Marxist theory as it is of all sociological theory: social differentiation generates distinct interests amongst those variously located in the structure of society" (1957a: 112).

A variety of social mechanisms help to articulate role-sets (1968: 425–433):

- differing intensity of role involvement among those in the role-set (some role relationships are central and others peripheral);
- differences in the power of those involved in a role-set;
- insulating role activities from observability by members of the role-set,
- observability by members of the role-set of their conflicting demands upon the occupants of a social status (this mechanism offsets 'pluralistic ignorance': the situation of unawareness of the extent to which values are in fact shared);
- social support by others in similar social statuses and thus with similar difficulties in coping with an unintegrated role-set;
- abridging the role-set (breaking off particular role relationships).

As well as providing for the examination of structured relationships between statuses, Merton attempts to analyse the emerging properties of social groups or

TABLE 4.1 Illustration of status-role analysis

Status	Role	Role-set
University teacher	Teacher	Student
	Researcher	Colleagues
	Administrator	Bureaucracy
'Housewife'	Mother	Children
	Wife	Husband
	Relative	In-laws

groupings which are built out of particular types of statuses. Embedded within his discussion of reference-group theory, Merton does attempt to sketch out a sociological analysis of membership groups. This is accomplished through an examination of the characteristics of group membership and through the listing of 26 properties groups are considered to possess. This discussion is recognized as an ad hoc and tentative stocktaking. But it is interesting that Merton avoids any premature attempt to develop a classification of types of groups, in order to first clarify the characteristics of groups in general.

Merton does not provide an easy transition between his theory of status-sets and role-sets and his theory of groups, except for a clue in a footnote to his later essay on sociological ambivalence. It is noted there that: "role-attributes are in some respects similar to properties of groups which are, after all, organised in the form of interrelated statuses and associated roles" 1976: 17, footnote 31).

Merton distinguishes between three different types of social formation: groups, collectivities and social categories. Social categories are aggregates of social statuses, the occupants of which are not in social interaction. While they have like social characteristics – of sex, age, marital condition, income and so on – they are not necessarily orientated toward a distinctive and common body of norms. Having like statuses and, consequently, similar interests and values, social categories can be mobilised into collectivities or into groups (1968: 353, 354). Collectivities are

> people who have a sense of solidarity by virtue of sharing common values and who have acquired an attendant sense of moral obligation to fulfil role-expectations
>
> *(1968: 353)*

> and in turn have a potential for group formation. A group is a number of people who interact with one another in accord with established patterns.
>
> *(1968: 339)*

and in addition, who define themselves as members and are defined by others as belonging to the group. Thus, groups have both objective (interaction) and subjective (social definition) aspects. This can be assembled (although Merton does not do so) into Table 4.2.

Merton also refers to 'non-membership groups' which are, essentially, the recruitment base for a group – sharing criteria of eligibility without actually being members. He continues his analysis of groups by listing their main properties (see Table 4.3; 1968: 364–380). The imagery behind the listing, which many of the posited dimensions point up, is of emergent group properties (properties not inherent in the individuals belonging to the group). These constitute an interplay between the extent to which members are involved with groups on the one hand, and on the other hand the capacity of the group to command the behaviour of its members in the short term, and in the long term to change in reaction to changing circumstances, respond to the wider social environment and so forth.

TABLE 4.2 Characteristics of three levels of social groupings

	Subjective		
	Similar norms (shared status)	Common norms	Shared definition and interaction
Group	X	x	x
Collectively	X	x	
Category	X		

TABLE 4.3 List of group characteristics

clarity/vagueness of social definitions of membership in the group
degree of (culturally prescribed) engagement of members in the group
actual (and expected) duration of membership in the group
actual (and expected) duration of the group
absolute (and relative) size of a group, or of component parts of a group
open/closed character of the group
'completeness' (ratio of actual to potential members)
degree of social differentiation
shape and height of stratification
type and degrees of social cohesion
the potential of fission/unity of a group
extent of social interaction within the group
character of social relations obtaining in the group
degree of expected conformity to norms of group (toleration of deviant behaviour and
  institutionalised departures from the strict definition of group-norms)
system of normative controls
degree of visibility/observability within the group
ecological structure of the group
autonomy/dependence of the group
degree of stability of the group
degree of stability of the structural context of the group
modes of maintaining stability of the group (and in relation to the structural context)
relative social standing of groups
relative power of groups.

Unfortunately, this approach is not linked to the terminology advanced in the useful Lazarsfeld and Menzel methodological essay (1961) on individual and group properties, although it is probably influenced by it. More systematic use of their typology of types of properties might have substructured this otherwise ad hoc listing. (For similar criticisms see Bierstedt, 1981: 482.)

Having provided a conceptual framework for describing the various elements of social structure, Merton then deploys a variety of conceptual frameworks which provide analytical purchase on how the social structure works, and especially, how it connects up with patterns of behaviour. The most well-known of these is 'reference-group theory' (first formulated by Herbert Hyman), but I have also located several other related theories.

Merton's reference-group theory is an attempt to show the mechanisms through which groups shape the behaviour of members. Perhaps the more interesting aspect, which Merton points up, is the way people are influenced by groups they are not members of and even by non-groups! (that is, fictional groups). What is socio-logically problematic is not so much that individuals are affected by social frames of reference, but which particular frames of reference are relevant in influencing them. In order to focus on this issue, Merton sifts through a plethora of scene-setting pre-liminary conceptual clarification of the way individuals are linked to groups:

- in-group v. out-group;
- groups v. quasi-groups or non-groups;
- positive v. negative groups;
- reference groups v. reference individuals;
- membership v. non-membership groups;
- normative v. evaluative contexts.

The theory of reference-groups consists in a scatter of propositions, for example (all from 1968):

- "non-membership groups are more likely to be adopted as reference groups in those social systems having high rates of mobility than in those which are relatively closed" (347), because in open systems such an orientation is more likely to be rewarded by membership;
- increasing intensity of in-group solidarity is often associated with hostility to out-groups, although the opposite process of allegiance to out-groups is even more sociologically interesting (352);
- individuals wishing to affiliate with a group are likely to adopt its values (359): designated 'anticipatory socialization';
- isolates in a group are more likely to adopt values of non-membership groups than those who are more centrally situated (359);
- "group affiliations which are matters of achievement, rather than of social ascription, tend to be more often relevant for the acceptance of values" amongst the upwardly mobile (383).

Another feature of Merton's conception of social structure is that it is a socially organised framework around which there is built social distributions of resources (opportunity-structure). He specifically notes authority, power, influence and pres-tige (1976: 124) and more generally means for achieving legitimate or illegitimate goals. (The concept of "opportunity-structure" was developed by Merton, but particularly taken up by Cloward and Ohlin, 1960.) This aspect of his work was particularly pointed up in his early essay on bureaucracy (1939a [1968: 250–251]) which makes the Marxian point (extended with a Weberian twist to cover wider arenas of social activity than the economy) that:

> With increasing bureaucratization, it becomes plain to all who would see that man is to a very important degree controlled by his social relations to the instruments of production. ... One must be employed by the bureaucracies in order to have access to tools in order to work in order to live.

Similar comments are made about the operation of 'Big Science' (Merton, 1973), and more generally in later work on patterns of accumulation of advantage and disadvantage.

An important property of social structures is the extent to which they shape information flows. As Stinchcombe points out, "Many of Merton's central concepts have to do with information" (1975: 20). He summarises these as involving three major mechanisms (cf. Merton, 1968: 373–376):

> First, sanctions depend on information. One person cannot sanction another for something he or she does not know the other has done. Second, information affects people's ideas about what choices they are confronted with. People do not choose alternatives they do not know about. Third, people use information in the concrete construction of successful activities, and success in an activity makes the activity more likely to continue. The collective competence of a science to solve scientific problems would be impossible if scientists could not find out the answers of other scientists to their questions.
>
> *(1975: 20–21)*

The way in which social structures motivate people through their reward structures is important in Mertonian analyses. Indeed, one of the central questions Merton poses in any context is to examine what kinds of signals for effort are given, and also what pointers of displeasure are conveyed so that the likely consequences for different categories of actors can be assessed. This is always a complex situation, as people's behaviour is not totally determined by reward structures but is mediated by their position in the social structure.

Alongside this concern with the way in which motivation for behaviour is shaped by reward structures, Merton places ideas about the way in which behaviour is constrained by mechanisms of social control. He has nicely pointed up the variability in the extent to which social norms are socially enforced in his alliterative formula of the 4Ps: prescription, preference, permission and proscription (1968: 187).

Merton has developed a theory of power, or more precisely, a theory of the maintenance and operation of power once structural power has been established. This stresses that authority is, in general, accorded by those who are prepared to obey as the exercise of power must meet with compliance. This in turn means that leaders must be sensitive to the norms of the group and have considerable information about the norms and group operation. Thus, leaders are, ironically perhaps, more trapped in the ongoing structure than their followers. However, leaders have a further responsibility to ensure adaptation to changes to secure long-term survival of the group, and this requires them to initiate or at least support change. But certainly, in Merton's theory, power is seen as necessary coordination function and a social resource whose exercise is closely limited by the followers. This is an image of power that operates only within a general consensus of values – however unenthusiastically held – and does not recognise a role for the application of violence which many other analysts see as a significant resource which underlies the wielding of power in at least some extreme contexts.

Finally, the various more technically analytical aspects of Merton's social structural theory can be set within a broader imagery of levels of social structure, and its overall mode of operation. Social structure is seen as being divided into two levels:

- the larger social structure (for example, the class or political structure of a society); and
- the social milieu (the patterns of interpersonal relations in which individuals are directly involved: 1955: 26, 27).

The pressures of the larger social structure are mediated through these social milieux, later referenced as 'microenvironments'. Merton suggests that there is a tendency in sociology to concentrate on the milieu, if only because of an interest in the meanings articulated by actors, which leads to a relative neglect of the larger social structure. This is an interesting comment, given that Merton's own emphasis often is on milieu rather than the larger structure (see 1973: 374).

But despite this emphasis, both structural levels are involved in many Mertonian analyses: for example, in examining role conflict he points to difficulties which might arise from the different social backgrounds of different members of the role-set; and in his analysis of deviance different social class situations are more likely to lead to particular modes of adaptation. It is a central feature of Merton's sociology that he connects up macrostructure with more immediate social organisation, and one of the prime analytical strengths of status-and-role theory is that it provides an understanding of the intervening channels through which macrostructures shape behaviour. (This linkage is particularly pointed up in the quotation used above (Chapter 3), that links characteristics of European sociologists of knowledge with American attitude surveyors.)

Either milieux or larger social structures may be characterised as being in a condition of organisation, disorganisation or unorganisation. "In unorganization a system of social relations has not yet evolved, while in disorganization acute or chronic disruptions occur in a more or less established system of social relations" (1976: 27). Social disorganisation is considered to be an accumulation of social dysfunctions (1976: 37). More specifically, Merton identifies four sources of social disorganisation (1976: 26–27):

- conflicting interests and values;
- conflicting status and role obligations;
- faulty socialisation;
- faulty social communication.

It is clear that in this model, there is a strong image of social groups as requiring a cultural structure and institutional structure that operate to dampen down the inherent conflicts and divergences to at least an operable level. The model assumes widespread consensus, within which there is considerable, but not unlimited, room for dissensus. Social disorganisation arises only when the normal coping mechanisms are overwhelmed. However, there is some room for innovation and long-term change, as his central image of social structure (([1968: 176] quoted in Chapter 2) which indicates that strains may stretch a social system, leading to social change, although such change too is limited, so that "When social mechanisms for control are operating effectively, these strains are kept within such bounds to limit change of the social structure".

This tension between routine and creative aspects of deviant behaviour is captured elsewhere in Merton's writings in the contrast between aberrants ("who have nothing new to propose and nothing old to restore, but seek only to satisfy their private interests or to express their private cravings" (1976a [1982a: 74]) and nonconformists ("who thrust towards a new morality or a promise to restore a morality held to have been put aside in social practice" 1976a [1982a: 74]).

Merton's work in both reference-group and role theory has attracted considerable commentary and discussion, although it is difficult to come to a rapid assessment of the fate of Merton's contributions to these concepts. Both of these two related areas of work have been largely dominated by empiricist social psychologists or social interactionist sociologists. Much recent work in role theory has become caught up in very detailed classificatory exercises in which an array of terms is fitted into an overarching 'role' framework (e.g. Biddle, 1979). Alternatively, role terms are used often loosely to guide sociographic descriptions of roles or of social processes affecting them. Within these wide or loose formulations, the structural acuteness of the Mertonian approach becomes blunted or lost. However, several important contributions to structural role analysis were included in *The Idea of Social Structure* (Blau, 1975; Rose Coser, 1990) and a more recent discussion suggests the convergence, or rather the complementarity, between structural and interactionist views of roles (Turner, 1985). Indeed, one of the more important theoretical and research programmes influenced by a Mertonian framework has been Blau's more recent work on macrostructures (foreshadowed in Blau, 1975).

Developing the sociology of science

Whereas his earlier (1930s) work in the historical sociology of science had focused on the interrelationships between the social institution of science and other areas of society, Merton's later sociology of science centred on the key internal features of science as an institution. Merton later summarised his own later work in the sociology of science as follows:

> It was along such lines [i.e. the interaction between social and intellectual influences internal and external to the institution of science] that, during the later 1940s and intermittently in the next decade, I continued my work on problems of the normative structure of science and turned to processes involved in its social organization. Attention was first centered on the process of social and cognitive competition in what Michael Polanyi called 'the scientific community' Starting in the middle 1950s, this plan of work led to further inquiry into patterns of competition among scientists, the reward structure of science as related to the assessed significance of contributions to scientific knowledge and, most recently, to inquiry into the institutionalized processes of such cognitive assessment (as exemplified by refereeing).
>
> *(1977: 23)*

Merton's return to an interest in sociology of science was launched through the highly visible forum of his 1957 Presidential Address to the American Sociological Society. Reportedly the address, although lengthy, held the audience spellbound. This address involved a reconceptualisation of the social structure of science aroused by a continued interest in the phenomena of multiple independent simultaneous discovery, priority disputes and the commemorative use of eponymy and other honours in science.

Key to this rejuvenated programme

> was the conceptualization that the institutionally reinforced drive for professional recognition, acquired almost exclusively in return for priority in scientific contributions and symbolized in the upper reaches of discovery by eponymy, constitutes the normatively prescribed reward for scientific achievement and thus the basis for a self-contained reward system of science.
>
> *(Storer, 1973: xxiii)*

Central to this image of science was the idea that scientific discoveries were given to the scientific community by the discoverers but in return for an acknowledgement (through citations) that the discovery was the symbolic property of the discoverer. Given the social pressures underlying the development of science discoveries are likely to be, in principle at least, *independent multiples* (likely to be uncovered by any of many competitors) and that the reward systems of science impel scientists to seek recognition of their discoveries by others in the form of citations which acknowledge intellectual debts. As a result of the fateful conjunction of these two principles, much of the energy of scientists becomes expended in attempting to secure their property rights to public recognition of their discoveries – if necessary, through occasionally clamorous 'priority disputes'. The prevalence of this is dampened by the norm of requiring humility, but this contrasting set of demands creates ambivalence often arising in the form of (deceitful) denial that priority is of any concern (often proclaimed in the middle of a priority battle!).

Indeed, Merton paints a picture of the *pure* motives of scientists being somewhat undermined by petty squabbles over priority and desire for the immortality of recognition. While many scientists work quietly at assigned puzzles, the motivation for intense scientific activity is the reward of recognition which flows from having been the first to make a discovery. The more significant the advance, the higher the prestige accorded the discoverer, and therefore with such high stakes, the more potent the likelihood of priority disputes. Moreover, if the pressure for discovery is too great, social pathologies in science may result. In particular, deploying his opportunity-structure-and-anomie framework Merton is able to indicate how such outcomes are likely given particular discontinuities between the cultural and social structures of science.

Much of his work from the 1960s on was in the Columbia programme in the Sociology of Science, supported by the National Science Foundation, with his students-colleagues Harriet Zuckerman, Stephen Cole, Jonathan Cole, later Thomas Gieryn and others. This programme included empirical studies of the evaluation systems across several scientific disciplines, of age structures and the differential effects of codification in science. Collaborative work has also meant that, while these essays retain the Mertonian stamp of theoretical argument coupled with an historically rich scatter of illustration, they also include extensive systematic empirical research support.

Interest continued in analysing the role of norms in science. Merton emphasises ambivalence in the operation of science. He makes sure that his portrait of key norms is offset also by counter-norms which also have some force. Scientists often have to mediate within the various pairs, sometimes in a cyclical pattern. The four Mertonian norms (often abbreviated as the CUDOS norms) can be summarised as:

- **communism**: all scientists should have common ownership of scientific goods (intellectual property), to promote collective collaboration; secrecy is the opposite of this norm;
- **universalism**: scientific validity is independent of the sociopolitical status/ personal attributes of its participants;
- **disinterestedness**: scientific institutions act for the benefit of a common scientific enterprise, rather than for the personal gain of individuals within them;
- **organised scepticism**: scientific claims should be exposed to critical scrutiny before being accepted: both in methodology and institutional codes of conduct.

As a balance to these norms, Merton later postulated counter-norms (as articulated by Mitroff (1974: although see Merton 1976 Chapter 3 'Postscript' for criticism of other aspects of Mitroff's work):

- **Solitariness** (secrecy, miserism) is often used to keep findings secret in order to be able to claim patent rights, and in order to ensure primacy when published;
  - **Particularism** is the assertion that whilst in theory there are no boundaries to people contributing to the body of knowledge, in practice this is a real issue, and in addition, scientists do judge contributions to science by their personal knowledge of the researcher;
  - **Interestedness** arises because scientists have genuine interests at stake in the reception of their research – well-received papers can have good prospects for their careers, whereas as conversely, being discredited can undermine the reception of future publications;
  - **Dogmatism** because careers are built upon a particular premise (theory) being true they may be fiercely held (and with his 'Phoenix phenomenom' Merton later suggested that often classic notions were retained despite frequent empirical invalidation).

The norms are expressed in the form of prescriptions, proscriptions, preferences and permissions. They are legitimatised in terms of institutional values. They are held out by statement and example and backed up by sanctions, including moral upset to transgressions, and to some extent internalised by scientists. The norms flow from the values embedded in a more generalised scientific 'ethos' and are carried as a moral consensus amongst communities of scientists.

Merton (1942) distinguished between technical and moral norms (also referred to as cognitive versus social norms: Zuckerman, 1988). Among the former, Merton identified two methodological principles (adequate, valid and reliable empirical evidence, as well as logical consistency) that guide and support the "extension of certified knowledge", which is "the institutional goal of science" (1942: 117). "Replication" is sometimes considered to be a "fifth norm". More recently, John Ziman suggested that "originality" be added as a norm and, sometimes in spelling out the acronym CUDOS, O is taken to stand for originality (Ziman, 2000), The moral norms likewise support this overarching goal, but in a different way: "The mores of science possess a methodological rationale but they are binding, not because they are procedurally efficient, but because they are believed right and good. They are moral, not technical, prescriptions" (118).

Do the norms (and counter-norms) adequately capture the overall normative system of science? The consensus is that they do not – nor could any finite list of normative principles represent the complex and evolving normative system of science. A significant implication of this approach is that it sets up science as a separate social institution, with its own internal 'property system' and mechanisms of peer recognition and control, ensuring that scientists are motivated to distance their activities from those fitting within other institutional spheres. (For example, recognition can be accorded by peers, not the general public.)

There have been a stream of empirical studies seeking to measure the extent to which scientists (1) agree with, (2) honour, and/or (3) see other scientists as honouring these norms. Many studies find they are formally honoured, but honoured 'more in the breach' in terms of actual behaviour (e.g. Andersen et al., 2007). But the scene has changed structurally. Many studies have endeavoured to track the putative change in norms as a result of commercialisation and increased competition amongst institutions. For example, Ziman (2000) identified norms characterising non-academic (or 'post-academic') research, namely Proprietary, Local, Authoritarian, Commissioned and Expert Work (PLACE). There has been a recent wave of research and writing on this topic. But research is necessary into the degree to which the norms are agreed among scientists and how they affect the level of competition, pressure to produce fraudulent findings, etc.

Moreover, the status of these norms in the Mertonian account is problematic: as it is not clear whether they are seen as 'necessary' for the advance of science (or even 'deduced' from an analysis of the requirements of science) or whether they have a causal force in their own right (see Gieryn, 1982: 295; Kuhn, 1977: xxii). It seems more than likely that the 'moral norms' of science have a multiple effect as *both* ideology and motivational driving force. Whilst some sociologists of science have suggested jettisoning norms in their analyses of science, coverage of norms makes sense as long as they are seen as ideals that:

- are counterbalanced by opposing norms;
- as a set are not exhaustive of the potential principles; and
- are indicative of what undoubtedly is a broader, far more complex, and largely unknowable normative system.

Having established this basic framework for analysing science, and organised a loose-knit research team, Merton was then able to raise and examine an array of subsequent questions, including:

- variation over time in the conditions under which scientific competition becomes intensified;
- the role of 'geniuses' in science as opposed to the total social determination of ideas ("It was precisely the great scientists, [Merton] points out, who prove to be most capable of exploiting the current state of the art – they are involved in many more multiples than others – so that the two theoretical perspectives actually complement each other": (Storer in Merton, 1973: 284);
- different theoretical and policy implications of the phenomenon of multiple discoveries;
- the stress and inner conflict induced in scientists by the complexities and trade-offs involved within the normative structure of science;
- the consequences for the operation of science of the accumulation of recognition by the scientific elite;
- an examination of the actual working of the system of evaluating the quality of scientific work, through the refereeing system and other structural modes of organised scepticism;

- the consequences for scientific activity of differences in the organization of knowledge in a discipline (its degree of codification);
- the impact of demographic structure (age and gender) on the social organisation of science.

The general thrust of this rapid exploitation of his own paradigm has been to explore further the various components of the internal structure of science in order to detail its workings. As well, Merton (and his research programme) considered a range of other aspects of science. Some conceptualised scientific work itself: for example, the idea of basic science with 'potentials of relevance' for a third way of science work between pure and applied science. He rejected the 'storybook' image of science that publications emerge in a final form bereft of the scaffolding which built them, and which provide the background data necessary for sociological analyses: "Typically, the scientific paper or monograph presents an immaculate appearance which reproduces little or nothing of the intuitive leaps, false starts, mistakes, loose ends, and happy accidents that actually cluttered up the inquiry" (1968: 4). Various intuitional arrangements within science were considered: e.g. vigilance systems, communications, reward systems, resource allocations. The historical evolution of institutions within science necessary for carrying out various functions were examined, such as the evolution of the journal and peer-review systems. Opportunity-structures were added to the analytical toolkit. One implication of opportunity-structures is that there can be heightened competition around boundaries: those just under a barrier may be particularly motivated to breach it, or it can create a 'ceiling effect'. One manifestation of this is the metaphorical '41st chair' which is reference to the 40 chairs in the *Académie Française*, but with worthy candidates lying just outside. Rather, it symbolises those who could be judged worthy of membership yet who are not elected. Merton notes that "the phenomenon of the 41st chair is an artifact of having a fixed number of places available at the summit of recognition" (1968: 2). Finally, there has been progressive examination of each of a set of different axes of differentiation (gender, age, etc.) within science and different parts of the institutional complex of science in order to build up a more complete picture.

Alongside the development of Merton's later sociology of science, and especially in the 1960s and since, there have been a range of other developments in the study of science:

- Kuhn's work on cognitive change in science (especially his ideas of paradigms which structure 'normal' scientific work, and 'revolutions' in which old paradigms are overthrown in favour of newer ones which better handle 'anomalies');
- Derek J. de Solla Price's modelling of the growth of scientific knowledge and the communication networks (the 'invisible colleges') through which scientists work;
- Polanyi's essays on the 'republic of science';

- Eugene Garfield's development of citation indexes for science (and later for social science and the humanities, in which the linkages between scientific papers can be traced).

American work in the sociology of science, including the Columbia University Programme, drew on several of these developments. The Mertonian school was able to achieve a rapid breakthrough by harnessing the quantitative analyses of productivity, and especially the quality of scientific production using citation indices, fitting them into models of stages of scientific growth extended from Price. Having established measures of the apparent meritocratic order of scientists, the American sociologists of science then examined whether science, and especially its reward systems, operate in the 'objective' interests of science as a whole. Against this meritocratic model, they examined whether particularistic characteristics, such as age, gender, position in the stratificational order of science, or the academic institution scientists are based in, intrude into the production of scientific knowledge. In general, this programme of investigation has found that the actual operation of science cleaves fairly closely, but with some jarring, to this meritocratic model. In the work of the Mertonians, this then can become broadly explained in terms of a 'functional' model of stratification, in which the internal stratificational order (which they usually express as three strata of scientists of the first, second or third order) is seen as more or less correctly mirroring the distribution of talent, and thus being functional for the ongoing progress of science.

Although Merton and his school sees the operation of science as largely fair, there are some deviations such as the 'Matthew effect' in which already eminent scientists capture disproportionate recognition when collaborating or if involved as one of multiple independent discoveries. Less significant researchers become invisible. In developing this notion Merton particularly drew on the empirical research of Harriet Zuckerman. (She has pointed out that this is not an instance of the Matthew/Matilda effects: 2011: 130.) An extension of this is the 'Matilda effect' (coined in 1993 by science historian Margaret W. Rossiter referring to suffragist and abolitionist Matilda Joslyn Gage (1826–1898) which is a bias against acknowledging the achievements of those women scientists, whose work is instead attributed to their male colleagues. (Rigney (2010) has pulled together, at book length, much information about the operation of the Matthew effect across several realms.)

Merton then generalised this point into a 'Principle of Cumulative Advantage', briefly introduced in his earlier writings on science and he also pointed to its operation outside the realm of science. (The correlative is cumulative *dis*advantage, often mirroring the other in reverse.) Indeed, it lies at the heart of many large social problems as it is the causal mechanism for "income inequality growth, corruption growth, centralization of power growth, and hardening of class stratification". He (1988) described cumulative advantage as dealing with "the ways in which initial comparative advantage of trained capacity, structural location, and available resources make for successive increments of advantage such that the gaps between the haves and the have-nots … widen" (606). Merton contended that CAD processes are simultaneously *unfair* and *functional*, depending on the level of analysis upon which one focuses.

At the individual level, he emphasised the *injustice* of CAD from the vantage point of individual scientists – benefitting some individuals well beyond the value of their contributions while ignoring or minimising the equally meritorious contributions of others. However, he argued that this process had a different significance at the social-system level of the scientific enterprise taken as a whole. At that level, Merton argued, the same CAD process is *functional*, because it reflects an efficacious process and a positive result for the collective enterprise of scientific productivity. It has the overall effect of organising communications to maximise the distribution of ideas among key intellects (without regard for who is actually contributing the ideas), aligning junior talent with the proper nodes in the communication system of science according to their potential, and enabling all scientists working in a given area to recognise which ideas are most promising. Thus, Merton's overall analysis brought the argument home for functional analysis after all: the Matthew effect is a systemically valuable set of processes, despite its unavoidable costs for some individuals.

If a scientist secures an initial advantage, this is likely to be further built on. The PCA applied as well to institutions which are in competitive races. Institutions can be primed to reward precocity, i.e. those maturing quickly. Success is rewarded with better access to rewards, better placement in supportive institutions and recognition generally, but this may particularly disadvantage slow-off-the-mark late-bloomers. On the other hand, those doing less well initially may struggle to obtain the resources and other support needed to compete.

However, such processes are unlikely to continue to grind away unabated, and countervailing forces may kick in. Cumulative advantage may be offset with limiting factors: e.g. although highly talented, being swamped in an over-talented situation. The CAD processes satisfactorily provide the conceptual muscle needed to understand stratificational processes, and although there is ample empirical evidence, it needs to be more directly related to the theory.

But, a European/British located alternative 'constructivist/relativist' school of analysis developed from the 1970s in considerable opposition to the Mertonian programme (see e.g. Gieryn, 1982; Zuckerman, 1988). The 'strong programme' Sociology of Scientific Knowledge (SSK) in part opposed a 'weak' sociology of *scientists*. The constructivists often focused on laboratory studies or on the discourse of scientists, and broached the usual demarcation between scientific content and social content. Systematic research into research was usually avoided in favour of in-depth case studies. However, more recently the fierceness of debates between these approaches has abated as it has become realised that each complements the other.

In sum, The Columbia programme yielded several major and many minor empirical books and papers but also led to a coherent and wide-ranging model for analysing science.

Linking deviance theories

Although Merton was largely concerned with developing his own theoretical analyses, he also often played a role in showing how different theories can complement each other. Keeping up with the developments of new models in criminology, Merton was several times able to link these to his own evolving programme. In a comparison of four alternative theories of deviance, Merton (1976: 31–37) shows how each highlights a particular area of phenomena while leaving other aspects in darkness (see Table 4.4). While some theories can be combined, others clash or give rise to competing hypotheses and others 'talk past each other'. In my view, this is a splendid example of a paradigm, although not recognised as such by Merton.

With a rising tide of concern with crime and juvenile crime the applicability of appropriate theories became salient. The anomie-and-opportunity approach provided some justification for the ways the Great Society programme attempted to open up channels for achievement.

Sociological ambivalence and social psychology

From the mid-1950s through to the mid-1970s a Merton theme has been 'sociological ambivalence' (better: *social* ambivalence). In several essays written in the mid-1950s (including his 'Preliminaries to a Sociology of Medical Education' 1957a and his 'Priorities in Scientific Discovery' chapters (1957b) Merton noted that ambivalences arose as individuals were subject to various forms of cross-pressure from the complex social structure they were placed in. In 1963 this theme was taken up in an essay on 'sociological ambivalence' which a decade later became the anchoring point for several other inquiries all collected into one part of his book with this title (1976).

He suggests that the core-type of ambivalence involves ambivalence being embedded in particular statuses and status-sets, together with their associated roles (1963 [1976: 7]), but also in rather different language that "the major norms and

TABLE 4.4 Relationship between different theories of deviance

Theory	*Problem*	*Ignores*
differential association	cultural transmission of deviance	original development
anomie-and- opportunity structures	structural sources	cultural transmission
labelling theory/societal reaction	formation of deviant careers	subsequent careers
conflict theory	formation of legal rules	differing rates

minor counter-norms alternatively govern role-behaviour to produce ambivalence" (1963 [1976: 17]).

Merton then lists a hierarchical series of different types of ambivalence:

- (in the most restricted sense) it is the "incompatible normative expectations incorporated in a *single* role of a *single* social status (for example, the therapist role of the physician as distinct from other roles of his or her status as researcher, administrator, professional colleague, participant in the professional association, etc.)" (1976: 6);
- conflicts of interest or values between different statuses (i.e. status-set) occupied by a single person;
- conflict between several roles associated with a particular status (e.g. between teaching, research, administration etc. for a university person or scientist);
- contradictory cultural values (e.g. sacred family values v. business needs);
- "disjunction between culturally prescribed aspirations and socially structured avenues for realizing these aspirations" (1976: 11);
- 'marginal men' (such as immigrants or more generally the socially mobile) who have been subject to two sets of cultural values (in sequence, or through holding a reference orientation to a group of which one is not a member).

It is clear that it conveys an important *image* of social reality, that ambivalence is built into the complex way social structures are constructed, as opposed to images that social reality is a smooth facade of consensus. In presenting this image, Merton distances himself from Parsons who has indicated that in his understanding, societies can only tolerate a very limited amount of ambivalence and strain. Further, the discussion of sociological ambivalence serves to *summarise* several themes that run through Merton's writings:

- the importance of maintaining an interest in the experiential psychological level of analysis, while focusing particularly on the social structural contexts of that level;
- the varying ways and levels in which cultural and social structures are arranged and are variously integrated and malintegrated;
- the varying ways in which ambivalences flow from divergent tendencies in sets of cultural goals (and counter-goals) and are then amplified or contracted by structural means;
- the continuity between conformity and change;
- the consequences for institutional structures of the ambivalences they generate, through the amplification and diffusion of components of ambivalence.

Many other studies refer to sociological ambivalence although few investigate – Room (1976) who discusses its relevance to the explanation of alcohol problems is an exception. As with Merton's SEDs (see below), while these were later developments in his approach, they are integral to it.

Theoretical pluralism and structural analysis

At some point between 1968 (when the third edition of *Social Theory and Social Structure* was published) and 1975, Merton located his 'functional analyst' label within a broader '*structural analyst*' branding. (The first clear use of the term 'structural analysis' seems to be in the essay on 'Insiders and Outsiders' (1972 [1973: 136] although Merton had long used the cognate term analysis of 'structural constraints'. In his 1975 formulation of structural analysis Merton refers to "that variant of functional analysis which has evolved, over the years, into a distinct mode of structural analysis" (1976: ix). As with his paradigm of functional analysis, Merton sketches out a programmatic framework, and also argues a stance in relation to several issues in structural analysis.

Merton contrasts structural analysis with symbolic interactionism, but sees them as complementary ("like ham and eggs", 1976: 119). Within structural analysis there are various approaches, and Merton contrasts the classical mode of structural-functional analysis with 'this' variant. Merton drives two main contrasts between 'this' variant and that of Parsons – an emphasis on "structural sources and differential consequences of conflict, dysfunctions and contradictions in social structure" (1976: 126) and a commitment to a 'theoretical pluralism'. But, the thrust of 'this' variant of functional analysis' is limited by its lack of a clear imagery, as well as the lack of a name. For once, Merton's keen sense of naming seems to have deserted him, and this terminological lack may be a surface indication of underlying difficulty. (So, to exorcise this minor problem, I will refer to '*Mertonian* structural analysis'.)

The features of the Mertonian structural analysis is sketched out through a set of 'stipulations' which (1976: 120–126):

- emphasise its multiple ancestral lineages of thought;
- locate the main ancestral lineage as a convergence principally drawing from Marx and Durkheim;
- draw attention to the need to span both micro- and macrolevel analyses;
- identify the key microlevel process as (explicitly following Stinchcombe) as the "choice between socially structured alternatives";
- identify the key macrolevel structures as the "social distributions of … authority, power, influence and prestige" and the key macrolevel processes as involving "cumulation of advantage and disadvantage";
- posit that social structures generate social conflict;
- posit that sociological ambivalence is built into normative structures;
- posit that social structures generate differing rates of deviant behaviour;
- posit that social structures generate change within and of structure itself;
- posit that every new birth cohort modifies social structure as it passes through it;

- posit an analytical difference between manifest and latent levels of social structure;
- admit that structural analysis provides limited explanations.

Merton devotes little space to detailing this approach and gives no examples (perhaps due to space limitations) in very considerable contrast to the vigour of his earlier essay on functional analysis. Instead, readers are directed to several accounts as "having worked out the essentials of this mode of structural analysis, more deeply and more critically than I am prepared to do" (1975 [1976: 120]).

Interestingly, much of the essay is devoted to arguing a case for sociology as a multiparadigm discipline. The earlier image of a broad working consensus within sociology, containing a variety of approaches, is shaded over by a picture of sociology as consisting in a small plurality of complementary theoretical orientations. Whereas the earlier functional analysis essay did not draw any contrasts with any non-functional sociology, the later structural analysis essay explicitly suggests that there are other non-structural approaches to sociology. The 'functional analysis' component is retained: "it is analytically useful to distinguish between manifest and latent levels of social structure *as of social function*" (1976: 126, my emphasis).

Several of the points Merton makes in the 'stipulations' are interesting. No attempt at all is made to grapple with the offerings of French 'structuralism' which is unfairly dismissed (with negligible direct attention) as something of a newcomer within the broad stream of structural analysis. Indeed, the parvenu is seen as a "popular and sometimes undiscriminating social movement which has exploited through undisciplined extension the intellectual authority of … iconic figures" (1976: 121).

Another interesting point is that in this formulation the 'sacred trio' of sociology's founding fathers is split open, and a (unspecified) pairing of Durkheim and Marx is claimed as the underlying inspiration for structural analysis. And the dropping of Weber is surprising given the availability of structural readings of Weber (e.g. Turner, 1981) on the one hand, and on the other hand Merton's retention in his framework of structural analysis of Stinchcombe's model of the microprocesses, which strikes me as having a definite Weberian ambience. Surely, Simmel too, deserves a place in the sun as a precursor to structural sociology. While Merton validates Stinchcombe's interpretation of the *micro*processes underlying Mertonian structural analysis, he adds a *macro*sociological centrepiece of the accumulation processes (CAD) that are the mechanisms which build up stratification systems. While several of the points made in his 'stipulations' are interesting, they do not have the power of his earlier framework for functional analysis. This is largely because Merton is posting a framework around structural analysis, rather than capturing its core, through a clear statement of how a structural analysis might be accomplished. Perhaps it is this lack of specificity that has meant that reaction to this later essay has been negligible. Nevertheless, it is part of the backdrop for my own analysis of Merton's underlying mode which I develop in Chapter 6.

There seem to be few clues in Merton's own writings, as to the roots of this broader approach. However, the intellectual environment had been changing during the early 1970s with a heightened popularity of the term 'structuralism', while 'functional' analysis was being increasingly subject to critique. Whereas Kingsley Davis's 1959 presidential address to the American Sociological Association was on the myth of functional analysis, he had earlier been an enthusiastic functional analyst, who had published prominent and controversial functional analyses of prostitution and social stratification as well as a major textbook (*Human Society*, 1948). But in his 1959 address Davis denies any particular virtue in a uniquely functional mode of analysis, and argues that such virtues as functional analysis has, had already been incorporated into 'good sociological analysis'. This argument has been continued further by other writers, such as Goode (1973) in which he portrays functionalism as an empty castle, which critics continue to attack, seemingly unaware that the defensive positions have long been abandoned (if indeed they had ever been manned in the first place). Other sources unacknowledged by Merton in this essay may nevertheless have influenced his thinking. Gouldner argues that Merton's approach to a model of a social system "can be regarded as a strategy of minimal commitment" (1967: 143), and goes on to attempt to develop an underlying model of interchanges between partial structures which he glimpses within Merton's approach: he attempts to promote 'exchange' theory to a collective level, rather than its more usual lodgement at the individual level. Wallace (1983) makes a similar point in placing the Mertonian mode of analysis in his typology of theoretical approaches as a 'functional structuralism' alongside 'exchange structuralism' and 'conflict structuralism' but well separated from Parsonian 'functional imperativism'. The latter is seen as being concerned with the ways in which social systems are organised to cope with meeting systemic requirements, whereas the three forms of 'structuralism' share an interest in the explanation of social phenomena (patterns of behaviour and social interaction) in terms of the social structure of statuses of participants. The three structuralisms are organised in a hierarchy: "Whereas functional structuralism typically focuses on one side of a given social transaction, exchange structuralism attends to both sides" (Wallace, 1969: 28) and conflict structuralists examine situations of unequal exchange in which a benefit is traded for an injury. Charles Page's retrospective comment (1982: 262) that "Later I became interested … by the functional doctrine of the Mertonian, not the Parsonian variety" is an indication that the distinction between the two was becoming more widely recognised at this time.

As functional analysis wound down, structural analysis wound up. One direct source of influence was a series of articles by an Italian social theorist, Barbano (e.g. 1968). Merton himself draws attention to the point that this essay is subtitled 'the Emancipation of structural analysis in Sociology'. Barbarno is particularly concerned to drive a wedge between Mertonian structural analysis and Parsons's structural-functionalism. He seems to centre on the idea that Mertonian structuralism concentrates on the *item* rather than the *system*. However, neither of these sources develop their thinking much beyond these sketches. The main point that most of this group of commentators shared was the conception that Merton was a structural analyst rather than a functional analyst, but they do not then converge in their presentation of what a structuralist approach might involve. A final and very immediate influence may have come from Peter Blau, a former student of Merton's, at the time a colleague, and perhaps most importantly the organiser of the plenary session presentations to the 1974 Conference of the American Sociological Association at which Merton's 1975 essay was presented. The aim of these sessions (and the subsequent collection) was to "juxtapose various theoretical conceptions of structural analysis" (Blau, 1975: 2). This context, and the terminology used in it, may have itself exerted some pressure towards the adoption of the structural mode of analysis. This is particularly reinforced by Blau's comment on Merton's community influentials paper that: "Although this paper was published in 1949, the same year as the functional paradigm was, it does not present a functional but a structural explanation of why influential citizens in a community exhibit two contrasting orientations to issues" (1975: 118).

Intimations of the sociological semantics programme

Alongside these programmes of study, Merton produced in the late 1950s two erudite volumes which later became ingredients for a latterly emergent programme on 'sociological semantics'. One book draft (written with Elinor Barber) analysing *Serendipity* became a 'time capsule' and lay unpublished for several decades and so is covered in Chapter 6. The other, *On the Shoulders of Giants* (OTSOG) was fairly quickly published and joined *STSS* as Merton's favourite amongst his works. Although *Serendipity* was completed before turning to *OTSOG*, the latter allowed the full potential of the Shandean mode to be elaborated. In turn though, this writing success seemingly displaced finishing work on the *Serendipity* text.

OTSOG was written in a vortex of ongoing activity chained to his desk but supplied by assistants with relevant library material, published in 1965 and republished as a Vicennial edition in 1985:

> Origins are one of Mr. Merton's compulsions: a letter to a friend on the origin of an aphorism attributed to Isaac Newton – 'If I have seen farther it is because I have stood on the shoulders of giants' – ended up as a 290-page book and earned him a footnote in *Bartlett's Familiar Quotations.*
>
> *(Cohen, 1998)*

The book is something of a literary 'detective mystery' sleuthing the historical trajectory of the uses of this metaphor over time. The study is couched in a delightful zigzagging 'Shandean' mode, a revered model for Merton since his youth. The book is blessed with dazzling erudition and adorned with many entertaining digressions. Most authors attribute the saying to Newton, whereas Merton was able to show that Bernard of Chartres in the twelfth century originated the aphorism. In doing so Merton also corrected those who tried to dignify the phrase by crediting it to (sometimes non-existent!) ancient authors. The book is also a serious inquiry into the phenomena of scholarly referencing and citing, the development of reputations and the place of science amid humane knowledge.

Merton deployed some of this material in his two new (1968) *STSS* chapters in discussing the relationship amongst different manifestations of the aphorism. He continued to address the relationship between the first and mature appearances of ideas and why they might be taken seriously. This might be because the 'prediscoverer' lacked stature, or because the context wasn't ready, because a crucial connection wasn't made, or because an empirical or practical test wasn't identified. Merton argues that the 'shoulders of giants' aphorism is a key metaphor through which the humility required of scientists is expressed; and that there is a non-linear development of science.

Summary

This period is notable for more sustained attention to a few theoretical and empirical research areas. This produced excellent research, and explored important, ideas, some of which were translated from the sociology of science site where they were formulated into more general theoretical ideas. Relaxing Merton's general theoretical stance allowed better conciliation with other approaches, but at some loss of a distinctive thrust and any opportunity to pull together a synthetic framework was lost.

References

Andersen, Melissa S.; Brian C. Martinson & Raymond De Vries (2007) Normative Dissonance in Science: Results from a National Survey of U.S. Scientists. *Journal of Empirical Research on Human Research Ethics*, 2 (4): 3–14.

Barbarno, Filippo (1968) Social Structures and Social Functions: The Emancipation of Structural Analysis in Sociology. *Inquiry*, 11: 40–84.

Biddle, Bruce (1979) *Role Theory: Expectations, Identities, and Behaviors*. New York: Academic Press.

Bierstedt, Robert (1966) *American Sociological Theory*. New York: Academic Press.

Blau, Peter (1975) Structural Constraints of Status Complements. In Lewis Coser (ed.) *The Idea of Social Structure*. New York: Harcourt Brace Jovanovich: 117–138.

Cloward, Richard & Lloyd Ohlin (1960) *Delinquency and Opportunity*. New York: The Free Press.

Cohen, Patricia (1998) An Eye for Patterns in the Social Fabric; Patriarch of Sociology Sees His Insights Become Just What Everyone Knows. *The New York Times*, Section B: 9.

Cole, Stephen (1979) *The Sociological Orientation: An Introduction*. Chicago, IL: Rand McNally.

Coser, Lewis (ed.) (1975) *Approaches to the Study of Social Structure*. New York: Free Press.

Coser, Rose Laub (1990) Reflections on Merton's Role-Set Theory. In Jon Clark, Celia Modgil & Sohan Modgil (eds) *Robert K. Merton: Consensus and Controversy*. London, New York & Philadelphia, PA: The Falmer Press: 159–176.

Davis, Kingsley (1959) The Myth of Functional Analysis as a Special Method in Sociology and Anthropology. *American Sociological Review*, 24 (6): 757–772.

Davis, Kingsley (1948) *Human Society*. New York: The Macmillan Company.

Friedrichs, Robert (1970) *A Sociology of Sociology*. New York: Free Press.

Gieryn, Thomas (1982) Relativist/Constructivist Programmes in the Sociology of Science: Redundance and Retreat. *Social Studies of Science*, 12: 279–297 (and ff).

Goode, William (1973) *Explorations in Social Theory*. New York: Oxford University Press.

Gouldner, Alvin (1967[1973]) *For Sociology*. London: Penguin.

Gouldner, Alvin (1970) *The Coming Crisis of Western Sociology*. London: Heinemann.

Hunt, Morton M. (1961) How Does It Come to Be So? Profile of Robert K. Merton. *New Yorker*, 28 January: 36: 39–63.

Kuhn, Thomas (1977) *The Essential Tension*. Chicago, IL: The University of Chicago Press.

Lazarsfeld, Paul & Herbert Menzel (1961) On the Relation Between Individual and Collective Properties. In Amitai Etzioni (ed.) *Reader on Complex Organizations* (2nd edn). New York: Holt, Rinehart and Winston: 499–516.

Levine, Donald; Ellwood B. Carter & Eleanor Miller Gorman (1976) Simmel's Influence on American Sociology. *The American Journal of Sociology*, 81 (4): 813–845.

Merton, R.K. (1984) Socially Expected Durations: A Case Study of Concept Formation in Sociology. In W.W. Powell & Richard Robbins (eds) *Conflict and Consensus: In Honor of Lewis A. Coser*. New York: Free Press: 262–283.

Merton, R.K. (1982) *Social Research and the Practicing Professions*. Cambridge: Abt Books.

Merton, R.K. (1957a[1982]) Preliminaries to a Sociology of Medical Education. In *The Student-Physician: Introductory Studies in the Sociology of Medical Education* (edited with George G. Reader and Patricia L. Kendall). Cambridge, MA: Harvard University Press: 135–198.

Merton, R.K. (1976) *Sociological Ambivalence*. New York: The Free Press.

Merton, R.K. (1973) *The Sociology of Science: Theoretical and Empirical Investigations*. Norman Storer (ed.). Chicago, IL: The University of Chicago Press.

Merton, R.K. (1957[1968]) *Social Theory and Social Structure*. New York: Free Press.

Merton, R.K. (1965) *On the Shoulders of Giants: A Shandean Postscript*. New York: The Free Press.

Merton, R.K. (1957b) Priorities in Scientific Discovery: A Chapter in the Sociology of Science. *American Sociological Review*, 22 (6): 635–659.

Merton, R.K. (1957c) The Role-Set: Problems in Sociological Theory. *British Journal of Sociology*, 8: 106–120.

Merton, R.K. (1955) The Socio-Cultural Environment and Anomie. In H.L. Witmer & R. Kotinsky (eds) *New Perspectives for Research on Juvenile Delinquency*. Washington, D.C.: Government Printing Office: 24–50.

Merton, R.K. (1942) A Note on Science and Democracy. *Journal of Legal and Political Sociology*, 1: 115–126.

Merton, R.K.; Leonard Broom & Leonard S. Cottrell, Jr. (1959) *Sociology Today: Problems and Prospects*. New York: Basic Books.

Merton, R.K.; Jerry Gaston & Adam Podgorecki (eds) (1977) *The Sociology of Science in Europe*. Carbondale, IL: University of Southern Illinois Press.

Merton, R.K. & R. Nisbet (eds) (1961[1976]) *Contemporary Social Problems*. New York: Harcourt, Brace & Wilson.

Merton, R.K. with George G. Reader & Patricia L. Kendall (eds) (1957) *The Student-Physician: Introductory Studies in the Sociology of Medical Education*. Cambridge, MA: Harvard University Press.

Mitroff, Ian (1974) Norms and Counter-Norms in a Select Group of the Apollo Moon Scientists: A Case Study of the Ambivalence of Scientists. *American Sociological Review*, 39 (4): 579–595.

Page, Charles (1982) *Fifty Years in the Sociological Enterprise*. Amherst, MA: University of Massachusetts Press.

Rigney, Daniel (2010) *The Matthew Effect: How Advantage Begets Further Advantage*. New York: Columbia University Press.

Room, Robin (1976) Ambivalence as a Sociological Explanation: The Case of Cultural Explanations of Alcohol Problems. *American Sociological Review*, 41: 1047–1065.

Rossiter, Margaret W. (1993), The Matthew/Matilda Effect in Science. *Social Studies of Science*, 23 (2): 325–341.

Simonson, Peter (2010) Merton's Skeptical Faith. In *Refiguring Mass Communication: A History*. Urbana, IL: University of Illinois Press: 123–162.

Stinchcombe, Arthur (1975) Merton's Theory of Social Structure. In L. Coser (ed.) *The Idea of Social Structure*. New York: Harcourt Brace Jovanovich: 11–34.

Storer, Norman (1973) Introduction to R.K. Merton. *Sociology of Science*: i–xxiii.

Turner, Bryan (1981) *For Weber: Essays on the Sociology of Fate*. Boston, MA: Routledge & Kegan Paul.

Turner, Jonathan (1985) Unanswered Questions in the Convergence Between Structuralist and Interactionist Role Theories. In S.N. Eisenstadt & H.J. Helle (eds) *Perspectives on Microsociological Theory*. London: Sage: 22–26.

Wallace, Walter (1983) *Principles of Scientific Sociology*. New York: Aldine.

Ziman, John (2000) *Real Science: What It Is, and What It Means*. Cambridge: Cambridge University Press.

Zuckerman, Harriet (2011) The Matthew Effect Writ Large and Larger: A Study in Sociological Semantics. In Elkana et al. (eds) *Concepts and the Social Structure* Budapest: Central European University Press: 511–574.

Zuckerman, Harriet (1988) The Sociology of Science. In *Handbook of Sociology*. Newbury Park, CA: Sage (Chapter 16): 511–574.

5

LATER YEARS

Introduction

The 1980s decade saw Merton's gradual withdrawal (after 1984) from active teaching. Merton worked largely from his Riverside apartment, but also was a resident fellow at Russell Sage Foundation (a day a week) where he was the first Foundation Scholar, mentoring many visiting scholars, until his retirement at the end of the decade. (In 2003, the position was renamed the Merton Scholar.) He was also an adjunct faculty member at Rockefeller University over this period. (RU is a private graduate university in New York City which focuses primarily on the biological and medical sciences.)

Much of his writing in this period is in a 'reminiscent' vein – often in the form of invited festschriften or obituary material for colleagues he had (somewhat to his own surprise) outlived – together with some rear-guard action defending (but also clarifying and extending) parts of his earlier writings against recent criticism or commentary, and some writing tasks which flowed from his 'elder statesman' position – e.g. writing forewords/prefaces for books. Honours descended (see Chapter 1). Those remembered through a more substantive essay included Paul Lazarsfeld (1979, 1998), Talcott Parsons (1980), Ludwick Fleck (although they'd not met –1981), Alvin Gouldner (1982), Florian Znaniecki (1983), Louis Schneider (1984c), George Sarton (1985), André Cournand (1988a), David Sills (1988b), Herbert Hyman (1988f), Franco Ferrarotti (1988c), Pitirim Sorokin (1988e), Peter Blau (1990b) and James Coleman (1997b) and Eugene Garfield (2000) – while being unable (much to his regret) to write concerning Juan Linz and others. Merton's reminiscent material is often interesting in fleshing out the social context of various portions of his intellectual career, and this is enlivened by his inclusion in such publications of portions of his correspondence. Where relevant, material from these publications is inserted in earlier chapters. The strongly emotive tone of much of this writing throws light on that side of many of these intellectual-friend relationships.

Merton also revisited the history of the 'career' of various of his concepts: SEDs (1984a), the Kelvin dictum (1984c), focus groups (1987b), reference groups (1988f), the Matthew effect (1988d), unanticipated consequences (1989), Science, Technology & Society (STS: 1990), Durkheim's 'division of labour' (1994a), opportunity-structure (1995a), and the Thomas Theorem and Matthew effect (1995b). As well as documenting aspects of his earlier work, these items were often able to be incorporated as case studies in the emergent study of sociological semantics, which is the key feature of this phase of his work.

Some personal vignettes

Some word portraits have been useful for giving a granular picture of Merton.

> These days, Mr. Merton works mostly out of his Riverside Drive apartment. His narrow, overstuffed office is barely three paces from wall to desk. Rows of black-and-white photographs – of Freud, of his first publisher, Alfred Knopf, of his former neighbor the sculptor Jacques Lipchitz – solemnly gaze out over greetings from some of his nine grandchildren and his Macintosh computer. Mr. Merton's face has grown thinner, and his jawline juts out sharply against his slender neck; his hands have an ever-so-slight tremor. But at 88 he is still a lanky six feet with a patrician bearing and a passion for conversation.
>
> *(Cohen, 1998: 9)*

> Mr. Merton's vast collection of books now fills six libraries, including the ones in the Upper West Side and East Hampton homes.
>
> *(Cohen, 1998)*

> I interviewed Bob Merton on September 27, 1983, in his apartment overlooking Riverside Park and the Hudson River. The late afternoon sun streamed into his book-lined study. One long wall of the study contained a work-table along most of its length. Above the table hung photographs of famous scholars, teachers, and other creative intellects Merton knew and admired: Alfred North Whitehead, Paul F. Lazarsfeld, George Sarton, Pitirim A. Sorokin, Talcott Parsons, L.J. Henderson, Corrado Gini (Merton was his assistant for a year), W.I. Thomas and Dorothy S. Thomas, Sam Stouffer, the sculptor Jacques Lipchitz, the chemist and philosopher of science Michael Polanyi, the publisher Alfred A. Knopf, the physiologist André Cournand, the physicist and mathematical statistician E.B. Wilson, the physicist-biologist Leo Szilard, the entomologist William Morton Wheeler, the anthropologist A.L. Kroeber, the novelist and essayist Elizabeth Janeway, and the classicist Gilbert Murray. There was also a portrait of a great psychologist he did not know: Freud. Seeing these pictures made Merton's adopted phrase, 'standing on the shoulders of giants' come alive.
>
> *(Persell, 1984: 355)*

Scholars at the Russell Sage Foundation, where Merton long served as senior savant, often heard the rapid staccato of his manual typewriter in the knowledge that one of them would soon receive an impeccably typed, elegantly phrased, and often uncomfortably acute point by point review of a recent paper, presentation, or conversation. They also knew that if he attended their session of a seminar, Merton would remain silent through most of the discussion, then deliver a telling review of argument and evidence coupled with concrete suggestions for (a great deal of) further work, as well as an invitation to a private parley.

(Tilly, 2003)

There were many events Merton addressed. An interesting anecdote (relayed by former RA Tom Gieryn) showing up Merton's character occurred at Bloomington airport when in 1978 Robert K. Merton arrived to deliver a lecture at Indiana University. Tom Gieryn, who had studied the sociology of science with Mr. Merton, could wait outside while his guest stepped off the plane. As they stood catching up by the chain link fence, they could hear the puddle jumper Mr. Merton had flown in on groan to life. "He said, 'My bag is still on the plane,'" Mr. Gieryn remembers. Don't worry, Mr. Gieryn assured him; after all, how could he be certain that the baggage handlers hadn't removed his suitcase? But Mr. Merton was insistent. A few moments later, the plane began rolling forward. In an instant, the rangy Mr. Merton bounded past the gate, across the tarmac and onto the runway. "He walks out in front of this plane that is beginning to move," Mr. Gieryn said. "I was scared that he was going to die." Confronted by the formidable Mr. Merton, however, there wasn't much choice. The plane stopped. "He insisted they open it up," Mr. Gieryn continued, "and sure enough, the bag was in there."

(Cohen, 1998)

In his early 70s Merton thought it was time, given his likely lifespan, to restrict the carrying out of other tasks, thus writing the following (Robert K. Merton as cited in Bonitz, 2004: 19–20):

SELF-EMANCIPATION PROCLAMATION

On this 22nd of February, 1982, I have completed 12 volumes (to be written, edited, or revised) and some 20 articles since I emerged from the hospital in 1972. This represents the full discharge of an inordinate stock of moral (not legal) obligations which I had accumulated over the years, as I discovered in taking inventory after my release from the hospital.

On this day, therefore, I issue this Self-Emancipation Proclamation;

TO REMOVE AT LONG LAST the albatross hung about my neck in the form of ever-urgent deadlines,

I HEREBY DECLARE that I shall not again agree to write, revise, or edit a book; deliver a public lecture; contribute to a symposium; write an article, review essay, or book review; or incur any of the other like moral obligations which so easily accrue in the course of academic life,

UNLESS

I have already written, revised or edited that book, prepared that lecture, or written any of the other sundry pieces referred to in the antecedent of *this* Proclamation;

AND TO GIVE more precise definition of intent and boundaries,

AND TO GIVE added spiritual force to this much-too-long-delayed edict by identifying the hypothetical limiting case,

I FURTHER DECLARE that should the editor of a Festschrift in honor of my oldest and closest friend invite me to contribute a piece to that altogether deserved honorific volume, I shall sadly but resolutely decline to do so,

UNLESS

it should come to pass by the time of the designated deadline that I happen to have a manuscript judged suitable for the occasion; and

BE IT FINALLY UNDERSTOOD that this Self-Emancipation Proclamation shall remain in effect until the end of my days, in the fervent hope that until then I shall have nothing but joy (along with those inevitable patches of suffering) in my work.

Writings

When offered a biographical slot in the *Annual Review of Sociology*, Merton (1987a) projected forward the broad pattern of his work on a range of patterns of scientific practices. This hints at his own practice of accumulating a variety of material (e.g. quotes) from reading and other material which were then filed away in a set of notebooks or folders which could later be drawn on in writing chapters or papers. The agenda is divided into three parts:

- Patterns of scientific practices. (e.g. OBI in science);
- Patterns in transmission change and growth of scientific knowledge (e.g. insiders/outsiders);
- Neologisms as sociological concepts – history and analysis (e.g. origins of the term 'scientist').

Quite a few of the 48 items on this agenda were subsequently published (at least in part). To gain some impression of their content we can turn to the 1987 article which provides an exposition of three of these items:

- establishing phenomena, the injunction to make sure the phenomenon exists before studying or explaining it);

- Specifying ignorance: processes for specifying what needs to be known (in effect following up on Merton's 1959 essay on problem selection);
- Selection of strategic research sites/material (which best reveal the operation of the phenomenon in question, even if it might seem that phenomenon is trivial).

In this era of Merton's scholarly work, his 'scholarly service' component involved a lengthy project with David Sills to put together a 19th volume of the *Encyclopedia of Social Science: Quotations Supplement* (1992a). Compiling this was a huge and complex task since the volume covers 773 authors shepherded by 238 advisers (not to mention other suggested quotations that were not included). As usual, Merton couldn't let the opportunity pass without noting patterns: that quotations were then echoed, parodied, or reversed when repeated by others (Merton & Sills, 1992b). (Merton himself appears with four quotations: SFP, Matthew effect, UCA and the four institutional imperatives of science.)

Some work was rear-guard action in relation to earlier publications: in particular, answering (1984b: 1092) Becker's critique of his early work on Pietism and Science, by constructing an appended database but also by developing a methodological argument concerning the 'fallacy of the latest word':

> That fallacy rests on three common but untenable tacit assumptions: (1) that the latest word correctly formulates the essentials of the preceding word while being immune to the failures of observation and inference imputed to what went before, (2) that each succeeding work improves on its knowledge base, and (3) that theoretically derived hypotheses are to be abandoned as soon as they seem to be empirically falsified.

Indeed, Merton terms this last fallacy the Phoenix phenomenon:

> the continuing resiliency of theories or theoretically derived hypotheses such as Durkheim's on rates of suicide ([1897] 1951) or Max Weber's on the role of ascetic Protestantism in the emergence of modern capitalism ([1904–5] 1930) even though they have been periodically subjected to much and allegedly conclusive demolition ('falsification').
>
> *(1092)*

One of the more memorable addresses by Merton and subsequent publication was his 'Life of Learning' delivered on the occasion of his Charles Homer Haskins lecture to the annual meeting of the American Council of Learned Societies, Philadelphia, April 1994. Merton felt particularly honoured because he was the first sociologist to be invited to such a humanities-orientated event. The lecture was a vivid account, illustrated by photos from a family album, taking the reader through Merton's childhood, college and early Harvard University days. Given that the lecture was given in his own hometown gave the presentation an extra flavour. Merton suggested (340) that "my life of learning has been shaped by a long series of chance encounters and consequential choices, and not by anything like a carefully designed plan". He also suggested since the child is father of the man, this justified the inclusion of considerable material on his youth.

Socially expected durations

A later addition by Merton to his structural analysis was in the area of 'socially expected durations' (SEDs), which makes explicit a theme that had been touched on from time to time throughout his writings (including 1940s housing studies). In an early article with Sorokin (1937) the concept of 'social time' is reviewed, and in later work the differential social structuring of time is teased out. SEDs are

> socially prescribed or collectively patterned expectations about temporal durations imbedded in social structures of various kinds: for example, the length of time that individuals are institutionally permitted to occupy particular statuses (such as an office in an organization or a membership in a group); assumed probable durations of diverse kinds of social relationships (such as friendship or a professional client relation); and the patterned and therefore anticipated longevity of individual occupants of statuses, of groups and of organizations.
>
> *(1984a: 265–266)*

There are at least two sociological implications of SEDs: at the individual level they affect behaviour, and at the collective level they help link social structure and individual behaviour (Merton, 1984a; Di Leillo, 1985).

Time can be seen as a means of social coordination (1936) or as a property of groups and organisations, and particularly status sequences. It is also basic to the social frameworks within which people make their choices about action. As in cost-benefit analysis, so in decision-making, different time preferences lead to rather different decisions. Those in some social locations prefer instant gratification, while those in other social locations use their ability to postpone their requirements to stack up more in the way of long-term resources. In their choice of timeframe, individuals are not simply able to choose, but are required to fit in with multiple, collectively determined timeframes. An obvious extension would be 'socially expected spatial arrangements' about how people view the spatial ordering of their lives, but this is at best implicit in Merton's work.

The research programme of sociological semantics (SS)

In his last few decades, the focus of Merton's work was increasingly directed towards cultural aspects and particularly to an evolving programme in what was eventually termed 'sociological semantics'. (Maybe just 'social' would have sufficed, although Merton saw that it was important to signal that serendipity wasn't just a psychological phenomenon but occurred in social settings.)

This work programme was only made explicit after the event (see Afterword in 2004) and with the posthumous assistance of commentators all published in Calhoun (2010) – notably Harriet Zuckerman, Cynthia Epstein, Charles Camic and Peter Simonson (who recruits Merton as an unrecognised exponent of the ancient discipline of rhetoric). The raw material for the programme were two major studies in the history of ideas that had been written in the late 1950s, but Merton's consideration of a broader framing took much longer to unfold. The occasion of the publication of the much earlier drafted *Serendipity* (*The Travels and Adventures of Serendipity: A Study in Sociological Semantics and the Sociology of Science* co-written with Elinor Barber) provided an opportunity to retrospectively consider this as a research programme. Harriet Zuckerman (2010) includes in her account of Merton's programme some 17 papers and three books – to which could be added the compendium *Social Science Quotations*. And indeed, appropriate material is threaded through most of Merton's work. Cynthia Epstein's claim, though, that Merton is "ultimately a theorist of cultural sociology" is likely going too far (2010: 79). This programme seems yet to have much resonance with the sociological community.

This interest in SS goes back to Merton's childhood interest in the dictionaries at his local library and the purchase of a set of *OED*s as a student (see above), followed by his acquisition of many dictionary sets. Merton's love of words has been quite renowned, although, until this programme developed, this interest was not explicitly specified. Interest in the circulation of 'culturally strategic' words as a strategic research site was mentioned in various writings, including *STSS* in 1949. Social theory, particularly in Europe, began a major 'cultural turn' from the 1980s, but Zuckerman refutes any claim that Merton's work in this area was shaped by these writings. Beyond laying out some of the wider parameters of the SS approach, Merton does not develop much theorisation: rather the framework is projected to be filled by examples which will then be reaped for identifying patterns. The objectives of this programme include interests to

> track who coined particular words, under what circumstances, for what purposes, and how their use changed or if they disappeared altogether.
> *(2004: 245–250)*

Why is this, perhaps somewhat trivial-appearing topic, scientifically important? Merton comments on the functions new words provide in the humanities/social sciences (2004: 67):

> the use of a new characterizing word or phrase, the drastic redefinition of an old word, or the resurrection or a term fallen into disuse is an integral part of the development of new perceptions and interpretations.

These points can be assembled into an analytical paradigm of the career of words/phrases, which would variously look at (Zuckerman, 2010: 256–257):

- the origins or particular words and phrases and the social standing of their originators;
- the social patterning of their use;
- the changing meanings attached to them, that is, their evolution;
- their modes of diffusion;
- the consequences, intended and otherwise of their use; and
- the conditions of their survival or disappearance.

Another angle concerns the cross-language transmission of loan words. For example:

> Who else but Merton, for example, would think of connecting the three loan-words esprit de l'escalier, Schadenfreude, and chutzpah to the loan-word that serendipity has become since its invention in 1754? All four words, Merton points out, travel well from language to language because they so nicely identify an experience widely shared across cultures that no competing term captures so deftly. In yet another coining of a memorable Mertonian phrase, Merton calls that sort of term a 'niche-word'.
>
> *(Tilly, 2005: 452)*

The new specialty would require some tools. Procedures to be used would include "archival forays, the content analysis of texts and quantitative and qualitative analyses of particular words or phrases in all manner of writings in one language and in multiple languages where appropriate". The material focused on might include: "Simple phrases, aphorisms, dicta – their ability to summarize, epitomize, exemplify, or even create complex programs of research or action – has long been known" (Merton & Sills 1984: 319). And further (Zuckerman, 2010: 256):

> slogans, niche words, loan words, vogue words, nonce words, idioms, eponyms, neologisms, epithets and compliments, words that are profane and words that are sacred, and words whose history, use and meanings, both lost and acquired would tell much about social life

Sources would include dictionaries but also text databases. Dictionaries are often careful repositories of current use as well as being normative. The fate of a word is that it is eventually consecrated (or not) in dictionaries. A sign of newness of a word is that authors feel the need to provide a definition as they use a word, whereas well-known words don't need definition.

Over the last few decades technology has facilitated this specialty: unfortunately, in the main too late for Merton who was remarkable for carrying out laborious searches which might have been aided by machine-searchable text databases, although he was quick to turn to their use in his article with Wolfe in which Nexus/Lexis was used to identify public use of sociological terms (1995c).

Merton splits the relevant characteristics of a word into its (2004: 95) meaning and the associations to that meaning and the word as a collection of sounds making a sensory impact: its 'psycho-aesthetic' characteristics comprised denotative or con-notative qualities. In sum, sound v. sense. Qualities favouring use of a word may include users who like it, see it as apt, are struck by its un/familiarity or find it attractive. An example: the term 'scientist' was introduced in 1834 by William Whewell (Merton, 1997a) but aroused opposition partly because it was a hybrid of a Latin root and a Greek suffix. After several attempts, Whewell was finally successful in finding acceptance of his word as there clearly was a need for it. Merton notes several interesting features associated with the word: that Whewell had to weather much rejection (and hardly used the term himself after he had first suggested it), and that although the term itself is degendered, dictionary and other definitions of it linked it to 'man of science'. Merton also points to debates about the scope and nature of science which also embroil the term 'scientist'.

A more extensive investigation into 'serendipity' (Merton & Barber, 2004: 65) showed that the word emerged in the correspondence of Walpole. Since then:

> Over a span of some 200 years, then, the genre has changed consider-ably: After an initial rejection, the word was given very limited currency amongst a few literary erudites; it gradually attained wider currency in more diversified literary circles; and finally it became popular in the world of science and among those journalists who describe the progress of science to the general public.

Camic (2010) points out that Merton grounds his explanations in terms of the different effects of different socio-cognitive microenvironments in which people are located or have access to. The example of Kuhn is referred to (see Merton, 1977) as having access to advantageous (e.g. 'serendipity-prone') microenvironments. The social form of a 'microenvironment' may be quite different in different instances, but usually lies somewhere in scale between an organisation (e.g. a uni-versity) and an interpersonal team. As well as particular effects from particular microenvironments, it is also necessary to trace the trajectories of items across successive microenvironments as these can reinforce/suppress the effects of prior microenvironments.

Other writers have extended this. Epstein (2010) takes the widest picture in reassembling Merton's contributions to cultural sociology. She argues that, as a Durkheimian, Merton was in part grounded in Durkheim's *Elementary Forms of Religious life* but also points to Merton's early inspiration by the Thomas Theorem. Of course, Merton's cultural sociology is closely mated with his structural sociology and is threaded through this. She points to the general workings of the pairing (Epstein, 2010: 61):

> The sociologist is required to consider the cultural web in which individuals are embedded, the social structure that causes them to make certain choices

and to act in concert with others because the share or are persuaded by social conventions that lodge them in institutional frameworks, which in turn circumscribe their options.

In particular, Epstein sees the cultural aspect of Merton's work as pointing to the need for individuals to be provided with and/or develop a cultural map through which they navigate their way through the social structure. Through anticipatory and contemporaneous socialisation, people must be observers of their situation, learning how to occupy status/roles and future status/roles. Compared to Marx's views, reference orientations are not just 'false consciousness' – although they may have elements of this. Epstein argues that the (evolving) names and cultural understandings of roles/statuses – e.g. scientist, doctor – have a considerable importance in shaping role behaviour of those occupying such roles. Given widespread clashes between values, this can lead to conflict amongst statuses and compromise will be necessary in order to cope. Despite their importance, cultural factors are often ignored, Epstein citing the example of Merton finding only infrequent mention of studies on the cultural factors influencing creativity amongst the vast literature on creativity.

Simonson (2010) attempts to retrospectively recruit Merton as a supporter of the study of rhetoric, with his evidence including that Merton had studied some of the classic rhetoric texts and had used appropriate quotes (e.g. from Aristotle) as heading quotes in his *Mass Persuasion*. Merton clearly saw rhetoric as a tool to be used in studying propaganda, which colours in another aspect of Merton's work.

Merton also covers the social arrangements and mechanisms involved: such as 'invisible colleges' but also (Camic, 2010: 287) 'socio-cognitive microenvironments' each of which

> is an 'opportunity structure' which furnishes differential access to ideas, concepts, information flows, and other resources to those actors who self-select or are institutionally selected into such a milieu and who differentially make use of the socio-intellectual possibilities that its reward system encourages or discourages. In addition different local microenvironments differ in the extent to which they are the sites of the process … of institutional serendipity, practices of oral publication, socially organized skepticism etc.

Merton extended his cultural analyses into the public use of sociological terms – as revealed by the Lexis/Nexis database. Merton and Wolfe (1995) make a bold and broad attempt to assess the extent to which there has been social and/or cultural incorporation of sociology (witnessed by use of terms originating from sociology) within society more generally. They distiguish between *cultural* incorporation of lamguage and *social* incorporation of methods and findings by other instituions. Thus, their study focuses not on how sociology is produced but how social knowledge is consumed. Since consumption is more particular than the universalistic production of sociological knowledge, their work is confined to a case study of the USA. Looking first at incorporation of sociological vocabulary, they used the online Nexis/Lexis to search for the use of some 200 sociological terms in major newspapres across 1991–1993. A wide range of useage was revealed. They suggsted that terms more related to psychology might be more likely to tranfer although they found that microsociology terms were not particularly prominent. Noting comments that sociology tends to enter public space as a debunker, they found that this point was confrmed by their results, since more negative terms predominate: to the contrary, upward mobility was mentioned more than downward mobility and Marxist terms received lower attention. (Other societies where a marxist ideological culture has been more predominant would doubtless have more attention to such terms: e.g. civic society.) Resonance of a term is more important, whereas jargon-sounding terms repel. Looking at changes over time, they suggest that once a term enters popular culture it tends to stay.

Widening their lens, Merton and Wolfe suggest that whereas economics has a hospitable home in media busiess sections, sociology can be located in media 'lifestyle' sections. Surveys and polls are often cited in the media although this has varied over periods. Yet another signal of incorporation is the extent to which sociology professors are invited on presidential commissions (cf. Merton, 1975) – this is a mere handful. Historically, public support for sociology has waxed and waned with ideology, with right-wing presidents less supportive and indeed often attacking the subject. Summing up, they conclude that incorporation is a mixed blessing. The downsides are that sociology terms can be seen as boring, concepts wander from their sociological meaning, and jargon induces distrust. Perhaps scientific sociology needs some barriers to the diffusion of its terms.

Finally, a methodological argument is pointed out by Camic. Merton has overcome in the book his earlier strongly marked distinction between history rather than systematics of theory, by developing a descriptive history of episodes in the career of an item, together with identifying the "mechanisms responsible for turning such episodes in the directions that they took historically" (Camic 2010: 285). This even becomes an understated argument about how historical sociology might proceed, through showing causal patterns apparent in particular parts of any historical situation. Another link to Merton's earliest work in the historical sociology of science is that SS retains, even extends, the broad sweep of tracing cultural themes across long periods of time that pertained in his work of the 1930s, in particular.

In sum, Merton's programme on cultural sociology/sociological semantics has sketched a useful analytical framework (i.e. analytical paradigm) to guide the development of this area of study and has indicated some of the methodological tools which might be pressed into service in pursuing studies in it. In carrying out this work Merton reached out to humanities concerns in scholarship while retaining a systematic approach and continuing to anchor his analyses in social structural analyses. Unfortunately, because it hasn't been sufficiently visible, there seems little prospect of this programme gaining much traction in the near future, which is a pity as it could readily generate a myriad of analyses. (Beyond the batch of reviews of the book, the term does not appear in *Sociological Abstracts*.)

Summary

Merton's writing in sociological semantics over this period was accomplished alongside a small stream of other work. While something of this new field was sketched out, nothing further by way of syntheses in other areas of writing appeared. A massive shift in sources of social theory swept sociology, but was almost entirely ignored by Merton, apart from a few negative side comments. Instead, quite reasonably, he pressed on with his own work programme. While it was largely drafted 50 years before, the final publication of *Serendipities* was a crowning achievement – with Merton reviewing the English-language publication pre-copy shortly before his death.

References

Bonitz, Manfred. (2004) Self-Emancipation Proclamation and a Light-Hearted but Nevertheless Deeply-Felt Exception. *Scientometrics*, 60 (1): 19–24.

Calhoun, C. (ed.) (2010) *Robert K. Merton. Sociology of Science and Sociology as Science.* New York: Columbia University Press.

Camic, C. (2010) How Merton Sociologizes the History of Ideas. In C. Calhoun (ed.) *Robert K. Merton: Sociology of Science and Sociology as Science.* New York: Columbia University Press: 273–296.

Cohen, Patricia (1998) An Eye for Patterns in the Social Fabric: Patriarch of Sociology Sees His Insights Become Just What Everyone Knows. *The New York Times*, Section B: 9.

Di Lellio, Anna (1985) Intervista a Robert K. Merton. *Rassegna Italiana di Sociologia*, XXVI: 3–26.

Epstein, Cynthia (2010) The Contributions of Robert K. Merton to Culture Theory. In C. Calhoun (ed.) *Robert K. Merton: Sociology of Science and Sociology as Science.* New York: Columbia University Press: 79–93.

Merton, R.K. (2000) On the Garfield Input to the Sociology of Science: A Retrospective Collage. In Blaise Cronin & Helen Barsky Atkins (eds) *The Web of Knowledge: A Festschrift in Honor of Eugene Garfield.* Mulford, NJ: Information Today, Inc.: 435–448.

Merton, R.K. (1998) Working with Lazarsfeld. In Jacques Lautman & Bernard-Pierre Lecuyer (eds) *Paul Lazarsfeld 1901–1976. La Sociologie de Vienne à New York.* Paris: L'Harmattan.

Merton, R.K. (1997a) De-Gendering 'Man of Science': The Genesis and Epicene Character of the Word *Scientist*. In Kai Erikson (ed.) *Sociological Visions.* New Haven, CT: Yale University Press: 225–253.

Merton, R.K. (1997b) Teaching James Coleman. In Jon Clark (ed.) *James S. Coleman.* London: Falmer Press: 351–356.

Merton, R.K. (1997c) On the Evolving Synthesis of Differential Association and Anomie Theory: A Perspective from the Sociology of Science. *Criminology*, 35 (3): 517–525.

Merton, R.K. (1995a) Opportunity Structure: The Emergence, Diffusion, and Differentiation of a Sociological Concept, 1930–1950. In Freda Adler and William S. Laufer (eds) *Advances in Criminological Theory: The Legacy of Anomie Theory.* New Brunswick, NJ: Transaction Publishers: vol. 6: 3–78.

Merton, R.K. (1995b) The Thomas Theorem and The Matthew Effect. *Social Forces*, December, 74 (2): 379–424.

Merton, R.K. (1994a) Durkheim's Division of Labor in Society: A Sexagenarian Postscript. *Sociological Forum*, 19 (1): 27–36.

Merton, R.K. (1994b) A Life of Learning: Charles Homer Haskins Lecture. *American Council of Learned Societies*, Occasional Paper No. 25.

Merton, R.K. (1990a) *STS*: Foreshadowings of an Evolving Research Program in the Sociology of Science. In I. Bernard Cohen (ed.) *Puritanism and the Rise of Modern Science: The Merton Thesis*. New Brunswick, NJ: Rutgers University Press, 334–371.

Merton, R.K. (1990b) Epistolary Notes on the Making of a Sociological Dissertation Classic: *The Dynamics of Bureaucracy*. In Craig Calhoun, Marshall W. Meyer & W. Richard Scott (eds) *Structures of Power and Constraint: Papers in Honor of Peter M. Blau*. New York: Cambridge University Press: 37–66.

Merton, R.K. (1989) Unanticipated Consequences and Kindred Sociological Ideas: A Personal Gloss. In Carlo Mongardini & Simonetta Tabboni (eds) *Opera di Robert K. Merton e la sociologia contemporanea*. Genova: ECIG: 307–329.

Merton, R.K. (1988a) André Cournand, 1895–1988. Memorial Service, Columbia University, 17 March. Luneberg, VT: Meriden-Stinehour Press: 21–26.

Merton, R.K. (1988b) Tribute to a Distinguished Career: Notes on the Retirement of David L. Sills. *Items*, Social Science Research Council, December: 97–98.

Merton, R.K. (1988c) Sociological Resonances: The Early Franco Ferrarotti and a Transatlantic Colleague. In R. Cipriani & M.I. Macioti (eds) *Omaggio a Franco Ferrarotti*. Rome: Siares: 83–91.

Merton, R.K. (1988d) The Matthew Effect in Science, II: Cumulative Advantage and the Symbolism of Intellectual Property. *Isis*, 79: 606–623.

Merton, R.K. (1988e) The Sorokin-Merton Correspondence on Puritanism, Pietism and Science, 1933–1934. *Science in Context*, 3 (1): 293–300.

Merton, R.K. (1988f) Reference Groups, Invisible Colleges and Deviant Behavior in Science. In H.J. O'Gorman (ed.) *Surveying Social Life: Papers in Honor of Herbert H. Hyman*. Middletown, CT: Wesleyan University Press: 174–189.

Merton, R.K. (1987a) Three Fragments from a Sociologist's Notebooks: Establishing the Phenomenon, Specified Ignorance and Strategic Research Materials. *Annual Review of Sociology*, 13: 1–28.

Merton, R.K. (1987b) The Focussed Interview & Focus Groups: Continuities and Discontinuities. *Public Opinion Quarterly*, 51: 550–566.

Merton, R.K. (1985) George Sarton: Episodic Recollections by an Unruly Apprentice. *Isis*, 76: 477–486.

Merton, R.K. (1984a) Socially Expected Durations: A Case Study of Concept Formation in Sociology. In W.W. Powell & Richard Robbins (eds) *Conflict and Consensus: In Honor of Lewis A. Coser*. New York: Free Press: 262–283.

Merton, R.K. (1984b) The Fallacy of the Latest Word: The Case of Pietism and Science. *American Journal of Sociology*, 89: 1091–1121.

Merton, R.K. (1984c) Texts, Contexts and Subtexts: An Epistolary Foreword. In Jay Weinstein (ed.) *The Grammar of Social Relations: The Major Essays of Louis Schneider*. New Brunswick, NJ: Transaction Books: ix–xiv.

Merton, R.K. (1983) Florian Znaniecki: A Short Reminiscence. *Journal of the History of the Behavioral Sciences*, 10: 123–126.

Merton, R.K. (1982) Alvin W. Gouldner: Genesis and Growth of a Friendship. *Theory and Society*, 11: 915–938.

Merton, R.K. (1981) On the Fleckian Sociological Epistemology and Structural Analysis in Sociology. Introduction to the Polish translation of *Social Theory and Social Structure*: 1–19.

Merton, R.K. (1980) Remembering the Young Talcott Parsons. *The American Sociologist*, 15 (May): 68–71.

Merton, R.K. (1979) Remembering Paul Lazarsfeld. In Robert K. Merton, James S. Coleman & Peter H. Rossi (eds) *Qualitative and Quantitative Research: Papers in Honor of Paul F. Lazarsfeld*. Free Press.

Merton, R.K. (1975) Social Knowledge and Public Policy. In *Sociological Ambivalence and Other Essays*. New York: Free Press.

Merton, R.K. & Elinor Barber (2004) *The Travels and Adventures of Serendipity*. Princeton, NJ: Princeton University Press.

Merton, R.K. (ed.) with Jerry Gaston & Adam Podgorecki (1977) *The Sociology of Science in Europe*. Carbondale, IL: University of Southern Illinois Press.

Merton, R.K. & David Sills (eds) (1992a) *Encyclopedia of Social Science Quotations*. New York: Macmillan.

Merton, R.K. & David Sills (1992b) Patterns in the Scholarly Use of Quotations. *Items*, 46 (4): 75–76.

Merton, R.K. with David L. Sills & Stephen M. Stigler (1984) The Kelvin Dictum and Social Science: An Excursion into the History of an Idea. *Journal of the History of the Behavioral Sciences*, 20, October: 319–331.

Merton, R.K. & Pitirim Sorokin (1937) Social Time: A Methodological and Functional Analysis. *American Journal of Sociology*, 42: 615–629.

Merton, R.K. & Alan Wolfe (1995) The Cultural and Social Incorporation of Sociological Knowledge. *The American Sociologist*, 26 (3): 15–38.

Persell, Caroline H. (1984) An Interview with Robert K. Merton. *Teaching Sociology*, 11: 355–386.

Simonson, Peter (2010) Merton's Sociology of Rhetoric. In C. Calhoun (ed.): 214–252.

Tilly, Charles (2005) Now that You Mention It. *Contemporary Sociology: A Journal of Reviews*, 34 (5): 451–453.

Tilly, Charles (2003) Robert K. Merton Remembered. *Footnotes*, 31(3).

Zuckerman, Harriet (2010) On Sociological Semantics as an Evolving Research Program. In C. Calhoun (ed.): 253–272.

6

REPRISE

Merton as discipline-builder, theorist, substantive sociologist and moralist

Having plotted various periods of Merton's writing in overview, this chapter now turns to some of the themes which permeate his whole oeuvre. Merton affected sociology by:

- sketching a methodology and way to build itself as a discipline;
- providing a wide-ranging theoretical apparatus,
- grounding his work in an understated values stance,
- contributing to specific areas of study, and providing a 'theory of society'.

Merton is not often thought to have contributed a 'theory of society' which is a macrosociological depiction of the key societal characteristics of the age, and the dynamics of their development: the section 'Merton's substantive contributions' below argues that he does.

Merton and the direction of sociology

In charting the role Sarton played in constructing the (sub-) discipline of the history of science, Merton and Thackray (1972: 145) delineate several features involved in the institutionalisation of any area of study:

> The most obvious is the set of shifts that a field of learning experiences as it changes from being a diffuse, unfocused area of inquiry, at best tangential to the true intellectual concerns of its occasional votaries, to being a conceptually discrete discipline, able to command its own tools, techniques, methods, intellectual orientations and problematics. This creation of a cognitive identity is only one facet … A set of shifts, which most often occurs at a later

period of time, revolves around the creation of a professional identity for the new enterprise.

They go on to suggest that historians of science too often concentrate on the latter, and they also draw a distinction between the provision of the infrastructure needed by an area of study (e.g. journals, databanks etc.) and the conceptual frameworks which energise it. Although Merton's own role in relation to sociology was set within a much more complex situation, likely diluting clear effects, his work had a major impact in shaping the contemporary face of the discipline, especially through the methodological stances he advocated. Much of Merton's discipline-building was in the 1940s in terms of his own work and in later decades in terms of more collective enterprises, and this has been presented in earlier chapters. (He was engaged in the operation of the BASR, the Sociology Department, ASA, ISA, the SSSS and the CASBS and contributed through many boards and committees.)

It was more through helping build up a broad body of ideas that Merton helped sociology establish itself, and gain self-confidence as a legitimate academic enterprise. Something of the scope of this is sketched in the useful synoptic statement developed out of a collaboration between Donald Levine and Piotr Sztompka (Levine, 2006: 240–241, and Sztompka 1996: 10–11):

> in working on the *Heritage of Sociology* volume about Merton, we articulated a series of specific practices that Merton propounded and modelled – practices that constitute a distinctly Mertonian program for theoretical work in sociology. This program includes:
>
> * Problem finding – defining scientific questions, finding rationales for them, and specifying what must be done to answer them.
> * Conceptual articulation and reconceptualization – advancing from an early, rudimentary, particularized, and largely unexplicated idea (proto-concept) to a genuine concept – an idea that has been defined, generalized and explicated to the point where it can effectively guide inquiry into seemingly diverse phenomena.
> * Conceptual clarification – making explicit the character of data subsumed under a concept and suggesting observable indices for conceptualized phenomena that cannot be directly observed.
> * Construction of middle-range generalizations – formulating generalizations that deal with limited aspects of phenomena or that apply to limited ranges of phenomena.
> * Functional analysis – specifying the consequences, positive and negative, of given social phenomena for the various social structures in which they are implicated.
> * Structural analysis – specifying the antecedent structural conditions that give rise to social phenomena.
> * Construction of typologies – systematizing the types of behavioral patterns found among actors in various domains.

- Codification – ordering the available empirical generalizations in a given domain, showing connections among generalizations in apparently different spheres of behavior, and tracing continuities within research traditions.
- Construction of paradigms (in a sense that antedates Kuhn's usage of the term) – systematizing the concepts and problems of a given domain of inquiry in compact form
- Formalization – deriving the implications of theoretical assumptions and postulates for other investigable properties of social phenomena (yet remaining aware of the danger of pursuing logical consistency to the point of sterile theorizing).
- Recasting theory – extending theoretical formulations in new directions in response to the appearance of unanticipated, anomalous, and strategic facts (serendipity) or the repeated observation of facts previously neglected.
- Specification of ignorance – expressly recognizing what is not yet known but what needs to be known in order to advance the pursuit of knowledge.
- Location in theoretical space – understanding the implications of theoretical pluralism for a given perspective or research program, including the fact that perspectival differences may entail complementary or unconnected as well as contradictory theories.
- Productive return to classics – mining the classics for crisper formulations, authoritative support, and critical rejoinders regarding current formulations, and for models of intellectual excellence.

This listing does not note the crucial term of 'evolving' to describe the trajectory of the research programmes – the not necessarily linear or swift, hard-won progression of an area of scientific activity.

Yet, developing a body of ideas is insufficient as influence on other sociologists relies on communication. An important way in which the ideas of a 'school', such as the 'Columbia Tradition', are disseminated is through publications. I have already noted (Chapter 4) Merton's role in organising two important published symposia (a general review of the state of the art in sociology and another on sociology and social problems). While Merton did not himself write any textbooks, he played an active role in shaping several exemplary introductory textbooks (most as editorial advisory consultant to Harcourt, Brace, Jovanovich):

> Kingsley Davis's (1948) *The Human Society*, Harry Johnson's (1960) *Sociology*, Stephen Cole's (1972) *The Sociological Orientation*, Alvin Gouldner and Helen Gouldner's (1963) *Modern Sociology: An Introduction to the Study of Human Interaction* and also Allan Johnson's (1986) *Human Arrangements*. More generally, Merton was able to place something of his stamp, through close editing and advice, on a wider set of influential texts that constitute a veritable

sociological library: including a set of sociological readings (*Sociological Theory: A Book of Readings*; Coser and Rosenberg, 1959); a history of social thought (*Masters of Sociological Thought: Ideas in Historical and Social Context*; Coser, 1977 [1971]) and a social research methodology text (*Sociological Research*; Riley, 1963).

But as well as helping to shape the 'form' of post-war sociology, Merton had a considerable influence on its 'content', with the two mutually building on each other. It is to an elucidation of this that this concluding reprise now turns. I discuss Merton's broad definition of social reality (and hence sociology) and then explore and extend the synoptic model provided by Stinchcombe which I take to be central to Merton's thinking as he agreed (see Sztompka 1996: 105)

Merton's sociology

Introduction: definition of sociology

It is difficult to find a clear and straightforward definition of sociology within Merton's writing. However, while addressing a wider audience through *The New York Times* in his 'The Canons of the Anti-Sociologist' (1976: 184) he suggests that:

> In the large, sociology is engaged in finding out how man's behaviour and fate are affected, if not minutely governed by his place within particular kinds, and changing kinds, of social structure and of culture.

At another point, sociology is referred to as the science of the group (1968: 363). At yet another point, Merton has provided a short listing of characteristic questions raised by sociologists (1957: 56):

- How is social organization to be conceived, what are its principal attributes, and how are these connected?
- Which properties and structures of social organization enable individuals to operate with greater or less effectiveness within their social setting?
- What processes in a social organization foster or curb the achievement of the goals of individuals within them, enabling these to be realized with greater or less stress?
- What are the regularities in the sequences of social status to be assumed by individuals within the organization or society? what are the effects of discontinuities and continuities in these sequences of status?
- The culture of society incorporates the values men in that society live by. How does the structure of the society facilitate or hamper the efforts of men, variously located in that structure, to act in terms of these cultural values?

Merton denigrated a biological view of mankind: see for example the introductory sentence to his essay on anomie (1938), and recognising both psychological and sociological perspectives can be in play, urged researchers to use both, but in particular to make sure that a sociological analysis was included, as often it is overlooked to a great loss in human understanding.

Boundaries of social phenomena

Before going on to further examine Merton's analytical system, some attention needs to be directed towards identifying its boundaries. Like other social theorists, Merton demarcates those features of human existence that are amenable to social inquiry from other features which are seen to be below the threshold of sociological attention. Whereas Weber contrasted 'meaningful' behaviour with mere biological behaviour, Merton demarcates between "standardized (i.e. patterned and repetitive)" (1968: 104) and presumably rather more ephemeral and idiosyncratic 'forms' or levels of activity. The units of analysis are expected to exhibit a degree of 'institutionalisation' of behaviour, although it is explicitly held that social patterns may include aspects that need to be observed as they are not culturally recognised, or recognised by the participants. It is, unfortunately, unclear as to what is involved with this residue of 'non-institutionalised behaviour' (perhaps including 'collective behaviour') or how it might be analysed. (Merton had no particular occasion to address the analytical issues of what this other social phenomenon might involve. He does not do so in his nearest attempt when writing an introduction [1960] to Le Bon's book on crowds. Instead, he provides an unjustly unknown tour de force in which Freud's reaction to Le Bon's analysis is examined.)

Merton's analyses all attend to the interaction between patterns of social life (often quite institutionalised) and social structure. However, one particular point where he analyses the interaction between institutional and 'pre-institutional' levels of social behaviour is his commentary on the effect of the self-fulfilling prophecy when runs on banks result in the very bank failures which investors fear (1948 [1968: 476–477]). In discussing this, Merton notes that, "The self-fulfilling prophecy, whereby fears are translated into reality, operates only in the absence of deliberate institutional controls" (1968: 490).

Stinchcombe adds to this definition, the criterion that in order to be of sociological interest, social phenomena should be 'institutionally consequent'. This adds to Merton's definition, by increasing the theoretical depth of interpretation. Stinchcombe's point emphasises the double-ended nature of social phenomena – they are both caused by social structure, and reproduce social structure. Thus, for example, in considering the choice of a political party to vote for, the range of choice amongst parties and even the possibility of voting are both affected by the person's position in the social structure, and in turn the act of choosing a particular party will have consequences in terms of the continued viability of that party and of the voting (electoral) system more generally.

Merton's general theory: latent theoretical stance

A latent theoretical stance

The previous chapters have shown that Merton's own definition of his contribution to social theory is circumscribed. Yet, Merton had in fact, in my view, and that of other writers, developed his own particular analytical apparatus, applied in a series of analyses and partly drawn out in developing theoretical articulations. But this general framework was never explicitly developed by Merton himself. Indeed, the very idea of having a general theoretical framework would be denied by his opposition to premature general social theories. Stinchcombe directly raises this difficulty and openly clashes with Merton's own theoretical modesty. Stinchcombe argues that:

> I do not agree with Merton's implicit diagnosis [of the usefulness of his theories] that it is because he works on 'theories of the middle range'. It seems to me that in the dialectic between Parsons and Merton, generality has been confused with woolliness. Merton, in taking up the correct position on woolliness, has tricked himself into taking up the incorrect position on general theory. The true situation is precisely the opposite. It is because Merton has a better general theory than Parsons that his work has been more empirically fruitful.
>
> *(Stinchcombe, 1975: 26–27)*

Some two decades later, after reviewing the debate about the general theory question, a more nuanced version of this argument is advanced by Kai Erickson (1997: 220):

> Whether or not Merton can be said to have presented us with a systematic body of general theory, I would argue that he has presented us with something far more important in the long term – a coherent *vision* of how the social order works and how one should go about studying it. I would further argue that the vision he has presented us has worked its way so deep into the sociological grain that it has become a permanent part of our way of looking at things. Even those who want to protest some view that Merton has proposed seem to do so using languages and concepts and logics and forms of argument that derive from him.

However, it is one thing to suggest that such a latent theoretical framework exists, and quite a different matter to make this explicit. In particular, we need some rules about how to proceed in order to most 'correctly' elicit this postulated underlying structure. In the following sections I have adopted three procedures:

- I have scanned and rescanned the array of Mertonian concepts to ensure that as many as possible are included in the framework;

- I have examined and reexamined various of Merton's key analyses (especially his key work on anomie and on scientific priorities) to ensure that the framework as I have constructed it can be seen to rigorously 'drive' these analyses;
- I have endeavored to make the framework as concise and internally coherent as possible.

Stinchcombe's model of Merton

Attention to the underlying analytical apparatus in Merton's theoretical work was first drawn in a penetrating exposition by Arthur Stinchcombe (1975) which codifies the key elements of this Mertonian theory of social structure. In further work, Stinchcombe is able to show that a similar model can be found embedded in the analyses of Tocqueville, Lenin and Bendix (Stinchcombe, 1978), although he himself chooses not to stress this continuity (indeed he does not refer to his earlier essay on Merton in his book devoted to this trio!).

I begin by summarising Stinchcombe's reconstruction, but because it does not adequately cover enough of Merton's working model, I then extend it further in the next section. The Stinchcombe version of the model centres on variation between people in their rates of choice amongst alternatives which are structurally produced, and in which the rates of choice loop back to affect the institutional patterns which had shaped the rates of choice 'in the first place'. People differ in their rates of choice amongst structurally given alternatives depending on their location in the social order. On the one hand, choices are 'causally' structured, and on the other hand, choices 'causally' influence the development of institutional patterns: the causal chain goes backwards and also forwards from the core process as the key phrase of 'choices with institutional consequence' nicely points up. For example, as Merton has shown, scientists are particularly concerned with the publication of research reports of original investigations, and the institutional pattern of science supports and motivates this. In turn, the importance of open publication rather than secrecy, and the continued availability of journals to publish in, is enhanced when scientists choose to publish their research work: a benevolent feedback loop.

The key relationships in Stinchcombe's model can be usefully sketched (see Figure 6.1; cf. Stinchcombe, 1975: 3).

Stinchcombe then thickens out this account by identifying three particular ways through which institutional patterns shape individual choice behaviour (through structurally induced motives, control of information, and sanctions), and also a causal loop in which the development of social character is influenced by choices and in turn affects the ways choices are made.

The first part of Stinchcombe's extension of the core model provides more detail about how Merton's theoretical work explains the linkage between institutional pattern and individual rates of choice. People in different social positions will have different goals or motivations, stemming from some mix of a range of structural sources – the cultural beliefs they have been socialised into, reward systems

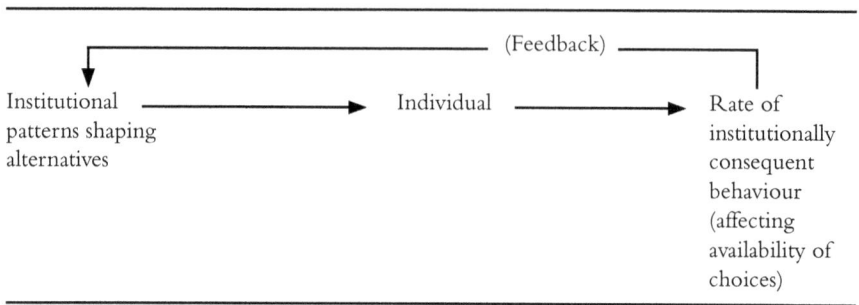

FIGURE 6.1 Basics of Stinchcombe's model of Merton's analyses

(including striving after status), seeking to affirm social identities valued by reference groups, and the need to maintain everyday life.

Another key mechanism linking institutional pattern and individual choice behaviour is the structural governance of information. The availability of information influences the knowledge of the range of choice (as well as, presumably, the person's weighing up of the costs and benefits of each alternative they are aware of). The flow of information may itself be a resource that affects the success in carrying out an activity (and in turn, success reinforces the choice of continuing in that activity). And the application of sanctions (rewards and punishments) is dependent on knowing when and whom to reward or punish. Further, a person's choice behaviour may be influenced by the social pressure which others bring to bear on them through their ability to reward or punish the person.

The last component which Stinchcombe adds into the model is a feedback loop involving socially patterned character or personality development. As a result of being placed in a particular social situation (for example, a bureaucrat), and making repeated similar choices, a particular social character is formed. This is further reinforced as it influences the style in which choice behaviour is carried out, which limits or changes a person's exposure to alternative sources of information or social pressure. Thus, a style of operating becomes cemented in. It should be noted that 'feedback loops' has rather a mechanical air, and that in reality these are embedded in fully fleshed social practices.

In this analytical reconstruction, Stinchcombe usefully draws on a wide range of Merton's specific analyses: especially the essay on anomie, but also Merton's analyses of bureaucracy, behaviour amongst scientists, the political machine, the cosmopolitan/local distinction and his analysis of the structural position of engineers. However, a range of other work by Merton, and especially his more theoretical essays, is only lightly drawn on. There is little to fault in what Stinchcombe says about Merton's work: indeed, there is a complimentary, if passing, endorsement of it by Merton (1976: 120–124), who notes that Stinchcombe's model is couched at a particularly analytical level, but specifies that it only reconstructs the microprocesses underlying Mertonian structural analysis. More deserves to be added from Merton's works.

An extended structural model of Merton

Stinchcombe's account, consonant with his earlier 'theory-constructionist' approach stresses processes rather than structures, He is rather too ready to show how Merton sees the 'social machine' as working, and not careful enough to show how Merton sees the components and organisation of the 'social machine' in the first place. Along with this is an overemphasis on the microsociological or social psychological components rather than the structural levels of analysis Merton was so keen to clarify. Yet, Merton is a theorist particularly concerned with the essential properties and types of social structure, as well as the detailed ways in which they work. The exposition of Merton's theory of social structure which follows is intended to complement and extend the basic insights laid out by Stinchcombe. His work should be able to be neatly located within my broader model.

There are five key elements in this extended version of Stinchcombe's core model. Two of the elements in his model are repeated, one is new, while the other two consist of a subdivision of one of his elements. I also develop the mapping of relationships amongst these elements.

Choice of starting point in this presentation is the actor and their agency (will). Perhaps it is easiest to begin with the individual choosing amongst alternatives on the one hand, and linked to this, patterns of behaviour resulting from these choices. In this I follow Stinchcombe's presentation, although relaxing somewhat his narrowing of patterns of behaviour to only those which are consequent for institutions: it seems to me important to attempt to retain the analytical possibility (laid out in the concept of 'non-functional consequences' in Merton (1949 [1968b: 105]) that not all behaviour patterns are institutionally consequent (cf. Boudon, 1981), and some affect other institutions.

Where I depart from Stinchcombe rather more substantially is in building forward from choices into Merton's views of the social environment shaping those choices. The social environment needs to be subdivided into 'cultural structure' and 'social structure' with a further extension to 'opportunity structure'. A brief textual analysis can readily substantiate that Merton used these terms to represent quite different aspects of social reality. Broadly, cultural structure consists in the shared ideas and symbols which shape people's images of social reality, provide motivations and ideological justifications for institutional patterns and cultural products. On the other hand, social structures are patterned social relationships amongst people who are embedded in various interlinked social positions. The means of achieving individual and group goals are conceptualised as the "opportunity structure" which designates the scale and distribution of conditions that provide various probabilities for acting individuals and groups to achieve specifiable outcomes. From time to time, the opportunity-structure expands or contracts, as do segments of that structure. However, location in the social structure strongly influences, though it does not wholly determine, the extent of access to the opportunity-structure (Merton, 1995). Although it may include other aspects, opportunity-structure includes various resources (what Bourdieu terms 'capitals') and is often subject to processes of the accumulation of advantage or disadvantage. Social structures, through the ways they shape differential access to various elements of the opportunity-structure, mediate between cultural patterns and choices and the behaviour patterns resulting from choices. Whereas the cultural structure provides goals (albeit selectively reinforced by social arrangements), the socially structured opportunity-structure provides the means for making and implementing choices. (As Merton points out, there may be marked disjunctions between aspects of cultural and social structures, and congruence should not be assumed.)

Lastly, 'mode of adaption' needs to be considered. This it seems to me is the (subjectively held) more strategic and longer-term frame within which more tactical choices are made, and as a result more likely to affect an actor's 'social identities'. Of course, such general orientations may be complex and not all choices unproblematically flow from them. It is important to note that this schema is not structurally deterministic, with many opportunities for subjective and individual-level factors to intrude, such as variance across individuals of perceptions of opportunities or expectations of particular roles. To a considerable extent, these distinctions repeat the orthodox introductory sociology textbook exposition (although this of course is not uninfluenced by Merton!). Nevertheless, they are useful distinctions. One of Merton's major theoretical accomplishments was a systematic codification of how to go about analysing cultural and social structures, as well as analysing their linkage to behaviour patterns and the choices behind them.

A related aspect of many of Merton's analyses which Stinchcombe underemphasises is the three-layer model in which macrostructures, especially social class, on the one hand and 'microenvironmental situations' such as a research laboratories, are seen as 'working behind', and through, intermediate social structures to influence social practices. In his earlier writing, Merton did not give much explicit attention to the microcontexts of interaction in which people's behaviour is set. However, this is explicitly addressed in his later work, and so will be treated as a separate element in the extended model. Organisations and communities are other meso-level social units which are important. Merton's most recent theoretical writings featured analysis of 'socially expected durations', and this – plus (my addition of) the related notion of 'socially expected spaces' – also needs to receive discrete attention.

Finally, in dealing with the consequences of behaviour for the maintenance and change of the institutional structures (which induce and shape the behaviour in the first place), an important distinction which is buried within Stinchcombe's reconstruction and the above diagram must be brought out. Behaviour (or practices) will have consequences not only for the institutional structures in which it is directly embedded, but also for *other* institutional structures. An obvious example of this is the 'Merton thesis' that the puritan ethos legitimated a concern with nature and technology. So, 'feedback' effects need to be separated from 'leakage' effects. Both may be unintended and unanticipated, but feedback effects particularly so. An outline of the more structural framework I suggest is shown in Figure 6.2.

The following sections separately delve into each of these components.

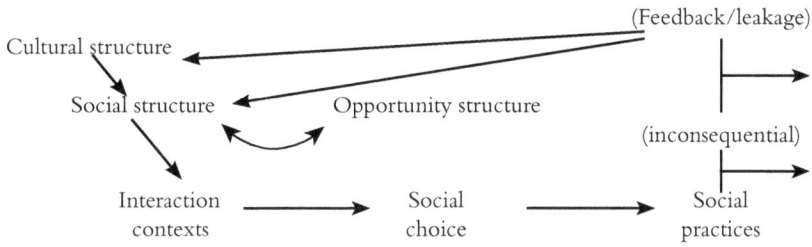

FIGURE 6.2 Extended model

Cultural structure

For Merton, as for Durkheim, culture is a collective phenomenon imposing on people externally, but also carried by them. "Cultural structure may be defined as that organized set of normative values governing behaviour which is common to members of a designated society or group" (1968: 216). Merton's model of cultural structure is conducted with a very considerable eye to the social bearing of beliefs, or knowledge or values and their consequences. This contrasts with more analytical concerns with the internal interrelationships within cultural structures themselves which so dominate the attention of French 'structuralists', and a variety of other more recent approaches in social theory. Nevertheless, there are several crucial distinctions which Merton deploys in constructing descriptions of cultural structures.

A major distinction is made between 'core values' – also variously expressed as 'Creed' (in the analysis of American race ideologies) or 'Code' (in the analysis of the value structure of pure science) or 'Cultural Goals' (in relation to the 'American dream') or 'Ethos' (as in 'Ethos of Science') and 'institutional norms', which are the more detailed forms in which the core values are 'operationalised' to influence social behaviour.

Much emphasis is placed on the built-in complexity of normative structures. This can be portrayed in part as patterns of norms and counter-norms, in which each norm is 'balanced' by its opposite, although the two seldom receive equal weighting. (Reference is made to the hierarchical ordering of the importance of values and norms, but procedures for examining this aspect of cultural structure are not developed (however, compare *Studies in Radio and Film Propaganda* (1943 [1968: 563–582]) and the discussion of Holton's conception of 'themata': 1975).

Another distinction is made between the more technical and the more social components of cultural structure. The former covers beliefs, knowledge and values concerning material production and the latter concerns, beliefs, knowledge and values in relation to society. In an early essay Merton used Alfred Weber's pair of terms 'civilisation' and 'culture' to differentiate between these two aspects. However, this nomenclature was subsequently downplayed (although briefly footnoted in 1968: 24), even though the conceptual distinction is continued unremarked in some actual analyses. Merton argued that these two different aspects of culture are each governed by rather different 'laws', and especially that the former has a capacity to cumulate in ways that the latter is resistant to. This distinction recurs later in Merton's work in his discussions of differences in the growth patterns of the natural sciences compared to the social sciences. In addition, Merton (1958) points to 'value climates' which are experienced by students and others in organisations: these are an aggregate effect much in the eye of the beholder. Merton's later 'sociological semantics' extended his analytical tools for consideration of culture much further, with separation of the ideas v. particular terms expressing them and the difference between symbolic and physical effects. He also added in consideration of the social production of culture, looking at the social contexts within which cultural items are generated, diffused, modified and indeed extinguished.

Part of the relative lack of sophistication in Merton's treatment of cultural structure arises in the absence of a clear suggested methodology for investigating it. In actual analyses, Merton was quite careful to attempt to provide an empirical basis in his descriptions of cultural structures, so that it is possible to extract something of a methodology. This is accomplished through quotation from written comments, and to a lesser extent through the citation of 'commonplace sayings' (sometimes as sanctified in dictionaries etc.). This, of course, is similar to Weber's approach to the same methodological problem. The sociological justification of this approach flows in large part from the recognition of the importance of pronouncements by key cultural entrepreneurs in affecting the beliefs of others. As well, it has the practical advantages of convenience, and perhaps even the advantage of allowing the display of an apparently almost effortless erudition! Although he himself seldom used survey data on attitude structures (with the exception of his study using ethnic 'opinionnaires': 1940 in his media reception studies and in later debates concerning the extent of conformity to 'success goals'), he cited with approval such studies carried out by others. However, it was important to Merton that the empirical studies be carefully carried out: they should particularly attempt to measure individuals' perceptions of commonly held cultural values rather than rely on the individual's own values (see Merton's critical comments [1976: 59–61] on Mitroff's sins in this regard). But people's assessment of, and commitment to, commonly held values is important too.

Much of Merton's interest in the sociology of knowledge was an attempt to explore the relationships between culture and social structure, but this was largely confined to review work, although essays on insiders and outsiders and conflict axes within national sociologies extended this. Given Merton's sustained interest in the sociology of knowledge it must have been a continuing disappointment that this area has been slow to show a cumulation of middle-range theories (cf. Barber, 1975). However, some of Merton's review work is pregnant with rich possibilities, when for example, he suggests the hypotheses

> that societies with sharp social cleavages, as allegedly in France, are more likely to cultivate sociology intensively than societies with a long history of

a more nearly uniform value-system, as allegedly in England; that a rising social class is constrained to see the social reality more authentically than a class long in power but now on the way out; that an upper class will focus on the static aspects of society and a lower one on its dynamic, changing aspects that an upper class will be alert to the functions of existing social arrangements and a lower class to their dysfunctions; or … that socially conservative groups hold to multiple-factor doctrines of historical causation and socially radical groups to monistic doctrines.

(1961[1973: 47–48])

Social character

Personality or character structure is occasionally deployed by Merton as an intervening 'variable' between cultural and social structure on the one hand and social choices and social practices on the other. There are several places, in particular, where Merton includes a personality 'level of analysis': the bureaucratic personality (1968: 259) with the propensity to adopt a ritualistic mode of adaptation, leadership capacities (1968: 402–404), and the talents and self-reassurance of *eminent* scientists (1973: 458–459). But, as a sociologist, Merton rightly shuns too close attention to character structure. Whenever 'personality' is invoked in explanation it is seen as both being shaped by social circumstances and in turn shaping patterns of behaviour (and especially in amplifying further, social tendencies already in train).

Sociological analyses can often assume that personality is a 'random' variable, merely creating background noise in the explanatory system. Merton points out that, at least in some situations, the individuals' choice amongst alternatives is further narrowed by socially constructed personality characteristics. Through repeated exposure and consistent choice, grooves of repeated information-handling are laid down, and this in turn becomes a further factor built into the ongoing situation and thus reinforcing the social structure. Character structure laid down during earlier socialisation, especially during childhood, which varies by social strata, may be particularly influential in later social situations. Merton's early comments, in his essay on anomie, on the role of the family in socialisation and especially the way in which the underlying structures of language and social perceptions are latently absorbed by the child, are prescient (1968: 212–213).

In more recent writing Merton referred to cognitive and social identities as a partial substitute for personality, for example in particular fields of science. But these may refer to individuals or to the self-characterisation of a collectivity or collectively held by each of its members.

Interaction contexts

Although Merton only accorded this 'level' explicit attention in his last phase of work, an interest in the microsociology of interaction is a continual thread throughout his work. In further formulations of his anomie theory ([1968: 233–235];

1964: 231–235), Merton makes it very clear that he considers that the interaction context plays a significant role either in amplifying or damping-down the vulnerability of individuals to anomic strain and their likelihood of converting this into deviant behaviour. This same interest threads through other work: in particular, the analysis of the network position of community influentials, the concomitant work on the dynamics of friendship links, studies of author–referee pairs, and the importance of social interaction if scientists are to sharpen their scientific ideas (1973: 347). As his programme of sociological semantics developed, more emphasis was placed on analysing the effects of 'microenvironments' although these were usually institutional settings, rather than necessarily smaller face-to-face groups. This level of analysis bridges the structural concerns more common in Merton's analyses with the smaller-scale settings in which social life is lived day by day. (The potential interface between the group theory called upon in guiding focus groups and a more general group dynamics is not developed.)

Social choices

At the centre of the Mertonian analytical system is the action of individual people in making choices amongst structurally given alternatives. This component in the schema provides its 'model of man' (or social psychology or philosophical anthropology: cf. Wrong, 1961). The actor is only partly socially determined in the Mertonian schema, and is conceptualised as having room to manoeuvre within structurally imposed constraints. The flesh-and-blood individual is also recognised as actively manning the positions in the social structure. By standing at the centre of often-diverse status-sets, the individual 'pulls together' the various strands and complexities of the social structure. In turn, the impulses and strains affecting an individual are structurally channelled along the lines of the social structure. As Merton commented on Homans's doctrine of 'bringing men back in' – they never left.

Despite the central place of the actor (as status occupant) in Merton's system of theorising, it has been a relatively unexplicated component, with rich descriptions yet to be more abstractly examined. Nevertheless, we can draw on two discussions – the early treatment in the essay on 'The unanticipated consequences of purposive social action' (1973 [1936]) and the recapitulation by Stinchcombe (1975).

Stinchcombe depicts Merton's conceptualisation of the core process as the:

> choice between socially structured alternatives ... [which] differs from the choice process of economic theory, in which the alternatives are conceived to have inherent utilities. It differs from the choice process of learning theory in which the alternatives are conceived to emit reinforcing or extinguishing stimuli. It differs from both of these in that ... the utility or reinforcement of a particular alternative choice is thought of as socially established, as part of the institutional order.

> *(Stinchcombe, 1975: 12)*

A later passage in the same essay contrasts Merton's model of choice with symbolic interactionism ("the choice determined by definitions of the situation") and Parsonian theory ("choices about inherent value dilemmas determined by cultural values": Stinchcombe, 1975: 14). Criticising symbolic interactionism, Stinchcombe points out that because of wider social frameworks which impinge on people, they cannot define situations as they please (1975: 15). Criticising Parsonian theory, Stinchcombe argues that value dilemmas indicated by the 'pattern variables' are pitched at too general an analytical level for the theory to be able to show how they affect people's choices.

Other aspects of Merton's 'model of man' can be gleaned from other parts of his writings. A central point in Merton's 'model of man' is the importance of the cognitive element. This is particularly pointed up in his publicising of the 'Thomas Theorem': "If men define situations as real, they are real in their consequences" (1948 [1968: 475]). In his essay on functional analysis this aspect has echoes in phrases such as unanticipated and unintended consequences. Merton was also sensitive to the build-up of emotional commitments to choices, especially scientists often thought to be emotionally neutral: their institutionally proscribed detachment wars with their emotional commitment to hypotheses, findings etc. The values of science at an institutional level are also described as 'affectively toned'.

As several writers have noted (e.g. Taylor et al., 1973), Merton departs from the biologically based 'model of man' in Durkheim's anomie theory, in which social structure must control the animating primitive urges. In fact, Merton is rather less concerned with this, and more with distancing himself from a Freudian intellectual embrace. However, this does not extend to his holding a 'rational' model. Merton has pointed out that his framework does not assume that people's choices are necessarily utilitarian or rational, but may incorporate less-considered action, such as that associated with some forms of juvenile delinquency, but nevertheless still arising out of socially structured stresses (1968: 232).

Rose Coser (1975: 239) has argued more aggressively that Merton holds a rather more active 'model of man':

> Merton has stood Durkheim on his head; rather than have the individual confronted with ready-made social norms that are external, coming down *in toto*, so to speak, for Merton individuals have to find their own orientations among the multiple, incompatible, and contradictory norms.

In sum, Merton's 'model of man' is complex, but compatible both with social analysis and with a vision that people have a considerable degree of autonomy, and much of that autonomy comes from the complexity of each person's status-set.

Social patterns

Description of the behavioural pattern resulting from the choice amongst the structured options is always a carefully crafted part of a Mertonian analysis. To grasp how Merton tackles this aspect of his schema, reference will be made to several examples detailed above, and then the more general principles will be elicited from these examples: Modes of adaptation and his prejudice typology.

Although these two typologies are particularly explicit examples, similar (if unrecognised) typologies underlie other Mertonian analyses. For example, in his work on the behavioural patterns of scientists there lurks a typology which is built around the tension between the concern for recognition and concern for the advancement of scientific knowledge. And applied researchers face a trade-off between long-term intellectual development and short-term policy relevance.

Several general methodological principles can be developed from these examples. One point is that the focus is on a whole complex of behaviour rather than on a simple dependent variable such as voting. Secondly, this complex of behaviour is conceptualised at an abstract level, so that it involves a general strategy of behaviour, which might subsume a wide variety of different tactics. Third, in order to capture much of this diversity of behaviour, Merton develops typologies (somewhat akin to Weberian ideal types) that are based on logical distinctions around a few key principles. This is clearly an analytical device which greatly simplifies the empirical diversity and gradations of 'real life', and the analytical skill lies in first of all setting up the main underlying dimension in the schema of logical possibilities, followed by careful logic in then expanding the framework of categories. Finally, it should be noted that behavioural patterns include both what might otherwise be termed (subjective) 'attitudes' on the one hand and (objective) 'behaviour' on the other.

The different terminologies which can be used in discussing this component of Merton's model create some difficulty. The term 'behavioural pattern' under-emphasises the attitudinal aspect which is also central to Merton's conception. The term 'social practice' or, better, 'alternative social practices' may capture the meaning more appropriately (moreover, it is at least partly legitimated by Merton's own reference to 'practice' in his work on discrimination (1948 [1976])).

Once set up, a typology may be useful in descriptive sociographies. For example, Merton suggests empirical research to determine the proportion of the four prejudice–discrimination types in various geographic areas and amongst different social classes, major associations and nationality groups (1976: 210). However, the main purpose of the typology is to then model different explanations of the social structural sources that differentially shape individual's choice of one or other of the prejudice–discrimination alternatives available to them. Moreover, policy initiatives would work differently depending on the spread of these types in particular communities.

Feedback and leakage loops

Some of Merton's essays have examined mechanisms of social dynamics and change – in general unanticipated consequences, and specifically the self-fulfilling prophecy, the self-defeating or suicidal prophecy – and at an institutional level, latent and manifest functions. This part of the schema is concerned with how the social practices resulting from social choices fold back to affect structures. The examples that bring this out include the way in which the practice of publishing (rather than non-publishing) then leads to the continuance of journals, and the way in which the practice of voting for a particular political party (rather than non-voting or voting for another party) will more likely result in the persistence of that political organisation. Thus, contributors and voters not only choose amongst options, but by making a particular choice they help to keep open the possibility of that option continuing to be available. This element of the overall model has already been presaged in the discussion of the conflict between alternative structures in Chapter 5 where it was noted that it is central to Stinchcombe's (1968) discussion of the causal imagery of functional analysis. It has also been adopted by sociologists such as Boudon (1981) as a framework for the tracing of 'perverse effects' at the aggregate level that flow from individual decisions. (Note that this point also relates to the discussion about the relationship between the institutional and 'pre-institutional' levels of behaviour above.) Consideration of linkages is particularly important in the study of social dynamics and change.

Although Merton was particularly interested in these feedback mechanisms, he did not publish work on their operation in detail. However, some of the examples he deploys in drawing attention to their operation are widely regarded as classic contributions. He defines a self-fulfilling prophecy as "a false definition of the situation evoking a new behaviour which makes the originally false conception come true" (1948 [1968: 477]). The examples he offers include the collapse of banks under 'runs' and the way in which people in minority groups have, in the past at least, not been allowed access to institutions and then been damned because they pursued alternatives. The suicidal prophecy involves changing the course of behaviour such that the prophecy fails to be brought about. Merton is careful to point out that there are social mechanisms that can intervene in such vicious cycles and that institutional controls are often able to quell rumours and panics that feed at the informal interactional level of operation.

In addition to the feedback effects specified by Merton, Stinchcombe and Boudon there is another class of 'social practice effects' on structure that can be designated as 'leakage effects'. This is where social practices affect the development of 'neighbouring' structures other than those which generated the behaviour patterns in the first place. The obvious example of this is Merton's hypothesis that the puritan impulse may have led to the increased pursuit of scientific knowledge. Leakage effects are not randomly sprayed around from their source, but are contained by the status-sets that people are simultaneously placed within. Often, however, this leakage effect will be unanticipated and unintended by the actors involved. It is a consequence of the way social structures are complexly organised.

The most obvious way in which consequences affect institutions is through building or collapsing the social support for a particular institution over against its rivals – the structural alternatives. However, the relationship may be more varied than this. For example, as a result of scientists' productivity, scientific work may accumulate into massive flows of articles. The resultant growth may in turn have effects on individual behaviour (e.g. the types of literature-citing practices needed to cope with the volumes).

Summary

Having sketched out Merton's multilayered analytical account, it is important to show how this is then 'set in motion' or made to 'work'. Herewith is an interesting passage where Merton pulls various items together: 1995: 60, 61 from 1979 – while this passage is clearly applicable in the immediate instance to the social structure of scientists, it has broader applicability. (I have minor quibbles, especially where institutional and organisational are run together and more might have been made of 'fields of activity'.)

Processes of individual self-selection and institutional social selection interact to affect *successive probabilities of access to the opportunity-structure in a given field of activity*. When the role performance of individuals measures up to demanding institutional standards, and especially when it greatly exceeds them, this imitates a *process of cumulative advantage* to which the individuals acquire enlarged opportunities to advance their work (and the rewards that go with it), even further, since elite institutions have comparatively large resources for advancing work in their domains, talent that finds its way into these institutions has the heightened potential of acquiring *differentially accumulating advantages*. The systems of reward, allocation of resources and social selection thus operate to create and maintain a class structure in science by providing a stratified distribution of chances amongst scientists for enlarging their role as investigators. Differentially accumulating advantages work in such a way that … unto everyone who hath shall be given and he shall have an abundance, but from him that hath not shall be taken away even that which he hath. *Mutis mutandis, cumulative advantages accrue for organisations and institutions as they do for individuals*, subject to countervailing forces that dampen exponential cumulation.

Merton places much emphasis on abjuring mere typologies, and requires that theoretical work posit 'causal' connections. This means that any full-blown Mertonian analysis must involve each of the components sketched out above. At this point we can again draw on some of the discussion presented by Stinchcombe. At the centre of the schema is some pattern of choices faced by actors, and this is seen as constrained and often routinised in continually repeated patterns, but still with a solid spark of 'free will'. However, the repeated acts of choice are the result of a variety of sources – both psychological and sociological. Merton's sociological analytical apparatus focuses on the structuring of choices and motivation, so that the actor as status-incumbent and chooser plays a key role in the system.

To a considerable extent, Merton's analytical schema locates the seat of energy in the cultural structure, but as mediated, reinforced or dampened by the social structure in its linkage to the opportunity-structure. It is their *joint* effect that shapes the range of choice for individuals. While the cultural structure provides the knowledge and values which circumscribe and motivate social action, these are variously effected by the opportunity-structure held in different areas of the social structure, not least through differential exposure to the cultural structure. At the centre of all Merton's analyses are social and opportunity structural features, which more specifically shape social practices, and which in turn differentially affect the development of culture and also feed back to gradually reshape the social structure itself.

It is difficult to evoke the imagery behind Merton's schema, although its explanatory bite is largely lost if we cannot conjure up a metaphor. Classic functionalism used the biological analogy of a homeostatic system, such as the blood circulation system of a body, in which any perturbation is fairly quickly restored back to equilibrium through the mechanisms which maintain body temperature. The more advanced versions of Parsons's thought might be likened somewhat to a very complicated energy-exchange motor system (a very sophisticated car engine) in which a variety of fuels circulate and can be in part transmogrified into each other although they are in part quite compartmentalised. Lukes has pointed out that in Durkheim's writing much is made of imagery drawn from thermodynamics and electricity (1973: 35). The imagery behind Merton's approach is different, but equally complicated. It seems to me that Merton's structural analysis might be imagined as centered on an actor, influenced and energised by various cultural elements, but who is embedded within a complex intermediate structural situation (in terms of positions and of resources) which variously amplifies, dampens down and certainly complicates this pull. The actor has some, albeit limited, control over the cultural and social system. This image conveys the idea of the distant and multidirectional pulling-power of the cultural structure, and of the limited but significant role of the actor in maintaining the balancing act of resolving in their performance some of the conflicting demands thrust upon them, or open to them. It also conveys an appropriate image of both the pressure towards conformity in behaviour as it is continuously enacted, but also the precariousness of this performance and the continual pressures to diverge into alternative paths. A difficulty with this imagery is that it is not too easy to fit in the typology of choices, although it is possible to glimpse some possibilities.

This imagery has several attractive features (compare the account given in Stinchcombe, 1975: 26–31). The scale at which the analysis is cast 'brings men in', but also shows how their behaviour is culturally and socially shaped. There is a focus on regularity in human affairs but also attention to ambivalence, deviance and reaction, and the vulnerability of the accepted social order to change. Social structure is portrayed as being real in its effects, but it is seen as permeable rather than reified. Private troubles and joys are linked to structure, but structure is shown to grow out of individual behaviour in a nice interplay of the objective and subjective. The mix of handling the ordinary and the exotic, the obvious and the mysterious, is nicely grasped: Merton urges attention to the unobvious hidden side of the social which often only sociologists can reveal, but he also attempts to confront the commonplace by showing the limitations of common-sense assumptions. Nevertheless, the mundane is built into his sociology as much as the newly revealed. While the Mertonian system is clearly able to handle variety in human behaviour, its ability to explain change and its handling of power need closer examination.

In Stinchcombe's exegesis the feedback-looping is given a prominent place. But, as in Merton's work, examples of changing structures are present, not prominent: examples include

* the reciprocal influences of science and society and how each changes in response to pressures from the other;
* changes in the reward structure in science;
* changes on cognitive structures;
* change in opportunity-structures.

Consideration of these complexities is furthered by the central point in his version of functional analysis that structural equivalents might be expected to 'come in' once a particular structure is seen to be failing, and despite his concern that long-term viability of any social structure is dependent on mechanisms that induce change. Merton also clearly feels that his approach has a weak spot in this area and discusses this in later reflections on his essay on 'Social Structure and Anomie':

> Unless systematic consideration is given to the degree of support of particular 'institutions' by specific groups, we shall overlook the important place of power in society. To speak of 'legitimate power' or authority is often to use an elliptical and misleading phrase. Power must be legitimized for some without being legitimized for all groups in the society. It may, therefore, be misleading to describe nonconformity with particular institutions merely as deviant behaviour; it may represent the beginning of a near alternative pattern, with its own distinctive claims to moral validity.
>
> *(1968: 176)*

An interest in the role of power in creating or confounding change is included within his discussion of the postulate of universal functionalism.

> Far more useful [than this postulate] would seem the provisional assumption that persisting cultural forms have a *net balance of functional consequences* [Merton's emphasis] either for the society considered as a unit or for subgroups sufficiently powerful to retain these forms intact, by means of direct coercion or indirect persuasion.
>
> *(Merton, 1968: 86)*

Beneath the intricate but bland Mertonian facade there lurks a flavour of realpolitik that is seemingly suppressed elsewhere! It is through such mechanisms that the Mertonian analytical system is able to explain how the structure is itself able to induce structural changes, whereas the Parsonian system seems only to react to external changes. Merton briefly endorses the approach taken by Stinchcombe that change, even revolutionary change, can be broken down in repeated cycles of structurally induced changes, provided that the timeframe can be frozen sufficiently

(Merton, 1976). In joint work with Lazarsfeld, Merton had already developed a similar model of the process of development of a friendship (Merton and Lazarsfeld, 1954). At several points, he suggests that there is something of a 'social learning' process as the social structure develops an increasing ability to handle certain endemic difficulties (for example in handling stresses in status-and-role structures). However, Merton is more often than not taken with the irony that change or con-flict can feed back onto social order, as expressed in his almost triumphant citation of the Simmel–Ross theory of conflict:

> a society … which is riven by a dozen … [conflicts] along lines running in every direction, may actually be in less danger of being torn with violence or filling to pieces than one split along 'just' one line. For each new cleavage contributes to narrow the cross clefts, so that one might say that society is sewn together by its inner conflicts.
>
> *(Merton, 1973: 681 citing Ross)*

However, these areas of power and change remain a seemingly potential explanatory aspect of his system that has not been sufficiently developed, because analysis has not been focused on them. Because of this limited attention Merton's sociology is rather too trapped in the deficiencies which are held to afflict all Durkheimian-derived sociologies, although there is a core of interesting ideas to work up.

Review

I shall conclude this discussion of Merton's underlying analytical apparatus by attempting to evaluate the validity of his conception compared to alternative formulations of this time period, by reviewing criticisms of it, and by revisiting my earlier (see Chapter 2) account of early influence on Merton. How original is Merton's approach to sociology? Sorokin, with his charming insouciance describes the theory of reference groups as "a somewhat fragmented and cursory recapitu-lation of more adequate theories of social groups developed by several sociologists [unnamed!] of the preceding and present generations" (1966: 455).

Indeed, Merton worked within the general 'culture, society, personality' trinity of central concepts. However, I feel that his schema possesses genuine originality in that it:

- is more specific about internal components of these three broad areas (for example, in depicting the latticework of statuses and roles which comprise social structures);
- is able to show the essential nature and 'relative autonomy' of each major com-ponent, and to specify some of the mechanisms through which each interacts with the other (for example, in suggesting that pressure towards deviant behav-iour is generated by the mismatch between cultural and social structure);

- links these three general 'explanatory' concepts to behavioural patterns or social practices (which include the feedback loop of reproduction or change in the structures generating the pattern), so that Merton always focuses on something to explain, rather than merely providing reified descriptive categories.

In sum, Merton took the 'culture, society, personality' schema, differentiated more finely within it, connected it up and set it to work on explaining behaviour. As with most other creative activities, the various materials for the extension of past work were at hand. But they needed to be activated.

Merton was an avowed functional analyst throughout his academic life (particularly during the late 1940s through to the early 1970s), and before this operated with a simplified and truncated version of this approach. In the mid-1970s he seemed to recast his overall approach, but did not enunciate in sufficient detail what was involved in the non-Parsonian structural 'variant' he now was prepared to accept, or clarify his attitude to his earlier work. In this book, I have argued that under the cover of, and while still retaining this functional framework, Merton in fact largely deployed a structuralist approach, in which behavioural outcomes and consequences are tied to structural sources. The top layer of Merton's functional analysis in some of his writings has unfortunately and confusedly sometimes distracted attention from the rather more important underlying structural analysis.

It is possible to revisit criticisms of his earlier work to show that they do not undermine his structural analyses. The difficulty with the functional mode of interpretation arose when Merton attempted to extend his earlier model of unanticipated consequences, to deal with the particular – but sociologically strategic – subclass of unanticipated consequences that affect the continuance of social institutions. The difficulty with explanations couched in these terms is that they can appear to 'explain' a social institution, or the continued existence of a social institution, in terms of its consequences. This not only unnecessarily reifies social structure, but appears to commit the aggregative fallacy of according social aggregates with intentionality and understanding. Only actors can act, although they often act collectively and may act in some part with a concern about the maintenance of social structure. Despite these philosophical difficulties, using the language of functions may continue to have a useful heuristic purpose in alerting social analysts to interlocking connections between diverse institutional phenomena, provided that at least in principle a translation into individual-level terms is possible. This is a version of the doctrine of 'methodological individualism'. Merton's 'functional interpretations' did not fall into the traps of 'functional explanations'. In each of his examples it is possible for it to be converted into such terms by showing that continuance or change in institutional patterns result from individual consequences – whether intended or not.

The challenge then becomes to show that Merton's classic examples of functional analysis can be reconstructed according to the above rule (i.e. recasting as a causal analysis and in terms of 'methodological individualism'). Merton has been criticised by several commentators (e.g. Matza, 1969: 59–60) for breaching his own methodological strictures by arguing that the "the functional deficiencies of the official structure generated an alternative unofficial structure to fulfil existing needs somewhat more effectively" (1968b: 127). That is, the continuity of the political machine proves its functionality. However, although such an interpretation of Merton's rather casual functional analysis of political machines can be made, a rather more careful reading of the complete passage indicates that:

- Merton establishes that there is a 'need' for services, such as those supplied by a political machine;
- Merton argues that political machines contrive to operate in the face of some opposition from decent citizens, and competition from alternative sources of supply for those services.

As argued above, Merton also holds a competitive (even 'conflict') perspective on the relationship between alternative structures. The brief analysis sketched by Merton can then be 'more properly' translated along the following lines: individuals have a choice in obtaining certain services from either legitimate or illegitimate sources, and for some groups with limited avenues for obtaining legitimate sources, illegitimate sources are especially attractive. When such people then choose to use illegitimate sources, the continuance of these sources is furthered.

A somewhat similar translation can be carried out for another central example: the Hopi dance ceremonial. In this example, there is presumably an individual need for reassurance in the face of environmental difficulties and a need for social involvement. But perhaps more important than this is the cultural imperative of the calendar of ritual practices, and the lack of competing alternative structures. Individual involvement in such patterns strongly tends to be self-reinforcing.

Merton's substantive contributions

In addition to his general work, as previous chapters show, Merton contributed to two main substantive areas and other areas with these contributions being further instances of the deployment of his characteristic approach. Indeed, one test of the correctness of my conceptualisation of Merton's general sociological structures is to find them embedded in his more substantive work. In addition, it might be expected that a close examination of more substantive work might reveal additional angles on his more general approaches. It might also be expected, that critics will obtain more leverage on Merton's substantive, rather than his general, statements, and that consideration of such concerns will more clearly reveal deficiencies and limitations.

It is not without significance that Merton has contributed to several areas of sociology which have at various times been central to the overall development of sociology, as crucial issues have been most visibly raised and fought over in these areas. In the late 1960s and through the 1970s, the area of sociology in which viewpoints (such as the labelling perspective) broadly deriving from a symbolic interactionist stance were most exercised, was the sociology of deviance. This was followed by arguments about deviance derived from a radical, Marxian perspective. Together they placed the sociology of deviance as an area which was the leading edge of theoretical development and debate in sociology.

About a decade later the sociology of science performed a somewhat similar role, although one less central to the whole of sociology. Fuelled by issues imported from the adjacent areas of philosophy and the history of science, many of the major theoretical debates affecting sociology as a whole have been played out within the sociology of science in a particularly intense form.

Media studies too has boomed in a media-saturated age, and cultural analyses have unveiled the ideologies which shape so much of our lives.

On the other hand, changes at the collective level of scientific specialties may have circumscribed Merton's legacy. Over the last few decades criminology has become its own discipline, overshadowing the broader sociology of deviance. Sociology of science too works across the more recently arising broader field of science studies or indeed 'science and technology studies' (STS: an acronym perhaps derived from Merton's 1930s thesis). Media studies, which Merton helped spur along in the 1940s, has also become a self-sufficient discipline although still remaining a branch within sociology. There are debates in each of these three fields about where they stand in relation to mainstream sociology with some sentiment that the fields retain few links. Such changes on the disciplinary front may have limited Merton's continuing influence, although arguably it may also give him a multitrack legacy now spanning a wider range of disciplines.

Merton's 'theory of society'

The resurgence of 'European' social theory has often taken the form of characterisations of the key features of modernity (e.g. the notion of 'liquid modernity') and is also related to macrosociological theories of broader societal-level structures and processes (e.g. globalisation). It is something of a gap that Merton did not come up with a relevant version, and for some sociologists this has dimmed their interest in his work. But, Merton does indeed supply the ingredients for such a 'theory of society'. He analyses the key features or institutions of modern society (although these analyses need to be linked together) and his historical sociology of science and (implicit) comparative sociology of deviance point to macrosocial dynamics. Quite a few of his concepts could be readily 'scaled up' to suit a macrosociological analysis. Merton never saw the need to do this himself, and perhaps would have been put off by such an enterprise, as hewing too closely to 'grand theory'. Comparative studies in the Mertonian spirit have been carried out on cross-national differences in deviance and related topics. A Mertonian macrosociology would paint a broader picture encompassing anomie and stresses, while also being focused on the operations of professions, scientists and bureaucracies. How emphases in values differ between societies would be studied, together with the extent of integrative fit amongst the institutions – their mutual interaction.

In describing the social structures of societies, some Columbian scholars (e.g. Rose Coser, Peter Blau) have already investigated different types of status-structures (e.g. simple v. complex) and cross-national differences in these might also facilitate explanations. Retrieving a Mertonian comparative/historical sociology couched at a societal level is an obvious opportunity that would be one of the ways in which his analytical work could be rounded off.

Merton's values

Finally, the level of values. In his *A Sociology of Sociology*, Friedrichs (1970) argues that the most important level at which paradigms operate involve the moral stances which undergird sociology, and he goes on to identify 'prophetic' versus 'priestly' modes of conducting sociology. A somewhat similar distinction, but one expressed at the conceptual rather than moral level, is made in other writings (e.g. Mills, 1959; Gouldner, 1970). As well as influencing the methodological and the theoretical stances of mid-century sociology, Merton also influenced its moral tone, and its stance towards the deficiencies of the existing social order. This was not systematically developed and involves limited passages and remarks.

Merton was a socialist in his earlier years (Merton, 1994), and was closely linked personally for several years with Granville Hicks who for a time was book review editor for a Communist cultural magazine *The New Masses*. Merton attended and helped support Hicks at a political debate between Hicks and Catholic right-winger Fa. Curran, president of the International Catholic Truth Society and a leader of the so-called Coughlinites: "Resolved, That Communism is the enemy of democracy." He broke with Hicks after Hicks had 'named' (as a communist) Merton's colleague Bernard Stern to the McCarthy investigation.

However, Simonson (2010) considers that Merton pulled back considerably by about 1950 from active political involvements and proclaimed he was an 'independent' in party terms. The student protests of the 1960s placed particular pressure on Merton and he did not appear to be too actively engaged, but broadly supported the establishment, while retaining a broadly center-left Liberal position. Merton supported the Humphrey campaign and was one of a group that corresponded with LBJ advocating getting out of Viet Nam.

In relation to sociology, Merton preached 'detached concern' (a concept coined in his medical school study) and his views – along with other social critics – about society more generally were similar: an adherence to a humane, evidence-based guardedly optimistic societal vision.

Merton is far too sensitive to the complex relationship between values and the scientific enterprise to take a simplistic stance on the social responsibilities of sociology. At several points in his writings, Merton is concerned that adequate sociological understanding must supersede naive moral judgements. In particular, he is concerned that simplistic social engineering bereft of an understanding of the complexities of latent dysfunctions might be ineffectual. However, this concern about the too-rapid involvement of sociology in social reform does not preclude concern with action. For example, Merton's essay on the self-fulfilling prophecy, with reference to racial discrimination, carefully argues for the role of social engineering, guided by soundly based social scientific knowledge, to combat its manifestations. Further, in his chapter on the 'Sociology of Social Problems' Merton (1976a: 26) develops an image of social criticism being built upon a "technical judgement about the working of social systems". This centres on the concept of 'social disorganisation' which refers to inadequacies in a social system that keep people's collective and individual purposes from being as fully realised as they could be. Social disorganisation is relative. It is not tied to any absolute standard, which would be Utopian, but to a standard of what, so far as we know, could be accomplished under attainable conditions. When we say that a group or community or society is disorganised, we mean that its structure of statuses and roles is "not working as effectively as it might to achieve valued purposes". Taylor et al. (1973: 95–96) develop their view that:

> Merton's ideal or perfect society would be one in which there was an accord between merit and its consequences. The means for achieving success would be respected, and the opportunities open to all those of sufficient merit. The motivation to compete and the opportunities to succeed would be in proportion to the degree of individual stratification *necessary* for the society to function. The competition for success, furthermore, would be enjoyed as an end in itself, and the cultural goals would be substantial and definite – rather than fetishistic and relativistic.

Although this model is developed out of Merton's writings on anomie, it is certainly also applicable to his implicit moral analysis of the deficiencies in rewarding merit within the institution of science.

Merton developed the outline of a moral stance for sociology, especially in the last chapter of *Mass Persuasion*. His alertness to the close links between technical problems and moral dilemmas is brought out in his argument that:

> the initial formulation of [any] scientific investigation [is] conditioned by the implied values of the scientist. Thus, had the investigator been orientated toward such democratic values as respect for the dignity of the individual, he would have framed his scientific problem differently … He would be, in short, sensitized to certain questions stemming from his democratic values which would otherwise be readily overlooked.
>
> *(1946: 188)*

In a later discussion Merton sees sociology as "link[ed] up with a critical morality as opposed to conventional reality" (1976: 38). Clearly, an activist value stance towards the recognition of social problems is preferred to a fatalist stance of passive acceptance of 'sadistic social structures' ("which are so organized as to systematically inflict pain, humiliation, suffering and deep frustration on particular groups and strata" 1976: 131) – if only because fatalism is frequently generated by such social structures and works in the class interests of the privileged against the depressed. This framework builds around the best ways of "serv[ing] the ultimate values of society" (1976: 40). However, this notion needs to be further developed.

Some aspects of Merton's image of sociology were to demarcate and defend professional sociology from confusion with political journalism, and he makes a point of separating C. Wright Mills's later polemical writings from his earlier scholarly work (Merton, 1968: 66). In his two main interventions in forums of sociology, 'Social Conflict in Styles of Sociological Work' (at an International Sociology Association Congress) and 'Insiders and Outsiders' (at the American Sociological Association conference and published in the *American Journal of Sociology*), he endeavoured to build complementarities from differences and to see lines of conflict as useful divisions of labour within the whole sociological enterprise. Indeed, in terms of his own sociology of knowledge (see above: Chapter 3), in which he suggests that views which emphasise the complexities and complications of social life tend to be held by conservative groups.

Several historians (Katznelson, 2002; Hollinger, 1983; Jaworski, 1990; also Simonson, 2010) have painted a broader generational picture in which Merton can readily be placed alongside other Columbia titans such as Trilling and Hofstadter. They shared a similar 'Columbia stance' of some detachmed aloofness in relation to American society, eschewing American triumphalism. They had experienced the horrors of a world gone mad in the convulsions of WW2, but had earlier been uplifted by the New Deal's rescuing of so many from poverty. Their secular faith was not based on any religious stance. However, they did not despair, but saw the possibilities for reform in smaller-scale social engineering. They were sceptical but hopeful. And they undertook some public activities to demonstrate this, and encouraged research and understanding.

Criticism

The immediate post-war decades required some guarding against the strictures of McCarthyism, and this period led into the heated 1960s and 1970s ideological disputes. Since then ideological concerns seem to have been more tempered, leaving sociology to progress without too much ideological vituperation until the millennium ushered in another wave of societal concerns. The critiques of Merton mainly arose in the conflictual era. The critics' concerns were in the way Merton handles issues of social class, power, exploitation, alienation, repression and the way Merton relates to the Marxian heritage of sociology. While I think these contrarian views are valuable in pointing to both real and imagined lacunae in Merton's work, they often are over-written and built on inadequate reading of Merton's work. Merton's analyses tended to be cool and technical whereas several critics have urged more vigorous vocabulary and critique. Often, Merton's writings have indeed covered points overlooked by critics, but the critics' vituperations may be salutary in suggesting stronger articulation on some issues.

Merton's exposure to Marxian thought was considerable. Coser refers to Merton's "continued focus on class factors which had been stimulated by his immersion in Marxian thought" (Coser, 1975b: 95), to his "profound knowledge of the Marxian canon" (Coser and Nisbet, 1975: 7), and to the considerable influence of the New Deal 'revolution' that captured the political imagination of that generation). Moreover, Merton had the courage to continue to use Marxian terms, even during a period when Barber felt that the term 'communism' used to describe one of the key norms of science, might be more tactfully replaced by 'communality'.

It is possible to develop a 'class reading' of Merton. The index to *Social Theory and Social Structure* reports references to class on 15 pages, and it is a thread running through several analyses. Class is central in his anomie/strain theory and in his sociology of scientists. 'Opportunity-structures', a concept particularly developed in later writings, should not be reduced to class, nevertheless refer to stratificational mechanisms. Gouldner interprets Merton's essay on 'Social Structure and Anomie' as using "Marx to pry open Durkheim" (Gouldner, 1970: 477). This refers to Merton's identification of the social class background which affects those taking up some modes of adaptation. In Merton's study of community influentials, class is seen as a base around which different forms of local influence are wielded. In later studies, the structure of stratification in science is at the centre of many analyses. Perhaps, most dramatically, the careful comparison of similarities between Marxian and functional analyses in Merton's 1949 essay on functional analysis is replaced in his 1975 essay on 'structural analysis' with an explicit if unspecified commitment to the Marxian theoretical approach as a central component in structural analysis. Further Marxian concern can be found behind Merton's sketch of a sociology of knowledge, and in his setting up of status-and-role analysis.

Despite this, in his critical review commentary on the Festschrift for Merton edited by Coser, Randall Collins argues that: "If there is a central theme that underlies virtually all of Merton's work, I would say it is the effort to de-fuse 'stratificational' issues. Structural inequalities are simply settings for the drama of social mobility" (Collins, 1977: 153). Collins argues that Merton holds a 'liberal' ideological stance and that the logic of his approach is to transform issues involving social conflict or political domination into abstract analyses that nicely show how such aspects really are part of a self-equilibrating status quo. This, he feels, might reflect something of the darkness of the McCarthy era during which many of Merton's ideas developed. There is a tension between meritocracy and elitism with Collins and Restivo arguing that Merton's later sociology of science consistently defends

> science against charges of unfairness or inefficiency … [by claiming] that any inequities at the individual level (where the achievements of established scientists are more readily recognized than those of obscure scientists) are compensated for by the gains to science as a whole that results from keeping research well organized around clearly defined goals.

The elite is valorised, but it is hard to see science operating without a hierarchy of talent. Thio (1975) also argues that Merton's analysis of deviance could be seen as stigmatising the lower class.

Even such a sympathetic critic as Stinchcombe points out that "aside from information determinants of this placement in the flow of rewards and punishments … Merton has not systematically analysed power systems and their implications" (Stinchcombe, 1975: 23). However, he does note that the development of "a systematic account of the implicit theories of power in a variety of Merton's structural essays would repay the effort".

A weaker version of this critique suggests that Merton's work operated with a more diffuse ideological tone that in particular had made too comfortable an alliance with established interests. Gouldner (1961) in his famous essay entitled 'anti-Minotaur, the myth of a value-free sociology' draws attention to differences he sees between 'professional' compared to 'intellectual' approaches to sociology by comparing the 'Columbia/Harvard' (and notably therefore Merton) and 'Chicago' styles of studying medical institutions.

> It is difficult to escape the feeling that the former are more respectful of the medical establishment than the Chicagoans, that they more readily regard it in terms of its own claims, and are more prone to view it as a noble profession. Chicagoans, however, tend to be uneasy about the idea of a 'profession' as a tool for study, believing instead that the notion of an 'occupation' provides more basic guidelines for study, and arguing that occupations as diverse as the nun and the prostitute, or the plumber and the physician, reveal instructive sociological similarities. Chicagoans seem more likely to take a secular view of medicine, seeing *it* as an occupation much like any other and are somewhat more inclined towards debunking forays into the seamier side of medical practice. Epitomizing this difference are the very differences in the book titles that the two groups have chosen for their medical studies. Harvard and Columbia have soberly called two of their most important works, *The Student-Physician* and *Experiment Perilous*, while the Chicagoans have irreverently labelled their own recent study of medical students, the *Boys in White*.
>
> *(Gouldner, 1961: 76–77)*

How did Merton actually use the Marxian canon? Coser is quick to point out that Merton carefully attempted to turn any Marxian ideological thrusts to analytical purpose, stripped of any value-laden freight. Upping the ante, Gouldner suggests that Merton "sought to make peace between Marxism and Functionalism precisely by emphasizing their affinities", and "thus make it easier for Marxist students to become Functionalist professors" (Gouldner, 1970: 335). (Merton protested in reply that "I had neither the far-seeing intent nor the wit and powers thus to transmogrify my students": 1976: 123). Gouldner attempts to capture this ambivalence:

The limits of Merton's work derive in part from its essentially 'liberal' bathos ... These limits do not derive only from Merton's *liberal* side but also from his 'rebel' side ... that is, Merton's limits derive as much from the *rebel horse* he rode, as from the liberal snaffle and curb with which he held it in check. ... In passing a serious judgement on Merton's work ... it should be seen *historically*, in terms of what it meant when it first appeared and made the rounds. ... Merton's work on *anomie* ... was a liberative work, for those who lived with it as part of a *living* culture and distinct from how it may now appear as part of the mere record of that once-lived culture.

There are several reasons for this. One is that Merton ... kept open an avenue of access to Marxist theory. ... Merton was much more *Marxist* than his silences on that question may make it seem. Unlike Parsons, Merton always knew his Marx and knew thoroughly the nuances of controversy in living Marxist culture. Merton developed his generalized analysis of the various forms of deviant culture by locating them within a systematic formalization of Durkheim's theory of *anomie*, from which he gained analytic distance by tacitly grounding himself in a Marxian ontology of social *contradiction*. It is perhaps this Hegelian dimension of Marxism that has had the most enduring effect on Merton's *analytical rules*, and which disposed him to view *anomie* as the unanticipated outcome of social institutions that thwarted men in their effort to acquire the very goods and values that these same institutions had encouraged them to pursue. In its openness to the internal contradictions of capitalist *culture* few Lukacians have been more incisive.

(*Gouldner, 1973: x, xi: this note includes contrasts with C. Wright Mills which have been deleted as they seemed unnecessary for present purposes*)

Another line of criticism has involved a rather more lofty annoyance that Merton's sharpening of analytical tools has vulgarised conceptualisations handed down from classic writers. Thus, for example, Bryan Turner argues that:

the bland Mertonian conception of 'unanticipated consequences' and 'latent functions' ... does not capture the evil ambience of Weber's theory of routinisation. It is not simply that purposive actions have consequences which are not recognised by social actors; the outcome of human actions often work against social actors in such a way as to limit or reduce the scope of their freedom.

(*Turner, 1981: 9–10*)

Similarly, Horton (1964) made the criticism that Merton's attention to anomie had confused the very different concepts of alienation and anomie. In sum, while Merton shares a careful critical view of (American) social reality this is more of an underlying pattern of thought than brought to the fore through explicit analyses. Merton tended not to engage with issues which are high on a Marxist agenda but on the other hand did not ignore them and his sociology has potential for more attention to them.

Conclusion, deep structures

There are some 'deep structures' to Merton's thought that bear reflection. He was placed or placed himself between alternatives:

> Merton was a complex figure: a social scientist with an ample humanist side, a modernist who sometimes anchored himself in history, an architect of objectivist sociology whose communication [and other] research had critical dimensions, and an outsider who became a consummate professional from his position at Columbia University.
>
> *(Simonson, 2010: 124)*

He had a lifelong concern with the dialectic between systemacity and ambivalence, change, chance and serendipity: the uncovering of patterns from their real-world complexities were hard-won. This too was reflected in his writing style: almost entirely quite formal and austere but punctuated by material in irreverent Shandian mode. Merton could not fully be described as reflexive, but he certainly saw sociologists within the frame and not sitting detachedly outside it, and he saw his work as often self-exemplary. These features can be summed up by Stinchcombe's rendition that:

> Merton clearly likes irony. He is most pleased to find motives of advancing knowledge creating priority conflicts amongst scientists, and hardly interested in the fact that such motives also advance knowledge. He likes to find political bosses helping people while good government types turn a cold shoulder. He likes to find Sorokin offering statistics on ideas to combat the empiricist bent of modern culture and to urge an idealist logico-meaningful analysis of ideas. He likes to range Engels and functionalists down parallel columns to show them really to be the same.
>
> *(Stinchcombe, 1975: 28)*

References

Barber, Bernard (1975) Toward a New View of the Sociology of Knowledge. In L.A. Coser (ed.): 103–116.

Boudon, Raymond (1981) *The Logic of Social Action*. London: Routledge & Kegan Paul.

Collins, Randall (1977[1981]) Merton's Functionalism. In *Sociology Since Midcentury*. New York. Academic Press: 197–203.

Collins, Randall & Sal Restivo (1983) Development, Diversity and Conflict in the Sociology of Science. *The Sociological Quarterly*, 24: 185–200.

Coser, Lewis A. (ed.) (1975a) *The Idea of Social Structure: Papers in Honor of Robert K. Merton*. New York: Harcourt Brace Jovanovich.

Coser, Lewis (1975b) Merton's Uses of the European Sociological Tradition. In. L.A. Coser (ed.): 85–102.

Coser, Lewis & Robert Nisbet (1975) Merton and Contemporary Mind: An Affectionate Dialogue. In L.A. Coser (ed.): 3–10.

Coser, Rose (1975) The Complexity of Roles as a Seedbed of Individual Autonomy. In L.A. Coser (ed.): 237–264.

Erickson, Kai (ed.) (1997) *Sociological Visions*. Lanham, MD: Rowman & Littlefield.

Friedrichs, Robert (1970) *A Sociology of Sociology*. New York: Free Press.

Gouldner, Alvin (1973) *For Sociology*. London: Penguin.

Gouldner, Alvin (1970) *Coming Crisis of Western Sociology*. London: Heinemann.

Gouldner, Alvin (1961[1973]) Anti-Minotaur: The Myth of a Value-free Sociology. *Social Problems* (*For Sociology*. London: Penguin).

Hollinger, D.A. (1983) The Defense of Democracy and Robert K. Merton's Formulation of the Scientific Ethos. In R.A. Jones & H. Kuklick (eds) *Knowledge & Society: Studies in the Sociology of Culture of Past and Present*. Greenwich: JAI Press, 4: 1–15.

Horton, John (1964) The Dehumanisation of Anomie and Alientation: A Problem in the Ideology of Sociology. *British Journal of Sociology*, 15: 283–300.

Jaworski, Gary (1990) Robert K. Merton as Postwar Prophet. *The American Sociologist*, 21 (Fall): 209–216.

Katznelson, Ira (2002) *Desolation and Enlightenment: Political Knowledge after Total War, Totalitarianism, and the Holocaust*. New York: Columbia University Press.

Lazarsfeld, Paul (1975) Working with Merton. In L.A. Coser (ed.): 35–66.

Levine, Donald N. (2006) Ambivalence Towards Autonomous Theory – and Ours. *Canadian Journal of Sociology/Cahiers canadiens de sociologie*, 31 (2): 235–243.

Lukes, Stephen (1973) *Emile Durkheim: His Life and Work*. London: Penguin.

McCaughey, Robert (2003) *Stand Columbia: A History of Columbia University*. Columbia University Press.

Matza, David (1969) *Becoming Deviant*. Englewood Cliffs, NJ: Prentice-Hall.

Merton, R.K. (1995) Opportunity Structure: The Emergence, Diffusion, and Differentiation of a Sociological Concept, 1930s-1950s. In Freda Adler & William S. Lauder (eds) *Advances in Criminological Theory: The Legacy of Anomie Theory*. New Brunswick, NJ: Transaction Publishers: vol. 6: 3–78.

Merton, R.K. (1976) *Sociological Ambivalence*. New York: The Free Press.

Merton, R.K. (1975) Thematic Analysis in Science: Notes on Holton's Concept. *Science*, 188 (25 April): 335–338.

Merton, R.K. (1973) *The Sociology of Science: Theoretical and Empirical Investigations*. Norman Storer (ed.). Chicago, IL: The University of Chicago Press.

Merton, R.K. (1969) Foreword to a Preface for an Introduction to a Prolegomenon to a Discourse on a Certain Subject. *American Sociologist* 4(2): 99.

Merton, R.K. (1964) Anomie, Anomia and Social Interaction: Contexts of Deviant Behavior. In Marshall Clinard (ed.) *Anomie and Deviant Behavior*. New York: The Free Press: 213–242.

Merton, R.K. (1961) Now the Case for Sociology: The Canons of the Anti-Sociologist. *New York Times Magazine*, 16 July.

Merton, R.K. (1960) *The Ambivalences of Le Bon's The Crowd* (introduction to Le Bon, The Crowd). New York: Viking Press: v–xxxix.

Merton, R.K. (1957) Some Preliminaries to a Sociology of Medical Education. In Robert K. Merton, George C. Reader & Patricia Kendall (eds) *The Student-Physician*. Cambridge, MA: Harvard University Press: 3–79.

Merton, R.K. (1949[1968]) *Social Theory and Social Structure*. New York: Free Press.

Merton, R.K. (1948) The Self-Fulfilling Prophecy. *Antioch Review* (Summer): 193–210.

Merton, R.K. (1940) Fact and Factitiousness in Ethnic Opinionnaires. *American Sociological Review*, 5 (1): 13–28.

Merton, R.K. (1938) Social Structure and Anomie. *American Sociological Review*, 3: 672–682.

Merton, R.K. (1936) The Unanticipated Consequences of Purposive Social Action. *American Sociological Review*, 1: 894–904.

Merton, R.K. with Richard Christie (1958) Procedures for the Sociological Study of the Value Climate of Medical Schools. In Helen H. Gee & Robert J. Glaser (eds) *The Ecology of the Medical Student*. Evanston, IL: Association of American Medical Colleges: 125–153.

Merton, R.K. with the assistance of Marjorie Fiske & Alberta Curtis (1946) *Mass Persuasion*. New York: Harper & Brothers.

Merton, R.K. & Paul Lazarsfeld (1954) Friendship as a Social Process: A Substantive and Methodological Analysis. In Morroe Berger, Theodore Abel & Charles Page (eds) *Freedom and Control in Modern Society*. New York: Van Nostrand: 18–66.

Merton, R.K. & Arnold Thackray (1972) On Discipline Building: The Paradoxes of George Sarton. *Isis*, 63, 219: 473–495.

Mills, C. Wright (1959) *The Sociological Imagination*. Oxford: Oxford University Press.

Mitroff, Ian I. (1974) Norms and Counter-norms in a Select Group of the Apollo Moon Scientists: A Case Study of the Ambivalence of Scientists. *American Sociological Review*, 39: 579–595.

Simonson, Peter (2010) Merton's Skeptical Faith. In *Refiguring Mass Communication: A History*. Urbana, IL: University of Illinois Press: 123–162.

Sorokin, Pitirim (1966) *Sociological Theories of Today*. New York: Harper & Row.

Stinchcombe, Arthur (1975) Merton's Theory of Social Structure. In L.A. Coser (ed.) *The Idea of Social Structure*. New York: Harcourt Brace Jovanovich: 11–34.

Stinchcombe, Arthur (1968) *Constructing Social Theories*. New York: Harcourt, Brace & Jovanovich.

Sztompka, Piotr (1996) Introduction. In P. Sztompa (ed.) *Robert K. Merton. On Social Structure and Science, The Heritage of Sociology*. Chicago, IL & London: The University of Chicago Press.

Taylor, Ian; Paul Walton & Jock Young (1973) *The New Criminology*. London: Routledge & Kegan Paul.

Thio, A. (1975) A Critical Look at Merton's Anomie Theory. *Pacific Sociological Review*, 18: 139–158.

Turner, Bryan (1981) *For Weber: Essays on the Sociology of Fate*. Boston, MA: Routledge & Kegan Paul.

Wrong, Dennis (1961) The Oversocialized Conception of Man in Modern Sociology. *American Sociological Review*, 26: 184–193.

7

MERTON THE MAN, HIS OPERATIONAL CODE AND INFLUENCES

Effects of personal characteristics and life on Merton's work

Ironically, there is little need for sociological exposé of Merton's life as, I would argue it bore only lightly on his intellectual career, above and beyond his highly strategic placing at Columbia University at the centre of the key city in American, and even world intellectual life. New York allowed better access to travelling scholars, publishers and funders but did not affect much the problems he investigated or the content of his theory and research on these problems. This setting provided the 'pulpit' but had little to do with the content of the sermons preached from it. Once established in his career there was likely considerable insulation from the wider social world and its vicissitudes.

The effects of changing times have been covered in previous chapters. There have been some speculative comments about the effect of Merton's humble origins on his subsequent career. But these beginnings were quickly overcome and Merton carried little anger about his benign background circumstances, albeit retaining a strong sense of social concern throughout his career. In terms of status-sequence, Merton moved from graduate student to professor (eventually becoming a senior and emeritus) without too much obvious difficulty (although he might have preferred to stay at Harvard) and with early stages achieved at considerable speed. Nor did his Jewishness seem to have much effect. (Merton was reportedly engaged when visiting Jerusalem, but only publically revealed his Jewish descent later in his life.)

Some consideration could be made of Merton's regular holidays (often to West Indies, Puerto Rico, Italy, although holidays might entail steady work on manuscripts) and periods as a visiting professor which must have widened his cultural experience. All may have influenced Merton and especially his year in 1973 at the Center for Advanced Study in the Behavioral Sciences where he worked with Zuckerman, Lederberg, Thackray and Lakatos on the sociology/history/ philosophy of science. Participation in many workshops and national committees involved the exchange of ideas. Although his musical tastes were classical, he was quite an American in terms of sports – playing tennis and enjoying watching the Knicks (New York's basketball team).

Some personalised comments may help build up a picture of Merton as a man. Some personal characteristics helped his success. Bourdieu saw Talcott Parsons, Paul Lazarsfeld and Merton as the 'Capitoline triad' ruling (American) sociology – although his French understanding of academic hierarchy may not be so pertinent in the USA. He later admitted he had earlier jumped too quickly to conclusions:

> When one is young … other things being equal, one has less capital, and also less competence, and so almost by definition, one is inclined to put forward in opposition to the established figures, and therefore to look critically at their work. But this critique can in part be an effect of ignorance. In Merton's case I was unaware not only of the context of his early writings … but also of his trajectory: the man I had seen – in an international conference where he was king – as an elegant refined WASP was in reality a recent Jewish immigrant who exaggerated an adopted 'British' elegance … and that disposition towards hypercorrectness, very common in first-generation immigrants undergoing integration and eager for recognition, was probably also at the root of his scientific practice and his exaltation of the profession of sociology which he wanted to establish as a scientific profession.
>
> *(Bourdieu, 2004: 13)*

Donald Levine has been an interesting sociological writer on ambivalence (amongst other topics) and applies this perspective in remembering Merton:

> Using the term ambivalence in the title of a talk honoring the life and work of Robert K. Merton seems perfectly plausible. For one thing, the man himself was the object of considerable ambivalence. Evoking the (expectable) negative sentiment customarily directed against outstanding public figures, Merton was resented for ways in which he appeared to deploy an interest in others in manipulative ways and to pursue a seemingly insatiable agenda of self-aggrandizement. On the other hand, there were those, myself included, who were awestruck by the depth of his collegial goodwill and of his proactive generosity toward younger colleagues and students.
>
> *(Levine, 2006: 235)*

His writings anticipated so much, and he would remind people of that.

> During the 'science' seminars at Columbia, Merton would routinely step out of the room just as a visiting scholar was finishing up, only to return with a stack of books at least two feet high, mostly authored by Merton (from which

he would read a few anticipations, precursors, apercus, foreshadowings – but always dancing away from the sin of adumbrationism). But Merton could not anticipate everything.

(Gieryn, 2003)

Epstein (2010: 83) opines:

He was tall (a valued attribute in this culture) and attractive, and he soon adopted the manner of the perfect professor – pipe in hand, tweed jackets, edited words. It was not irrelevant that his knowledge of border crossings and symbolic capital … qualities that permitted or restrained the movement of individuals from one social class to another, led to his scholarly contributions.

She also reported: "Further, I found he knew how to respond intimately, but always respectful of privacy, when people were experiencing hard personal times". There were some authorial flourishes which marked out a Merton style, he:

- Used a red pen to write comments on others' drafts;
- Provided typically single-spaced typed notes of running commentary that went on for pages;
- Deployed titles tending to ambitiously profess an unqualified scope, and nearly always with a subtitle separated by a colon;
- Developed combination words (of three or more terms often joined by hyphens)
- Often referred to his book titles by their acronyms as short-hand;
- Used a green arrow rubber stamp to point to relevant parts of a document, and other stamps;
- Used a Sarton-derived dating system as a get around from the ambiguous American date format (e.g. 53.11.04 = 4 November 1953)
- Smoked a pipe when a good reception was then likely, whereas smoking a cigar was a signal of a bad mood (with mood often set by perceived writing progress);
- Was a devotee of good quality single-malt scotch, drinking butter-milk sprinkled with pepper during Columbia Sociology Department meetings;
- At home applied his analytical skills on baseball and other American sports.

Performance in the array of sociological roles

This section will briefly examine Merton's performance in various of the array of roles available to the status-occupant of any university teaching/research position: as scholar, editor, reviewer, teacher, organiser, consultant and social critic (cf. the list given by Merton, 1973: 519–522) ('Lover of words' is more of a 'latent role' or orientation). These characteristics span across the decades, and repetition of earlier coverage is avoided.

Scholar/writer

Merton had his early books published by the Free Press, a then new firm which actively published *sociological* work (see Chapter 4). His work has been widely translated (for example, *Social Theory and Social Structure* has been translated into a dozen languages) and frequently reprinted (for example, *Social Structure and Anomie* has been reprinted some 40 times). Besides this, "for all his publications, Merton has a writing block" (Caplovitz, 1977: 143). He bequeathed several unpublished book manuscripts and many unpublished paper drafts, many in the form of notes for teaching or conference presentations. Indeed, Merton (1980) has drawn attention to the importance in his work, and that of others, of the advancing front of 'oral publications' which often precede printed scholarly form, and much of his teaching material didn't make the transition. But Merton was also careful to avoid publication of unworthy material, and did not regret some of his 'non-publications'.

Merton usually presented his work in the form of an essay, a form of writing over which he exhibited consummate control. It is probably fairly easy to recognise the particular style of a Mertonian essay, but it is rather more difficult to distinguish analytically its key characteristics. (For rhetorical analysis of some of Merton's writings see Bennett, 1990; Simonson, 2010b.) Merton departs from more austere forms of essay-writing in deploying headed sections and he uses listings, emphases, tables and other devices to enumerate points or to point up interrelationships. Another hallmark of his writings is an abundance of reference notes designed:

> to place American sociology... in the mainstream of worldwide scholarship … [since] Merton wrote in an intellectual climate in which sophisticated scholarship could not be taken for granted.
>
> *(Coser, 1975: 89–90)*

However, the dense thicket of historical and contemporary references seems sometimes diverting, and even Coser pointedly remarks that Merton's abundant footnoting has a 'functional autonomy' of its own! Simonson suggests (2010a: 125) that Merton's [footnotes] are a thing of beauty … and remind[ed him] of a kind of Talmudic disputation carried on beneath the main text and running parallel to it". Calhoun (2003) commented that

> Indeed, Merton was among the clearest and most careful prose stylists in sociology. He edited each essay over and again, and left behind added footnotes and revisions both large and small to a host of his writings. It was easy to imagine that he might have been a professional editor had he not been an academic.

Coser's codification of the ways in which Merton attempts to relate his work to the European tradition, is also a useful *general* picture of his essay-writing approach:

> When choosing a problem for investigation, Merton seems most of the time to have been stimulated by (1) a public issue that was salient at the time; or by (2) a theoretical formulation by a previous thinker …; or by (3) general scholarly interest in a particular area of inquiry. The execution of the project, in turn, led him to either (a) use previous scholarship to buttress his argument; or (b) use that scholarship in order to suggest formulations, refinements and reformulations; or (c) use that scholarship to suggest new lines of inquiry.
>
> *(Coser, 1975: 91)*

Merton is very careful in his attribution of concepts and terms to predecessors, at the risk of being accused (cf. Sorokin, 1966) of merely repeating the work of others. Yet concepts were seldom used without imparting to a novel twist.

Merton frequently worked closely with collaborators and research assistants (often, it appears, partners or partners-to-be of colleagues). Beyond his immediate working environment, Merton was been particularly supportive of other scholars, drawing widely on their work and providing encouragement. Merton seldom engaged in any extended polemic or even exchange of views, although from time to time he firmly and carefully commented on the work of others where he felt it was insufficiently scholarly: Dahrendorf, Dubin, Feuer, Mills, Mitroff – and others – were subject to vigorous critique (e.g. Chapter 3, *The Ambivalence of Scientists: A Postscript* in his 1976).

Other critics have been ignored. An unfortunate consequence of this could be that Merton's own sociology became detached from trends, and he didn't engage with newer perspectives. Stephen Cole (2004) has argued that had Merton commented on the 'new sociology of science', it would have helped proponents of the Mertonian approach. Instead, Merton kept his writing energies focused on his own programme.

Editor

A major, but largely invisible, role that Merton discharged has been his close and active editing of other scholars' writings. Merton estimated he edited 250 books and 2,000 articles. Caplovitz argues that these tasks of reading and commenting have taken up much of Merton's professional life, and have severely cut into his own publishing performance.

> Merton became engaged as an editor in four different ways. Early in his career, he was frequently asked by publishers to evaluate manuscripts that they were considering publishing. Second, he edited the papers of the various contributors to collections of essays that he edited, notably *Sociology Today* and *Contemporary Social Problems*. Third, some twenty-five years ago he became the sociological editor for Harcourt Brace and thus evaluated all the social science books they considered publishing; and finally he receives each

year a large number of unsolicited manuscripts from former students and colleagues for his opinions of their work.

(Caplovitz, 1977: 146)

Much of Merton's contribution in 'close' editing work lay in offering reformulations and additions of arguments, as well as in showing how prose can be sharpened or highlighted and needless words omitted. Merton's 'rough' editing cleared up and structured the presentation of arguments (Caplovitz, 1977). His editing for Harcourt Brace Jovanovich – as well as many other books – often involved highlighting and summarising key themes through an introductory preface. However, Merton appeared in his editing work to not attempt to restructure the writer's manuscripts along lines that suited his own theories, although undoubtedly many of his comments were based on his own work.

Reviewer

Merton was very active as a book reviewer, especially early in his career. Most of these were straightforward descriptive and critical notices, but in several (e.g. 1941) Merton actively summarised and developed the author's material, with Znaniecki being particularly pleased with Merton's extended review of his *Social Role of the Man of Knowledge*.

Humanist

A particular quality of Merton's writing was his love of words and language (Caplovitz, 1977) and in general, in a humanities approach. He chose evocative terms to sharpen and highlight concepts. Many of these terms were recovered from archaic usage, enhanced by his favourite reading, which was "not the *ASR* or *AJS*, but rather those eighteenth and nineteenth century literary magazines, *The Edinburgh Review, Notes and Inquiries* and *Athenaeum*" and because "he is a fond collector of rare books that he uncovers in out of the way second-hand bookstores" (Caplovitz, 1977: 44). Hunt (1961) provides an extended example of Merton's drawing on previous literature:

> Many of Merton's writings furthermore, are liberally flavored with apposite references to literature and history. An introduction he wrote to an anthology called *Sociology Today* either quotes or alludes to John Aubrey, Charles Darwin, Herbert Spencer, Seneca, Descartes, Hegel, and John Stuart Mill, and another of his books, *Mass Persuasion*, is sprinkled with choice morsels from Thomas Hobbes, Plato, Aristotle, de Tocqueville, Julian Huxley, and Kate Smith.

This love of words further extended to the coining, or more usually recovery, of some splendid terms, often culled from the *OED* which he would browse for entertainment. In a paper on the drift of sociological ideas into the vernacular, Merton has supplied a list of his own neologisms:

self-fulfilling prophecy, manifest and latent functions, the displacement of goals, retreatism (a social phenomenon become widely known a generation later as 'opting out'), opportunity-structures, role-sets and status-sets, local and cosmopolitan influentials, the Matthew effect, accumulation of advantage, theories of the middle range, homophily (friendships between people of the same kind, *not* as more recently proposed, a synonym for homosexuality) and heterophily, strategic research site, obliteration by incorporation, potentials of relevance and the acronym OTSOG (standing for the title of a book of mine, *On The Shoulders of Giants*).

(1982: 102)

His interest in words spilled over into the occasional use of poetry (sometimes suitably paraphrased for the purpose at hand) to drive home a particular point, and to a controlled scholarly wit (perhaps most clearly expressed in his little 'Foreword to a Preface for an Introduction to a Prolegomenon to a Discourse on a Certain Subject': 1969).

Merton's erudition has been supported by his command over several languages – Latin, French, German and Italian. However, this facility was not accompanied by an oral fluency.

Teacher

Merton taught a variety of courses and seminars, but since going to Columbia, only at graduate level (Persell, 1984). Besides lectures he ran seminars and tutorials. For many academics, their research interests are centred around their teaching duties: Merton was in a position to allow his general interests to shape his teaching. Several accounts of his teaching have been published and are referred to in previous chapters.

Organiser

Cole and Zuckerman note various organisational efforts Merton made in developing the sociology of science as a specialty, as he

encouraged the scheduling of sessions at ASA in the early 1960s, by agreeing to chair them or to prepare papers, and was one of the chief organizers of the ISA Committee [the International Sociological Association's Research Committee in the Sociology of Science].

(1975: 164)

But they go on to comment that Merton

does not find these activities congenial. He does not want to organize things or to run them. Unlike his teacher, George Sarton, who avidly devoted himself to establishing an elaborate organizational infrastructure for the history of science, Merton has set about most of these tasks reluctantly and has been far less effective than Sarton.

(1975: 164–165)

Nevertheless, Merton was prominent in a range of efforts to secure the infrastructure needed to underpin the development of social science research: for example, his active encouragement of Eugene Garfield's *Citation Indexes* (Zuckerman, 2018) or his support of Lazarsfeld in setting up graduate training for sociology students which led on to the establishment of the Advanced Center for the Behavioral Sciences for which Lazarsfeld wanted a European-type ranked set of incumbents; Merton preferred a non-hierarchical arrangement.

Merton early was placed in an informal leadership role, for example, mediating, through correspondence, between scholars Gerth and Mills (Horowitz, 1983). Merton's letter files reveal a mesh of correspondence that helped informally to pull together much of the American and world sociology establishment (see Dubois, 2014; St-Arnaud, 2014).

Although Merton claimed he held little power – in that era appointments were apportioned through 'old boys' networks' – his influence was considerable, and extended as well to other areas of scholarship where informal influence might be exerted.

Consultant

Lazarsfeld (1975) notes that Merton engaged in consulting, especially in relation to the Bureau of Applied Social Research, but only traces of this have surfaced in the published literature. (The account by Merton and Devereux, 1964, summarises a larger storehouse of material.) His later work as consultant to the American Nursing Association led to several short useful essays (e.g. 1966, 1970b) that explore areas of occupational and organisational sociology relevant to nursing, together with a footnoted admonition that improvement in the economic and social status of nurses might require wresting of at least some power away from doctors.

Social critic

Although as Hunt (1961) reports, Merton preferred to take an 'independent' political position, this did not preclude him from some involvement in liberal causes.

Correspondent

Merton's correspondence network was a large one (addressing at least 650 scholars throughout the world, whose letters run from 1930 to 2003: DuBois, 2014), accounting for the largest series in the collection of his papers. Merton's whole professional career is chronicled through these letters received from and sent to colleagues in the field of sociology, and individuals acting in a variety of scholarly fields, including philosophy, English, anthropology, mathematics and science. He would get his assistant to send a card asking for offprints for newly published articles, thus also bringing his own work to the attention of the recipient.

Research trajectory

A characteristically Mertonian question is to consider: what led to his changing foci of interest? (cf. Merton, 1938a [1970a: 6]). Coser (1975: 88, and also Bierstedt, 1981: 444) has applied Isaiah Berlin's image of the 'fox' ("who knows many things") to describe the complexities of Merton's research strategy (as opposed to the hedgehog "who knows one big thing" approach). Clearly, there have been complex threads of opportunistic reaction to possibilities made available, but also strong guidance from continuing theoretical and methodological themes. The skeins are less entangled at the beginning and then again at the end of his research career – the early focus on sociology of science, and the later return to this. In between there is a growing confidence in reacting less to opportunities which were made available, and instead using his growing prestige in generating research resources to pursue programmes of more central sociological interest.

A related question would be to consider whether Merton had notably changed his *theoretical* approach in tune with any phases in his research trajectory. For the most part, there had been relatively little change, since his basic sociological orientation was clearly laid down during the first decade of his writing and most of its basic features can be discovered within the set of his early set of essays and investigations. However, there have been changing emphases: the self-conscious concern with functional analysis dominated his '1940s' period, while by the '1970s' he worked under a 'structuralist' label. Another change seems to have been the social psychological approaches (see Nichols, 2016) more often involved with Bureau of Applied Social Research studies in the '1940s' which was complemented in several essays during the '1950s' with a more conscious 'social structure' level of analysis. Lazarsfeld detected a shift in the tone of Merton's writing, noting that in the early essay on the intellectual in the bureaucracy no sympathy is shown the latter, and that "The balanced tone of later papers is still absent" (1975: 37).

There was a reluctance to finally commit himself to definitive statements. A general tone in his work is 'work in progress', with final publications reporting studies yet to be completed. This reluctance is evidenced in his preparedness to take the active advice of editors (e.g. Storer, Rosenblatt and Gieryn) in collecting his material into books and Hunt's perceptive comment that:

> His friends hope he will soon settle down to the magnum opus they feel he is capable of producing – an integrating work, which will weave the scattered strands of theory into a sturdy fabric. On good days, Merton thinks that some of his unpublished manuscripts are the beginnings of such a work; on bad

days he is glumly certain that nothing of the sort can be written by anyone
for at least fifty years.

(1961: 62)

Having briefly examined the man, the next two sections extend this to look at
the influences on and influences from him.

Work pattern

Much of Merton's writing has taken the form of "programmatic essays" each of
which is a pioneering contribution opening up a particular area of sociological
study by specifying interesting research problems, sketching appropriate theoretical
lines of interest in engaging with these problems, and then (often with the provision
of some illustrative empirical material of his own) encouraging others to continue
research in this area. This means that the array of his essays is scattered, although
several collections have brought the more important of these together into accessible volumes. How these various components of Merton's work came together can
be evocatively presented in Harriet Zuckerman's (2011: 163) rendition of a

> prototypical Mertonian contribution. It exemplifies his eye for a telling social
> phenomenon which despite its generality goes unnoticed by others, his skills
> at laying out its distinctive properities, his ability to recognize and to eluci-
> date the mechanisms that bring it about and perpetuate it and then, not to be
> denigrated, his skill at inventing evocative terms that make the phenomenon
> visible, comprehensible and usable.

A similar account is provided by Lew Coser:

> When choosing a problem for investigation, Merton seems most of the time
> to have been stimulated by (1) a public issue that was salient at the time; or
> by (2) a theoretical formulation by a previous thinker …; or by (3) general
> scholarly interest in a particular area of inquiry. The execution of the project,
> in turn, led him to either (a) use previous scholarship to buttress his argument;
> or (b) use that scholarship in order to suggest formulations, refinements and
> reformulations; or (c) use that scholarship to suggest new lines of inquiry.

(Coser, 1975: 91)

These two passages give a good sense of the flow of a Merton project.

Intellectual heritage: influences on Merton

Merton has established his own official intellectual lineage in the acknowledgments
to his *STSS* (1949d [1968b]), building on those who influenced his PhD, where
he thanks:

- Charles Hopkins (his brother-in-law, friend and teacher);
- George Simpson (his undergraduate teacher);
- Pitirim Sorokin (his graduate teacher);
- George Sarton (historian of science and early sponsor);
- Talcott Parsons (graduate adviser and colleague);
- Paul Lazarsfeld (Columbia colleague).

The ways through which each influenced him have been depicted in Chapter 2. But these are only his 'masters-at-close-range': much of Merton's concern was, as Coser puts it a "self-conscious effort to ransack the whole house of European erudition" (1975: 89). Merton draws very widely, but less systematically, on a very wide array of European social theorists, many minor, but including several neglected by Parsons – Sim, Marx and Mannheim (cf. Coser, 1975: 88). Of all these European social theorists, Merton himself chose Durkheim as a role model, especially in following his open-ended train of inquiry across a scatter of topics. Besides Durkheim, Coser (see also Sztompka, 1995: 5–8) identifies Weber, Mannheim, Simmel and Marx as major sources drawn on by Merton. Durkheim was a major source in the development of the anomie theory of deviance, the functional mode of analysis, and more generally Merton's methodological approach; Weber in developing the 'Merton hypothesis' of the religious impetus to the development of seventeenth-century science and in work on bureaucracy; Mannheim in sociology of knowledge; Simmel on work on group properties and Marx for a concern about the operation of class. Also, the ideas of Pareto were exposed through the Henderson seminar at Harvard. Yet, Merton wrote systematically on the thinking of none of these classic theorists (apart from his early review essay on Durkheim, 1936b). Rather, each was actively used and reformulated in developing an approach to a particular theoretical problem. (To some extent, Coser's superb 1977 *History of Sociological Thought* presented some of Merton's thinking on the development of sociology.)

Although Merton's use of earlier American theorists is less remarked, he also drew on American sociological thought. For example, Gouldner notes, inter alia, "the extremely fruitful uses to which Robert K. Merton has put such classic theorists as C.H. Cooley, H. Spencer, W.G. Sumner, and above all, G. Simmel, in his recent essay on 'Continuities in the Theory of Reference Groups and Social Structure'" (Gouldner, 1973[1958]: 387–388). Further sources have been Anglo-American social anthropology (Linton, Malinowski and Radcliffe-Brown, Murdock), contemporary sociology, and a range of historians and social critics (for example, the second Festschrift, organised by Thomas Gieryn for the New York Academy of Sciences, includes a selection of "scholars and scientists other than American sociologists, whose work [Gieryn] knew Merton to admire" [1980: vii, viii]). Gieryn describes the list of contributors as including: "three sociologists; two based in England and one in Israel. The seven Americans come from eight disciplines: economics, physiology-and-medicine, psychology, philosophy of science, information science and statistics and history of science" (1980, preface). To these can be added the array of colleagues and students, many for whom he wrote appreciative pieces for Festschriften. Moreover, while Merton didn't devote much explicit mention of his colleagues at Columbia (and other contemporaries), it is clear that there was much interaction. But the influencers were chosen on his own terms and he never followed a master.

Intellectual legacy: influences from Merton

A major influence from Merton on the discipline-building of sociology lay through his methodological writing. But, in addition, there are several other aspects of his theoretical work which served to bring together some of the multifarious strands of post-WW2 American sociology. It is through these mechanisms, according to my analysis, that Merton played his role in helping shape the central directions of sociology.

Merton's laying out of a common mainstream methodological position to which most sociologists could actively adhere, was flanked with an active public defence of sociology (e.g. *The Canons of the Anti-Sociologist* (1961 [1973]). Several of Merton's formulations 'in support for sociology' were popular amongst sociologists; for example, Merton's insistence that:

> the distinctive intellectual contributions of the sociologist are found primarily in the study of unintended consequences (among which are latent functions) of social practices, as well as in the study of anticipated consequences (among which are manifest functions).
>
> *(1968: 120)*

Another useful point was his neat contrast of the (European) sociologists' knowledge banner "We don't know that what we say is true, but it is at least significant" against the (American) empirical researchers' claim that "We don't know that what we say is particularly significant, but it is at least true" (1968: 494).

Alongside his explicit methodological positions, Merton's theoretical stances were sympathetic with, and therefore attractive to, the development of empirical sociology. Most of Merton's work was carried out with a close connection to possible or actual empirical research investigations. This helped to link with a wide range of empirical researchers. For example, in two crisp sentences Merton nicely linked survey research into his theoretical concerns:

> The categories of audience measurement have been primarily those of income stratification (a kind of datum obviously important to those ultimately concerned with selling and marketing their commodities), sex, age and education (obviously important for those seeking to learn the advertising outlets most appropriate for reaching special groups). But since such categories as sex, age, education and income happen also to correspond to some of the chief statuses in the social structure, the procedures evolved for

audience measurement by the students of mass communication are of direct
interest to the sociologist as well.

(1968: 505)

Merton's influence on contemporary sociology is broad and pervasive. Although
Merton has worked with a range of collaborators on a sequence of projects, and
his work has inspired a series of research programmes, he has not groomed nor
attracted a *general* school of followers; there are only a few Mertonians, as is appropriate in any scientific field.

As the considerable slew of his biographical comments attest, very many sociologist had links with Merton, including a sequence of visiting scholars at Columbia
from many countries, especially European. Several were clearly affected by their
stay, as several published accounts attest (e.g. several in Elkana et al., 2011).

His influence has broadly affected much of what Mullins (1973) has termed
'Standard American Sociology', and within this the particular current of the
'Columbia School' ('Tradition' was the preferred title). Broadly, this characterisation
involves a conception of a Columbia–Harvard axis, ranged against 'the loyal opposition' of a continuing 'Chicago School' and more generally against those streams of
sociology particularly stressing the history of social theory, social criticism, empiricism and commentary on social problems. Pinning down the key characteristics
of Standard American Sociology and of its specifically Columbia mode is more
difficult: it would generally be held to involve a contemporary focus, a functional
theoretical approach locating social phenomena in their social structural contexts,
an interest in developing theory, a sophisticated empirical research approach, and a
considerable degree of moral and political detachment but concern.

The 'Columbia Tradition' is a *joint* product of both Merton and Lazarsfeld.
Throughout the 1940s, 1950s and 1960s Merton played a major role as both a graduate
teacher in training large cohorts of sociologists and as an editor in helping shape,
through editing, a wide range of the sociological writing from this group and more
generally other sociologists. Several essays have been written about graduate student
experience: e.g. James Coleman expressed his Columbia experience, "I worked with
Lipset, worked for Lazarsfeld, and worked to be like Merton" (1990: 31).

In addition to this general and diffuse impact, Merton did establish several
programmes that for a time shaped research in a particular area. Anomie theory in
the sociology of deviance had a strong Mertonian flavour in the 1940s and 1950s,
although Merton's role was solely as a theorist. Merton provided consequential
early studies of the media and propaganda. During the 1960s Merton developed
a research programme in the sociology of science that generated much research
material, and more broadly the Mertonian approach to analysing the social institution of science dominated. However, these programmes soon lost their distinct-
iveness and became merged with broader approaches. Although each of these were
'cutting edge' studies at the times of Merton's involvement, more recently there
have been signs of some withdrawal from mainstream sociology as each of criminology, media studies and science studies have formed their own interdisciplinary

TABLE 7.1 Overall pace of citation to Robert K. Merton's articles

Decade	Citations by decade
−1939	7
−1949	64
−1959	108
−1969	281
−1979	667
−1989	769
−1999	897
−2009	2,114
−2019	6,614
Total	11,297

Source: Web of Science Citation Index. (cf. Zuckerman, 2011)

field of study. On the other hand, these provide even wider platforms for Merton's work to be built on.

Given the empirical impetus Merton sponsored in sociology, it is appropriate that Merton's influence has been documented in a series of studies, most using various forms of citation count. Several studies of authors cited in American introductory sociology texts, or in major journals, have shown Merton at least level pegging with Parsons in textbook citations through the immediate post-WW2 period. Parsons and Merton dominate textbook citations over this period, although Wells (1979) found a slight tendency for a decline of their influence in the 1970s, and certainly found an increase in the extent to which "conflict theorists" and symbolic interactionists were cited. In a recent study of the sociology elite, using a considerable range of data sources, Korom (2019) placed Merton as third circa 1970 but ninth by circa 2010.

Interest in the work of Merton continues to increase. The *Web of Science* citation data can be organised to track the flow of citations up to and including 2019 citations to articles at least, which show marked increases: see Table 7.1. Plotting the influence of Merton or any other writer is complex and this table is intended as a broad characterisation only, needing much supplementary investigation. The pattern is clear: an exponential rise after about 2005. Beyond the influence exerted by name alone, there are the further influences of concepts/terms particularly associated with Merton and the range of times concepts/terms are used without being formally cited: as indicated by the concept of OBI (obliteration by incorporation). These need additional investigation.

Merton's earlier central role in providing a stock of useful theoretical ideas has been replaced by a wider variety of theoretical sources. Ben-David (1978) has made a useful point about the two-stage development of post-war American sociology that may help to indicate what the limits on Merton's *direct* influence have been. The first 'functional analysis' phase was particularly concerned with institutional description on a comparative basis. This, though, has become superseded by, or rather overlayered by, a quantitative mode of carrying out sociology. Although Merton's work may continue to have contemporary relevance, it is to some extent locked into the earlier phase of development in terms of its theoretical language and style of discourse. As the concerns of American sociology have changed, they have increasingly limited Merton's direct impact.

Some motivation to cite Merton has been to attack his stances (for example Campbell, 1982; Becker, 1984). This has the effect of raising attention to Merton's work, and sometimes provided an opportunity for its development. It is also possible, too, that Merton's writings may participate in a revival as sociologists review the recent history of their own discipline.

Envoie

Clearly, various terms-concepts developed by Merton continue to be used (often heavily used) and several lines of inquiry and fields of study in which he was a pioneer prosper, but the immediate overall relative significance of his work may have been declining. This book portrays much of the extent of Merton's work. In writing this reintroduction, I've been interested in how different analyses come together, once one explores their connections, and then figures out how they are related. There are more skeins of connectivity to be unearthed and synoptic accounts to be developed. It is hoped that this volume on *Reintroducing Robert K. Merton* will provide the reader with the arguments and evidence that justifies keeping Merton's entire range of work within the attention-space of contemporary sociology.

References

Becker, George (1984) Pietism and Science: A Critique of Robert K. Merton's Hypothesis. *American Journal of Sociology*, 89: 1065–1090.

Ben-David, Joseph (1978) Emergence of National Traditions in the Sociology of Science. In Jerry Gaston (ed.) *The Sociology of Science*. San Francisco, CA: Jossey-Bass.

Bennett, James (1990) Merton's 'Social Structure and Anomie': Suggestions for Rhetorical Analysis. In *The Rhetoric of Social Research: Understood and Believed*. New Brunswick, NJ & London: Rutgers University Press.

Bierstedt, Robert (1981) Robert K. Merton. In *American Sociological Theory – A Critical History*. New York: Academic Press: 443–489.

Bourdieu, Pierre (2004) *Science of Science and Reflexivity*. Chicago: The University of Chicago Press.

Calhoun, Craig (2003) Robert K. Merton Remembered in ASA Footnotes: www.asanet. org/sites/default/files/savvy/footnotes/mar03/indextwo.html

Campbell, Colin (1982) A Dubious Distinction? An Inquiry into the Value and Use of Merton's Concept of Manifest and Latent Functions. *American Sociological Review*, 47: 29–44.

Caplovitz, David (1977) Robert K. Merton as Editor: Review Essay. *Contemporary Sociology*, 6: 142–150.

Cole, Jonathan & Harriet Zuckerman (1995) The Emergence of a Scientific Speciality: The Self-exemplifying Case of the Sociology of Science. In. L Coser (ed.) *The Idea of Social Structure*. New York: Harcourt Brace Jovanovich: 139–172.

Cole, Stephen (2004) Merton's Contribution to the Sociology of Science. *Social Studies of Science*, 34 (6): 829–844.

Coser, Lewis (1977) *History of Sociological Thought*. New York: Harcourt Brace Jovanovich.

Coser, Lewis (1975) Merton's Uses of the European Sociological Tradition. In L. Coser (ed.) *The Idea of Social Structure*. New York: Harcourt Brace Jovanovich: 85–102.

Di Lellio, Anna (1985) Intervista a Robert K. Merton. *Rassegna Italiana di Sociologia*, fig. VI: 1–26.

Dubois, Michel (2014) 'Private Knowledge' and 'Disciplinary Program' in Social Sciences: The Correspondence of Robert K. Merton as a Case Study. *L'Annee sociologique*, 64 (1): 79–119.

Elkana, Y. et al. (eds) (2011) *Concepts and the Social Structure*. Budapest: CEU Press.

Epstein, Cynthia (2010) The Contributions of Robert K. Merton to Culture Theory. In Craig J. Calhoun (ed.) *Robert K. Merton: Sociology of Science and Sociology as Science*. New York: Columbia University Press: 79–93.

Gieryn, Thomas (2003) Eloge: Robert K. Merton, 1910–2003. *Isis*, 95 (1): 91–94.

Gieryn, Thomas (ed.) (1980) *Science and Social Structure: A Festschrift for Robert K. Merton*. New York: The New York Academy of Sciences.

Gouldner, Alvin (1973) *For Sociology: Renewal and Critique in Sociology Today*. New York: Basic Books.

Horowitz, Irving (1983) *C. Wright Mills: An American Utopian*. New York: Free Press.

Hunt, Morton M. (1961) How Does It Come to Be So? Profile of Robert K. Merton. *New Yorker*, January 28: 36: 39–63.

Korom, Phillip (2019) The Prestige Elite in Sociology: Toward a Collective Biography of the Most Cited Scholars (1970–2010). *Sociological Quarterly*, 61 (1): 128–163.

Lazarsfeld, Paul F. (1975) Working with Merton. In L.A. Coser (ed.) *The Idea of Social Structure*. New York: Harcourt Brace Jovanovich: 35–66.

Levine, Donald N. (2006) Merton's Ambivalence towards Autonomous Theory – and Ours. *Canadian Journal of Sociology/Cahiers canadiens de sociologie*, 31 (2): 235–243.

Merton, R.K. (1994) A Life of Learning: Charles Homer Haskins Lecture. *American Council of Learned Societies*, Occasional Paper No. 25.

Merton, R.K. (1983) Florian Znaniecki: A Short Reminiscence. *Journal of the History of the Behavioral Sciences*, 10: 123–126.

Merton, R.K. (1982) *Social Research and the Practicing Professions*. Cambridge: Abt Books.

Merton, R.K. (1973) *The Sociology of Science: Theoretical and Empirical Investigations*. Norman Storer (ed.). Chicago, IL: The University of Chicago Press.

Merton, R.K. (1970a) Sociology of Science: An Introduction. In Robert K. Merton, *Science, Technology and Society in Seventeenth Century England*. New York: Howard Fertig, Inc.

Merton, R.K. (1970b) The Ambivalence of Organizational Leaders in James F. Oates, Jr, *The Contradictions of Leadership*. New York: Appleton-CenturyCrofts: 1–26.

Merton, R.K. (1969) Foreword to a Preface for an Introduction to a Prolegomenon to a Discourse on a Certain Subject. *American Sociologist* 4 (2): 99.

Merton, R.K. (1966) Dilemmas of Democracy in the Voluntary Association. *American Journal of Nursing* (May): 1055–1061.

Merton, R.K. (1965) *On the Shoulders of Giants: A Shandean Postscript*. New York: The Free Press.

Merton, R.K. (1961) Now the Case for Sociology: The Canons of the Anti-Sociologist. *New York Times Magazine*, 16 July.

Merton, R.K. (1949[1968]) *Social Theory and Social Structure*. New York: The Free Press.

Merton, R.K. (1941) Florian Znaniecki's *The Social Role of the Man of Knowledge:* A Review Essay. *American Sociological Review*, 6: 111–115.

Merton, R.K. (1938[1970]) *Science, Technology and Society in Seventeenth Century England in Osiris: Studies on the History and Philosophy of Science and on the History of Learning and Culture.* George Sarton (ed.). Bruges: The St Catherine Press, 362–632. New York: Howard Fertig, Inc.; Harper Torchbooks, Harper &Row.

Merton, R.K. & Edward C. Devereux, Jr (1964) Practical Problems and the Uses of Social Science. *Trans-Action*, 1: 18–21.

Merton, R.K. (ed.) with Matilda White Riley (1980) *Sociological Traditions from Generation to Generation: Glimpses of the American Experience.* Norwood, NJ: Ablex Publishing.

Mullins, Nicholas (1973) *Theories* and *Theory Groups in Contemporary American Sociology.* New York: Harper & Row.

Nichols L.T. (2016) The Enduring Social Psychology of Robert K. Merton: Motivating Sentiments, Reference Groups and Self-Fulfilling Prophecies. *American Sociologist*, 47 (2): 356–381.

Persell, Caroline H. (1984) An Interview with Robert K. Merton. *Teaching Sociology*, 11: 355–386.

Saint-Martin, Arnaud (2014) Robert K. Merton épistolier, ou la gestion de l'influence par correspondence: https://hal.archives-ouvertes.fr/hal-01006253/document

Simonson, Peter (2010a) Merton's Skeptical Faith in *Refiguring Mass Communication: A History.* 123–162. Urbana, IL: University of Illinois Press: 123–162.

Simonson, Peter (2010b) Merton's Sociology of Rhetoric. In Craig Calhoun (ed.) *Robert K. Merton: Sociology of Science and Sociology as Science.* New York: Columbia University Press: 214–252.

Sorokin, Pitirim (1966) *Sociological Theories of Today.* New York: Harper & Row.

Saint-Martin, Arnaud (2014) Robert K. Merton épistolier, ou la gestion de l'influence par correspondence: hal-01006253https://hal.archives-ouvertes.fr/hal-01006253/document

Sztompka, Piotr (ed.) (1996) *Robert K. Merton on Social Structure and Science.* Chicago, IL: The University of Chicago Press.

Zuckerman, Harriet (2018) The Sociology of Science and the Garfield Effect: Happy Accidents, Unanticipated Developments and Unexploited Potentials. *Frontiers in Research Metrics and Analytics*, 3: 20.

Zuckerman, Harriet (2011) The Matthew Effect Writ Large and Larger: A Study in Sociological Semantics. In Elkana et al. (eds) *Concepts and the Social Structure.* Budapest: Central European University Press: 121–164.

INDEX

For Product Safety Concerns and Information please contact our EU
representative GPSR@taylorandfrancis com
Taylor & Francis Verlag GmbH, Kaufingerstraße 24, 80331 München, Germany